For the Childlike

George MacDonald's Fantasies
For Children

Roderick McGillis, Editor

The Children's Literature Association
and
The Scarecrow Press, Inc.
Metuchen, N. J., & London
1992

British Library Cataloguing-in-Publication data available

Library of Congress Cataloging-in-Publication Data

For the childlike : George MacDonald's fantasies for children / Roderick McGillis, editor.
    p.   cm.
    Includes index.
    Summary : A collection of essays discussing the work of the nineteenth-century Scottish author best known for his children's fairy tales.
    ISBN 0-8108-2459-0
    1. MacDonald, George, 1824-1905—Criticism and interpretation.
2. Children's stories, Scottish—History and criticism. 3. Fantastic fiction, Scottish—History and criticism.
    [1. MacDonald, George, 1824-1905—Criticism and interpretation. 2. Scottish literature—History and criticism. 3. Fairy tales—History and criticism.]   I. McGillis, Roderick.
PR4969.F67 1992
823'.8—dc20   92-8991

Copyright © 1992 Roderick McGillis
Manufactured in the United States of America
Printed on acid-free paper

For my Mother (1920-1989)
Without whom as always not
Also for Kate and Kyla

Acknowledgments

This book has been long in the making. I thank all those who contributed to it for their patience. Grateful thanks must go to the following for allowing us to reprint previously published essays: *Parabola: The Magazine of Myth and Tradition* for Nancy Willard's "Goddess in the Belfry," volume vi, 1981, 90-94; Durham University Journal for Roderick McGillis' "Language and Secret Knowledge in At the Back of the North Wind," volume 42 n.s., 1981, 191-198; and the *Children's Literature Association Quarterly* for Cordelia Sherman's "The Princess and the Wizard," volume 12, 1987, 24-28, and for Cynthia Marshall's "Reading 'The Golden Key': Narrative Strategies of Parable," volume 14, 1989, 22-25.

The essay by Stephen Prickett in this volume is a revised and enlarged version of an article which appeared in *North Wind: Journal of the George MacDonald Society,* number 2, 1983, 24-32.

Thanks, too, must go to Tony Manna, who has the kind of energy that is felicitous; without him this project may never have found a home. Members of the Children's Literature Association have also supported this project and deserve credit for their vision, and I especially reserve affection and gratitude for Perry Nodelman and Jill May. Finally, I sincerely thank Barbara McQuaid not only for typing the manuscript under a tight schedule, but also for friendship.

A Note on Texts and Titles

I have made no attempt to standardize the editions of MacDonald's works referred to by the various authors in this volume. For example, six editions of *The Princess and the Goblin* are referred to in these essays: Chatto & Windus, David McKay, Airmont, Dell, Puffin, Oxford. Not all of them are cited in the Select Bibliography at the end of this book. MacDonald scholars do not have standard editions (except for first editions, which are often difficult to find) of his works, and the Puffin editions, which are the most often cited versions of the "Princess" books, are unreliable as texts. The Puffin books take liberties with MacDonald's texts for purposes of audience; the editors obviously wished to make the books more accessible to modern child readers than they thought they were in their original format. I have not, however, changed references where authors have used the Puffin books because these remain the most easily obtainable versions. I suspect an examination of the various editions of MacDonald's works would reveal inconsistencies from edition to edition. We know the confusion that exists in versions of some of the adult novels such as *Robert Falconer* and *Adela Cathcart,* and little reason exists to think the same would not occur in the childrens' books. Clearly, the editing of MacDonald's works remains to be done.

A second inconsistency occurs in the titles of two of MacDonald's works. First, *The Lost Princess* has appeared under the following titles: *The Wise Woman: A Parable, The Lost Princess, or The Wise Woman, The Lost Princess,* and *A Double Story.* Second, *The Day Boy and the Night Girl* also appears as *Photogen and Nycteris.* I have chosen not to alter references to these works in the various essays. Mostly, the titles the authors use in these essays reflect the edition of the works he or she is working with.

A Note on Texts and Titles

My hope is that the reader does not find this confusing; certainly, those readers familiar with MacDonald's work will have no difficulty.

Table of Contents

Introduction **Roderick McGillis**	1
The Two Worlds of George MacDonald **Stephen Prickett**	17
The Fairy Tales of George MacDonald and the Evolution of a Genre **Michael Mendelson**	31
The Community of the Centre: Structure and Theme in *Phantastes* **Roderick McGillis**	51
The Goddess in the Belfry: Grandmothers and Wise Women in George MacDonald's Books for Children **Nancy Willard**	67
Social Conscience and Class Relations in MacDonald's "Cross Purposes" **A. Waller Hastings**	75
The Golden Key: Milton and MacDonald **Celia Catlett Anderson**	87
Reading "The Golden Key": Narrative Strategies of Parable **Cynthia Marshall**	99

Table of Contents

The Platonic Imagery of George MacDonald
and C. S. Lewis: The Allegory of the Cave Transfigured
Frank Riga — 111

Diamond and Kilmeny: MacDonald, Hogg,
and the Scottish Folk Tradition
William Raeper — 133

Language and Secret Knowledge in *At the
Back of the North Wind*
Roderick McGillis — 145

Old Wine in New Bottles: Aspects of Prophecy
in George MacDonald's *At the Back of the North Wind*
Lesley Smith — 161

Kore Motifs in *The Princess and the Goblin*
Nancy-Lou Patterson — 169

The Diamond in the Ashes: A Jungian Reading
of the "Princess" Books
Joseph Sigman — 183

The Princess and the Wizard: The Fantasy Worlds
of Ursula K. LeGuin and George MacDonald
Cordelia Sherman — 195

Duality Beyond Time: George MacDonald's
"The Wise Woman, or The Lost Princess:
A Double Story"
Melba N. Battin — 207

Select Bibliography — 219

List of Contributors — 229

Index — 231

Introduction

In his recent book on George MacDonald as a Scottish writer, David Robb notes that MacDonald's work for children has "attained the most sustained popularity—and availability in print—of all his writings" (111). Willing to offer an evaluation of this work, William Raeper writes: "his fairy-writing for children is probably the most significant in the English language as he is one of the very few British writers to write lasting fairy-tales and his imaginative power even today stands unrivalled" (309). This is high praise and perhaps overstates, but it is true that MacDonald wrote a sustained and coherent corpus of work in the faerie vein for children, much of it still readily available and in paperback editions.

As both Robb and Raeper imply in their discussions of MacDonald's children's books, these works are valuable as much for their difficulty as for their delightful evocations of fantasy and the fantastic. As early as 1869, when MacDonald had as yet produced only one book for children, *Dealings with the Fairies* (1867), H. A. Page (A. H. Japp) commented in the *Contemporary Review* that MacDonald "more than any other in our country, has raised child-literature to the level of high art" (23). High art, it seems, means challenging art or more specifically symbolic art. Page praises MacDonald's imaginative power, but notes that children will be impatient with the "shifting grasp of reality" evident in MacDonald's works (24). Another contemporary of MacDonald's, Edward Salmon, concurs; he credits MacDonald as a "really original worker," but he also asserts that he "soars above the intelligence of children of tender years" (173). We might conclude that such writers as Jacqueline Rose (*The Case of Peter Pan or The Impossibility of Children's Fiction*) and Zohar Shavit (*Poetics of Children's Literature*) are correct in suggesting that the children's writer only ostensibly writes for children, that the real audience is the adult who buys the books and who evaluates them. MacDonald's children's books are most often valued because of their spiritual insight and symbolic resonance. MacDonald himself accepts the idealization of the child as a metaphor for the pristine, pastoral, innocent creature prior to the corruptions of urban and industrial civilization that surrounds most of us with its prison-house shade. He offers his books to "the childlike, whether of five, or fifty, or seventy-five" (*Dish of Orts* 317).

The essays in this book implicitly concur. In essays that range over nearly all of MacDonald's fantasies for children, the writers in this volume discuss and develop such topics as MacDonald's Platonism, his theology, his mythopoeia, his psychology of the self, his social concerns, his reflections on literature and language, his influences, his Scottishness, and his universality. The MacDonald who emerges from these pages is a writer of impressive sophistication and subtlety, unlike the rather rustic and intuitive figure set before the public in C. S. Lewis's various descriptions of MacDonald. MacDonald's worth resides not only in his religiosity, but also in his literary skill. In this we may catch a hint of one of this book's dominant themes: MacDonald's deft ability to conjoin apparently disparate aspects. His work is both didactic and symbolic, clear and puzzling, realistic and fantastic, introverted and extroverted, personal and social. Such oppositions suggest MacDonald's dialectic method.

Stephen Prickett's "The Two Worlds of George MacDonald," as the title makes clear, sets out these oppositions. Prickett writes of MacDonald's life experiences in Scotland and later in England, and he connects biographical detail to MacDonald's use of myth and language in his fantasies *At the Back of the North Wind, The Princess and the Goblin,* and *Lilith*. Drawing on the work of the philosopher Douglas Berggren, Prickett argues that MacDonald stretches "us between literally impossible alternatives in order to discover a new meaning, which is neither." Prickett nicely introduces us to MacDonald the man and MacDonald the writer.

The second essay, Michael Mendelson's "The Fairy Tales of George MacDonald and the Evolution of a Genre," eschews biography in order to present an overview of MacDonald's fantasy for children. The emphasis is on the form of the stories, MacDonald's transformation of traditional motifs to conform to his unique vision. Mendelson argues that MacDonald both preserved and modernized the traditional fairy tale, and in doing so he created a "new mythus." Like Prickett, Mendelson is acutely aware of MacDonald's "double" thinking in his "blend of tradition and personalization." Although ranging over MacDonald's fantasy work, Mendelson focuses most closely on "The Light Princess," "The Golden Key," and *The Princess and the Goblin.* The third essay, my own "The Community of the Centre: Structure and Theme in *Phantastes,*" deals with this same theme of duality in a strictly formal sense. Form is meaning in *Phantastes.* I chose to include this essay because *Phantastes* is MacDonald's first fantasy and it contains virtually all the motifs and images that appear in his later works. I also note that the Everyman edition of 1915 places it among works "For Children."

The essay by Nancy Willard might seem to shift the focus to the mythic resonances of MacDonald's work, but this essay too examines MacDonald's "two worlds." In this case, the two worlds are the worlds of Christian piety and pagan deities. In her examination of the goddess figure in MacDonald's work, Willard touches on "The Golden Key," *The Princess and the Goblin, The Princess and Curdie,* and *The Lost Princess.* The next essay, by A. Waller Hastings, offers the only extended treatment we have of MacDonald's short story, "Cross Purposes." Also, Hastings's focus is social rather than psychological or spiritual; this is rare in studies of MacDonald. Informing this essay is Jack Zipes's contention that the condition-of-England question found a distinct discourse in the Victorian fairy tale (*Victorian Fairy Tales* xi), but Hastings finds the story problematic because it offers no specific vision of social change. Implicit in the discussion is an awareness of our theme: MacDonald's two worlds here are not only reality and fairyland, but also working class and upper class.

Whereas my essay on structure in *Phantastes* suggests a neatness to the book's ending, rounding as it does to the beginning, forming a closed circle, Cynthia Marshall's splendid essay on "The Golden Key" demonstrates MacDonald's parabolic method in which endings are deferred. Comparing "The Golden Key" with the parable of the hired laborers in Matthew (20:1-16), Marshall argues that MacDonald's story presents the reader with the means of interpreting its discourse and in the process teaches one to appreciate the experience of reading rather than reaching irritably after fact and meaning. The meaning is the reading experience itself, not some transcendental meaning exterior to the story.

In contrast to this exercise in the subversion of meaning, Celia Anderson's "The Golden Key: Milton and MacDonald" sets out to find a source for MacDonald's images and ideas in Milton's *Comus*. Anderson acknowledges the importance of the German Romantic writers to MacDonald, but she notes that commentators have paid little attention to the "pervasive influence" of Milton on MacDonald. Her focus is "The Golden Key" and *Comus*. After tracing the echoes of *Comus* in MacDonald's story, Anderson concludes that "The Golden Key" offers "an interpretation of Milton's masque that anticipates much modern commentary."

In his essay on the two worlds in MacDonald, Prickett briefly discusses MacDonald's Platonism. This topic receives extended commentary in Frank Riga's "The Platonic Imagery of George MacDonald and C. S. Lewis: The Allegory of the Cave Transfigured." Riga documents Lewis's debt to MacDonald and points out how their thought reflects Platonic ideas. As his title indicates, however, Riga is careful to show how both MacDonald and Lewis Christianize Plato's ideas, especially as they appear in the famous passage on the cave in *The Republic*. His desire is to show how the claims of the flesh and the spirit are reconciled in MacDonald and Lewis, and in this he hearkens to this book's recurrent theme: MacDonald's two worlds. He discusses the following works by MacDonald: "The Shadows," "The Golden Key," "The Lost Princess," *At the Back of the North Wind, Lilith,* and "The History of Photogen and Nycteris." And he discusses the following works of fiction by Lewis: *The Voyage of the Dawn Treader, The Last Battle,* and *Out of the Silent Planet.*

Following Riga's expansive essay are three on *At the Back of the North Wind*. The first is William Raeper's "Diamond and Kilmeny: MacDonald, Hogg, and the Scottish Folk Tradition." Raeper outlines Hogg's *Kilmeny,* one of three works MacDonald mentions in *At the Back of the North Wind* as providing glimpses of the country at North Wind's back (the other two are not works, but writers: Herodotus and Dante). Then he argues for the Scottishness of both Hogg's and MacDonald's imaginations; in doing this Raeper begins the work called for by David Robb in his book, *George MacDonald:* "Scottish critics still have to grapple with his fantasy works and works for children—becoming familiar with them and relating them to the longer reaches of Scottish writing" (131). The same cannot be said for my essay, "Language and Secret Knowledge in *At the Back of the North Wind,*" which analyzes the book as a book that deals with poetry as a way of knowing. The connection here is to Marshall's essay on "The Golden Key"; both deal with what we might refer to as MacDonald's prescient postmodernist spirit. The third essay on *At the Back of the North Wind,* Lesley Smith's "Old Wine in New Bottles: Aspects of Prophecy in George MacDonald's *At the Back of the North Wind,*" offers a nice contrast to the preceding two essays. Smith illustrates the connections between MacDonald's book and Old Testament prophecy, especially as it manifests itself in the Book of Daniel. Unlike either McGillis or Marshall, Smith sees MacDonald's work as fundamentally teleological; the book promises the reader, she argues, an end to strife and a future in which each shall rest.

The next two essays are about MacDonald's "Princess" books, and they offer contrasting views. The first, Nancy-Lou Patterson's "*Kore* Motifs in *The Princess and the Goblin,*" places the book in the context of the Persephone myth as it appears in the Homeric Hymns and argues that its theme is Irene's coming of age, her assumption of maturity and of her mother's identity. The daughter becomes the mother while at the same time she gains her independence. This contrasts with Joseph Sigman's Jungian reading of the "Princess" books as the story of Curdie's coming of age. Whereas Irene's individuation is accomplished within the unconscious and within the domestic sphere, Curdie's ego finds its identity in a balance between unconscious and social realities. The apocalyptic ending of *The Princess and Curdie,* far from being an indication of MacDonald's pessimistic view of mankind, is rather indicative of his sense of the integrated personality, the personality in which the ego unites with "the body of the divinity"; such integration is possible only upon the sacrifice of the ego. Such a view directly disagrees with the many writers who see *The Princess and Curdie* as a failure of MacDonald's imagination, as a sign that in despair MacDonald envisages evil triumphing in the end (e.g. Wolff 176).

The penultimate essay in this collection, Cordelia Sherman's "The Princess and the Wizard: The Fantasy Worlds of Ursula K. LeGuin and George MacDonald," argues for the similarity of worldview between the nineteenth-century Christian and the twentieth-century "non-Christian." Although their depiction of ego integration is similar, each has a distinct view of evil: for MacDonald, evil is interior and must be exorcised; for LeGuin, it is external and must be embraced.

MacDonald's spirituality is the subject of the final essay, Melba Battin's "Duality Beyond Time: George MacDonald's 'The Wise Woman, or The Lost Princess: A Double Story.'" This essay not only rescues "The Lost Princess" from the familiar charge that it contains too much cruelty, but it also turns once again to the theme of duality. Battin focuses on MacDonald's "concern with the inner and outer, the spiritual and the physical." Her interest is in how MacDonald reconciles the claims of these apparently opposed aspects of the self in order to clarify "some of the steps necessary for spiritual growth."

In total, then, the essays collected here touch on all but one of MacDonald's fantasies for children (I refer to "The Giant's Heart," although we have no discussion of "Little Daylight," a story included in *At the Back of the North Wind*). They begin with an overview of MacDonald's life in relationship to his work and an overview of his children's fantasy, and then proceed in a loosely chronological order from *Phantastes* (1858) to the "Princess" books (first book publication in 1872 and 1883) to *The Lost Princess* (1875). Implicit in all the essays is the sense that MacDonald wrote for a mature audience. Few of the writers here acknowledge the child reader of MacDonald's work; they implicitly suggest what Hastings states clearly: "The fairy tales were aimed at both middle-class children and the adults who bought or read the stories to those children." If, however, Jacqueline Rose is right in arguing that children's literature by its very nature views the child as an outsider (the child does not create the books he or she reads) and tries to draw him in, then we ought at least be able to discern MacDonald's attempt to seduce his child-reader (Rose 1-11). His appeal to the child is perhaps most evident in *The Princess and the Goblin,* where he uses many familiar techniques that connect his story to the oral tradition: questions to the reader, personal asides, sound effects, colloquial turns of phrase, and so on. In all this, MacDonald never pretends to close the distance between his adult narrator and his child reader the way Tolkien, for instance, does in *The Hobbit.* MacDonald's stories for children are spoken from an adult point of view which demands the child puzzle and think as he or she reads.

Introduction 7

As an example of MacDonald's method in writing for the young, I offer his story "The Giant's Heart," the one story for children not discussed in any of the essays in this volume. Wolff remarks on the story's "terrifying and cruel ideas and images" (125), and he concludes that it "must be voted nauseous" (126). Reis uses the word "repellent" in his very brief reference to this story (81), and Raeper finds it "uncomfortable reading" because of its violence and lack of coherence (316). It has always appeared to be one of MacDonald's lesser achievements, its importance lying in its clear connection to folklore. The story of a giant who keeps his heart hidden outside his body is familiar to students of folklore. As Wolff points out, Stith Thompson classifies this type of story as "External Soul" and numbers it "E710" in his *Motif Index of Folk Literature* (11, 493; *see* Wolff 398, n. 10). But the story has the virtue of showing clearly how MacDonald approached the children's story, and he also offers his own comment on it in its first appearance in his novel *Adela Cathcart* (1864).

Briefly, the story recounts the adventure of a brother and sister who find themselves unexpectedly in Giantland threatened by the giant, Thunderthump. What comes to mind is "Jack and the Beanstalk"; both stories contain a giant who likes a little human flesh for supper. With the help of the giant's wife and later a bird and many spiders, the children outwit the giant, and after finding his heart, they dispatch him when the boy, Buffy-Bob, stabs the heart with his knife. This very brief summary should show that the story conforms to many folklore tales: children are separated from home, confront threats from a villain (in this case the giant), use their wits in conjunction with help from nature, and defeat the villain. The success of the Brothers Grimm and others in reaching a child audience in the nineteenth century with similar stories must lead us to conclude that for MacDonald at least "The Giant's Heart" is a fairly typical story for children.

In tone, too, "The Giant's Heart" contains indications that the implied reader is a child. The narrator carefully explains the actions and details of the story and draws the reader in with the second person pronoun: "You would have thought you saw the whole earth through the door when he opened it, so wide was it; and when he closed it, it was like nightfall" (*Complete Fairy Tales* 66). He also meets implied objections from his audience: "I refer anyone who doubts this part of my story to certain chronicles of Giantland preserved among the Celtic nations. It was quite a common thing for a giant to put his heart out to nurse . . . " (70). Language and syntax are not difficult, and the similes throughout the story draw on that with which any child will be familiar. MacDonald also uses simile to relieve anxiety; when Tricksey-Wee first encounters a giant, she sees "a huge face, with spectacles as big as the round windows in a church" (65). Throughout the story, MacDonald's prose sounds with the rhythms of oral speech: "It stood in a plain alone, and shot right up, I don't know how many thousand feet, into the air, a long, narrow, spearlike mountain" (79).

But of course "The Giant's Heart" is not a folktale. One of the first things a reader of folktales notices is that the children in this story do not return home. No family reunion occurs. The two children, Tricksey-Wee and Buffy-Bob, do not cross the border back to their own land; the story ends in Giantland. Few folktales, if any, begin in one world and move to another. Here is the beginning of "The Giant's Heart": "There was once a giant who lived on the borders of Giantland where it touched on the country of common people" (65). "There was once" sounds comfortingly reassuring; this is a conventional fairy tale beginning which welcomes both child and adult reader. But what is this about the "borders of Giantland"? Where are these borders? In the story "Cross Purposes," MacDonald provides an answer: "No mortal, or fairy either, can tell where Fairyland begins and where it ends. But somewhere on the borders of Fairyland there was a nice country village, in which lived some nice country-people" (*Complete Fairy Tales* 188). If we assume for the moment that Giantland and Fairyland are the same, then we can conclude that the borders (why plural?) between this land and our reality do exist, people live near them, but no one knows where they are. Paradox. We might also conclude that Giantland's borders touch on the country of uncommon people as well as of common people. Who are the common people, and who are the uncommon people? Furthermore, what does the narrator mean by "common people"? Obviously one meaning is "ordinary folks" like you and me, the kind of people we meet everyday. The same cannot be said about giants and fairies. And yet MacDonald uses the word "common" elsewhere to mean of inferior quality or vulgar (see, for example, *The Princess and the Goblin* 12). Are the children in this story ordinary children, or are they vulgar and in need of improvement? To choose the latter possibility is to read the story as a rite of passage in which the two children, cut off from the familiar, mature and take control of their own lives. The allusion to Matthew 10:39 when Tricksey-Wee runs into the wood to look for her brother at the beginning of the story supports such a reading. But Tricksey-Wee and Buffy-Bob, true to the implications of their names, are pretty much the same at the end of the story as they were at the beginning; Tricksey-Wee is a trickster and Buffy-Bob is a buffeter, given to violence. At the beginning, she tricks him and he boxes her on the ear; at the end, she tricks the giant and he stabs the giant's heart. Still and all, I find it difficult to decide whether the children are more common than the giant, who will wear nothing but white socks on Sundays and who eats little children, albeit "*very* little ones" (65). Surely MacDonald's point has something to do with the commonness of such hypocrisy.

Finally, why does MacDonald begin his story with detail that suggests two different worlds and then not return the children to their world at the end? We might argue that the story is over when the giant dies and that the children obviously make their way home safely. But this is to conjecture beyond what the end of the story gives us. Both the beginning and ending depart from what we have come to expect from a fairy tale. This is the clue to MacDonald's method in all his stories: he creates situations with which we are familiar, and then he confounds our expectations. For example, many readers (many adult readers, that is) look for a moral in fairy tales in order to feel comfortable with such reading material for their young. "The Giant's Heart" complies with this expectation. In fact it does so several times with the result that the reader will have a difficult time feeling comfortable that this story offers a coherent and safe moral message for the young.

First we have the familiar folktale situation which presents two children, who loosely represent the "good" characters juxtaposed with the giant, who is the "bad" character. Also familiar is the character of the giant's wife who has sympathy for the children and tries to help them. In both sets of characters we have familiar gender-specific traits: Tricksey-Wee is the instinctive child, Buffy-Bob the aggressive one. Similarly, the giant's wife is gentle and domestic, the giant loud and brutal. The male is active, the female passive. MacDonald depicts these stereotypes often in his fiction: Curdie and Irene in the "Princess" books, Photogen and Nycteris in "The Day Boy and the Night Girl," and Mossy and Tangle in "The Golden Key," for example. But, as Cynthia Marshall has pointed out in her analysis of "The Day Boy and the Night Girl," MacDonald uses binary opposites in order to transcend the very thinking that such opposites suggest (*see* Marshall). Buffy-Bob may well be the more violent of the two children, but he is decidedly not the more active nor the more intelligent. Throughout their adventure, Tricksey-Wee takes the lead; she makes suggestions and decisions, while Buffy-Bob quietly goes along with his sister. The narrator tells us that Buffy-Bob "seldom said anything else than *All Right*" (71). In short, the female has the dominant role here, not the male. Further, the giant refuses to allow his wife to care for his heart, arguing that "the responsibility would be too much for *you*. You would no longer be my darling, light-hearted, airy, laughing Doodlem" (71). As his implicit metaphor suggests, the giant thinks of his wife as light-headed and frivolous, while we see her as a cooking and sewing domestic drudge careworn by the activities and eating habits of her husband. Clearly, the giant would have done well to have given his heart over to his wife for protection. MacDonald encourages us to reconsider our attitudes to sex roles and sexual stereotyping.

But what about the good guys and the bad guys? We are asked to support the two children and cheer the defeat of the giant. However, MacDonald complicates this neat moral duality in several ways. In an exchange between Tricksey-Wee and the giant's wife in which Tricksey-Wee's childlike innocence is apparent, the giant's wife remarks that her husband is "fond of little children, particularly little girls." Tricksey-Wee feels relief: "Oh, then he won't hurt me." To this the giant's wife replies: "I am not sure of that. He is so fond of them that he eats them up; and I am afraid that he couldn't help hurting you a little. He's a very good man though" (66). As a giant, Thunderthump cannot help hurting little girls; it is his nature to eat them. Like the spiders we meet later in the story, Thunderthump eats nothing "but what is mischievous or useless" (80). In a passage reminiscent of *Alice's Adventures in Wonderland* ("The Giant's Heart" has other hints of *Alice*), we learn that the giant's wife comforts herself by rationalizing that the children her husband eats are in reality "only little pigs pretending to be boys and girls" (67). The giant's wife assures Tricksey-Wee that her husband is a "good man." As a matter of fact, we have reason to believe this is true because a little later in the story we learn that he does not condone lying and that he "always kept his word" (69). The boys he eats have "fat faces and goggle eyes" and are wretched not simply because the giant has captured them, but because "they knew if they could only keep from eating, and grow thin, the giant would dislike them and turn them out to find their way home; but notwithstanding this, so greedy were they, that they ate as much as ever they could hold" (67). We might conclude that their fate is punishment for their greed. Not only this, but one of the boys informs the giant as to the hiding place of Tricksey-Wee and Buffy-Bob. When the giant cannot find them, he pops the tattle-tale into a pot of boiling water. The reader must experience some confusion about whether this boy is punished for telling on other children or for lying. In other words, which morality is preferable: the giant's, which finds lying unacceptable, or the narrator's, which condemns tattling? Or do we accept both moral positions? Whichever position we take, we must side with the giant who punishes the little blighter. Anyway, the question of lying does not end here. As Wolff notes, Tricksey-Wee and Buffy-Bob are "liars too: they obtain vital information from the unsuspecting lark only by telling her the exact opposite of the truth" (125). If they are not exactly "liars," as Wolff asserts, they do refuse to tell Mrs. Lark their secret after she has told them hers. In short, MacDonald complicates our response to the characters and action of the story.

We might set this kind of close scrutiny aside as unnecessarily picky, especially in light of the story's end in which the giant obviously speaks duplicitously in his attempt to have Tricksey-Wee and Buffy-Bob return his heart to him. Here the villain receives his just reward when Buffy-Bob "buries his knife" in the giant's heart (86). Before we dismiss the story so easily, however, we would do well to notice how the characters in *Adela Cathcart* respond to it. A child listening to the story in that novel thanks the narrator:

"Thank you, dear Mr. Smith. I will be good. It was a very nice story. If I was a man, I would kill all the wicked people in the world. But I am only a little girl, you know; so I can only be good."

The darling did not know how much more one good woman can do to kill evil than all the swords of the world in the hands of righteous heroes (quoted in Wolff, 125).

Wolff comments only that here MacDonald gives his story a moral. But what is the moral? The little girl appears to accept the conventional moral assigned to fairy tales: evil is and should be eradicated violently. She also appears to accept a patriarchal definition of herself as only a girl and in consequence she is good but ineffectual. MacDonald's narrator (not Smith, the narrator of the story in *Adela Cathcart*) challenges the girl's interpretation when he suggests that a woman might well be more powerful than a man. In other words, he implicitly criticizes Buffy-Bob, who wields the sword of righteousness in the story. The males in "The Giant's Heart" do not trust the females and the result is painful, even sad. When the giant dies, Tricksey-Wee "could not help being sorry for him, after all" (86). We might now understand that the children do not return to their home country because they are not ready to return. "The Giant's Heart" might well not be a story about maturation or ego integration or restored harmony or however we might like to articulate our sense of a fulfilled quest, a closed system.

And what about the tale's violence, thought so excessive by many commentators? Rather than simply a tasteless exercise in Victorian brutality, "The Giant's Heart" sounds to me like a delightful flaunting of convention. We all know the tales of the Brothers Grimm have offended conventional morality with their red-hot shoes and casks of nails and bleeding heels and sliced-off toes, but MacDonald takes such images and suggestions to the extreme. The giant likes his little children pickled, and he prefers them "crisp, as radishes, whether forked or not, ought to be eaten" (69). Just as the giant really sticks it to the goggle-eyed boys, MacDonald really sticks it to the reader, or at least to the reader who will wince at such descriptions. I suspect that MacDonald here is speaking to his child reader the way Roald Dahl speaks to his. Writer and child reader delight in the subversive use of violence. Glenn Sadler has suggested that this story is about "spiritual conversion," and that the giant is "made to repent" (375-376). A detail he does not notice, but one which might go some way to corroborating his interpretation, is MacDonald's use of the word *anoint* to describe Tricksey-Wee's use of the spider's juice to shrink the giant's heart (82). It is a strange anointment, however. It causes extreme pain. And of course the giant does not repent; he merely pretends to repent in order to get his heart away from the children. MacDonald's mood is playful, irreverent, and subversive.

I spoke earlier of the story departing from what we expect of a fairy tale; I want now to scrutinize this "we." Clearly, the story does speak to an adult audience in its satire of Victorian disingenuous piety and its parody of religious conversion. I'm not certain, but I suspect not many children would catch the pun on "stalked" when right after the children have hidden in what they take to be a "brake" (in reality, the giant's broom), the giant stalks into the room (66). And perhaps the most subtle of MacDonald's jokes will reach only a few readers. Near the end, when the children have the giant's heart and force him to release all the children in his possession, the giant complies and assures his tormentors that he has released every child. "That's a lie," squeaks a little voice from within one of the giant's pockets. Tricksey-Wee squeezes some spider juice on the giant's heart and remarks: "You're not a gentleman. You tell stories" (85). Gentlemen do not tell stories. What, then, does this say of George MacDonald, who tells the story "The Giant's Heart"? Also, how do we assess stories which are associated here with lies? Lies are shown to be unacceptable in this story, and yet stories are lies. MacDonald has fun not only with Victorian conventional expectations, but he also has fun at his own expense.

But this does not mean that the story is closed or does not speak to a child audience. It does. Most children will appreciate a story in which a child (or children) defeats an adult authority figure. The children's interaction with birds and spiders is also meant to capture the child reader's sense of wonder. Most important is the complicity between MacDonald the narrator and child reader that I spoke of earlier when I wrote of this story's use of violence. The story speaks of secrets, secrets both shared and kept. Although this story, like all stories, keeps some secrets to itself, it also shares others with its various readers. Those readers, both child and adult, will take from the story what they will; some will find the story either repellent or puzzling, others will find it comic and liberating. Only equals may laugh, and the child and adult who laugh at the histrionics of Thunderthump are equals. As Bakhtin tells us, "hypocrisy and lies never laugh" (95) and this is why neither the children nor the giant in "The Giant's Heart" laugh. They take themselves too seriously; we laugh at them.

Laughter, parody, and satire feature in many of MacDonald's children's works: "The Light Princess," the "Princess" books, and "Cross Purposes." They function to bring readers together into a community, a true community which exists without authority or power. Child reader and adult reader appreciate the release from fact and reason and the subversive commentary on the reality they inhabit outside the stories. Just as the reading experience in the Victorian household was often for the whole family, so are MacDonald's stories. His readership, MacDonald declares, is the childlike of whatever age. "Childlike" in this context means open to new experience, nonjudgmental, and dispossessive. MacDonald's stories, if listened to with unblinded ear, will delight, amuse, and perhaps even teach our children and their parents too.

Works Cited

Bakhtin, Mikhail. *Rabelais and His World.* Trans. Helene Iswolsky. Bloomington, IN: Indiana UP, 1984.

MacDonald, George. *Adela Cathcart.* 1864. London: Edwin Dalton, 1908.

_____. *Complete Fairy Tales.* Intro. Roger Lancelyn Green. New York: Schocken, 1977.

_____. *A Dish of Orts.* London: Sampson, Low, Marston, 1895.

_____. *The Princess and the Goblin; The Princess and Curdie.* Oxford: World's Classics-OUP, 1990.

Marshall, Cynthia. "Allegory, Orthodoxy, Ambivalence: MacDonald's 'The Day Boy and the Night Girl'," *Children's Literature* 16 (1988): 57-75.

Page, H. A. "Children and Children's Books," *Contemporary Review* 11 (1869): 7-26.

Raeper, William. *George MacDonald.* Icknield Way, Tring, Herts.: Lion, 1987.

Reis, Richard. *George MacDonald.* New York: Twayne, 1972.

Robb, David. *George MacDonald.* Edinburgh: Scottish Academic Press, 1987.

Rose, Jacqueline. *The Case of Peter Pan or the Impossibility of Children's Fiction.* London: Macmillan, 1984.

Sadler, Glenn Edward. "George MacDonald." *Writers for Children.* Ed. Jane Bingham. New York: Scribner's, 1988, 373-380.

Salmon, Edward. *Literature For the Little Ones.* London: Henry J. Drane, 1888.

Shavit, Zohar. *Poetics of Children's Literature*. Athens, GA: U of Georgia P, 1986.
Thompson, Stith. *Motif Index of Folk Literature*. Vol. 11. Bloomington, IN: Indiana UP, 1956.
Tolkien, J. R. R. *The Hobbit*. New York: Ballantine, 1966.
Wolff, Robert Lee. *The Golden Key: A Study of the Fiction of George MacDonald*. New Haven: Yale UP, 1961.
Zipes, Jack. *Victorian Fairy Tales*. New York and London: Methuen, 1987.

The Two Worlds of George MacDonald

By Stephen Prickett

"You would have me then understand, Mr. Raven," I said, "that you go through my house into another world, heedless of disparting space?"

"That I go through it is an incontrovertible acknowledgement of space," returned the old librarian.

"Please do not quibble, Mr Raven," I rejoined. "Please to take my question as you know I mean it."

"There is in your house a door, one step through which carries me into a world very much another than this."

"A better?"

"Not throughout; but so much another that most of its physical, and many of its mental laws are different from those of this world" (*Phantastes and Lilith* 220).

This idea of two worlds co-existing in time and space, superimposed upon one another, and yet—except for the occasional mysterious "doorway"—totally invisible to one another is one of the most persistent themes of George MacDonald's fantasy writing. It is central to the action of *Phantastes,* his first prose work, and it is no less important in *Lilith,* his last—from where the above passage was drawn. The passage from *Lilith* is interesting, not least for its technical functions both within the narrative and in the reader's relationship with that "world."

Mr. Vane, the protagonist, has discovered a manuscript written by his father in which he describes a conversation with Mr. Raven, the elusive figure who seems at one and the same time to be librarian, bird, sexton, and finally, our forefather Adam. The conversation parallels Vane's own conversations with Mr. Raven, but also goes beyond them in their metaphysical probing. Vane's father, for example, is more curious than his son about the relationship of the two worlds, but, as we have seen, the answers he receives are, to say the least, enigmatic.

This manuscript has several purposes in the narrative of *Lilith*. One of its most important is to assure Vane that he is not alone. Not unnaturally, the sudden discovery that he is poised in some mysterious way between this world and another, where in order to live he must sleep the sleep of death, is highly disconcerting. What the manuscript demonstrates to him is that this experience is neither as new, nor as unique, as he had at first supposed. Mr. Raven's contention that all men must sooner or later enter his house is substantiated by at least the knowledge that Vane's father did. Similarly, if we were typical Victorian novel readers, we would ourselves have borrowed the book from a library, so we are placed in an analogous position—poised between our own lives and the world of fiction in the book before us.

MacDonald himself was acutely conscious of being poised between two worlds in both his life and in his writings. If his peculiar gift as a writer was to see, and to make others see, that to live in two juxtaposed worlds is not an accident of spiritual geography or a psychological quirk, but part of man's normal conditions of existence, that insight was rooted simply enough in his own personal environment. England was, for him, a long way from home.

It is easy for a North American reader, used to the vast distances of the continent, to forget the even vaster cultural gulf between MacDonald's childhood home in Huntley, Aberdeenshire, and his environment as a writer first in Hastings, then on the Sussex coast, and then in London. Huntly and London are only five hundred miles apart, but they represent two nations, two cultures, and two religions. In the vivid phrase of a recent critic, MacDonald has grown up "in a traditional rural atmosphere, compounded of Calvinist hellfire, oatcakes, horsemanship, agricultural virtues, and exploration of neighbourhood ruins and wildernesses" (Reis 21).

MacDonald's upbringing was, in many ways, typical for a poor rural Scottish boy of the period. He grew up within a religious and educational system far removed from Anglican or English equivalents of the day. In one respect, at least, it was far superior to anything he would have been likely to have found in England. The

Scottish education system in the early and mid- nineteenth century was one of the best in Europe. Until the beginning of the nineteenth century Scotland had five universities to England's two. MacDonald was able to go on from his local school to the University of Aberdeen, where, in 1845, he gained his M.A. in Chemistry and Natural Philosophy (as Physics was then called).

Yet even within this background there were elements suggestive of the tensions and conflict that were to shape his life. Though his upbringing had been Calvinist, he did not wholly belong to the Calvinist ethos. His grandfather had been a Catholic, Gaelic-speaking Highlander—a representative of a very different emotional and intellectual tradition from that of either strict Calvinism or the more urbane Scottish Enlightenment. The ruins of the old faith and of clan warfare—the romantic abbeys and castles—were a part of George MacDonald's childhood landscape; and what, in the rest of his family, was no more than a slightly fey streak, was to blossom in MacDonald into a fully elaborated mysticism. But even here the contradictions obtrude themselves. The image of the poor-but-earnest scholarship boy entering university on a bursary is rapidly displaced by the record of financial extravagance that was to be a recurring problem throughout his life. If we are to read the accounts of similar situations in his novels as being autobiographical (as at least some of his biographers have done), his chronic overspending was helped by hard drinking and the Aberdeen brothels. Certainly we know that in 1842 he was forced to leave the university for a time in order to earn more money.

When, after some kind of spiritual crisis in 1847, MacDonald decided to seek ordination, it was not to the Scottish Presbyterians, but to England and the Congregationalists that he turned; and in 1848 he entered Highbury College, in London, as a theological student. In addition to his formal theological studies, he was also an avid reader of German, a rare accomplishment in England, where, only twenty years earlier, it was said there were only two men in the University of Oxford who could read it. This Scottish erudition was from the start to arouse the gravest suspicions of the elders of his first church at Arundel, in Sussex. In fact, it does not seem to have been German theology so much as German poetry that attracted him. His first published work was a translation of *Twelve Spiritual Songs* by the German Romantic poet, Novalis. He was also reading other mystics at this time, including William

Blake, and finding through the painting of Turner a visual confirmation in nature for his own growing mystical intuitions.

It was from this background, then, that George MacDonald came to Arundel in 1850. But before he could take up residence, one other event intervened which was to have a lifelong impact on him. He was discovered to have tuberculosis. It was the first of many such attacks, and though he was to live through all of them and finally die at a ripe old age in 1905, he was for much of his life a semi-invalid, always conscious of death as a more or less immediate possibility. Tuberculosis was the family disease. His father and two brothers eventually died of it, as did four out of his eleven children. The disease was to have, moreover, a lasting effect on his literary as well as on his private sensibility. Some have speculated on possible connections between tuberculosis and literary talent—certainly an impressive number of nineteenth-century writers did suffer from the disease—but more to our point is the way in which it served to reinforce MacDonald's Calvinist lesson that "here is no abiding city"; that he lived as a wanderer on borrowed time, which was a debt too precious (or too heavy) not to repay with interest.

Though Sussex apparently offered him the security and salary he needed to get married, he came as an outsider, a sick Scot of poetical and mystical leanings, to take charge of English dissenters, lower middle-class and commercial in outlook and as rigidly Calvinist as any of the congregations MacDonald had left behind him in Aberdeenshire. Even in the first flush of enthusiasm, the gap between himself and his new flock was dauntingly obvious. In an early letter to his father, he wrote:

> The people are a simple people—not particularly well informed—mostly tradespeople—and in middling circumstances. They chiefly reside in the town, which has between two and three thousand inhabitants. There are none I could call society for me—but with my books now and the beautiful earth, and added to these soon, I hope, my wife—and above all that, God to care for me—in whom I and all things are—I do not much fear the want of congenial society ... (*George MacDonald and His Wife* 139).

Within three years it was to prove (in spite of his pious hopes) a recipe for disaster. To social and cultural differences were added doctrinal ones. At the final showdown, the deacons of the church charged him with three areas of "heresy." First, that he had been unwise enough to speculate about salvation for animals—though he had, modestly enough, added that this was "for all he knew." Second, and far worse, he had followed up this piece of liberal agnosticism by suggesting that the same dispensation might even be extended to the heathen. Finally, turning away from specifics altogether, the deacons declared MacDonald to be "tainted by German theology"—by which, interestingly enough, they seem to have meant not the bolder speculations of Eichhorn, Feuerbach, and Strauss, which, at about the same time, had destroyed the faith of George Eliot, but of whom they seem never to have heard, but simply that MacDonald had been translating Novalis—whose work today looks unexceptionably pietistic.

Thus that sense of inhabiting two worlds, so characteristic of all MacDonald's fantasy, is rooted, at any rate at the most obvious level, in the facts of his own outward existence. Though circumstances may have made his an extreme case, it was by no means a unique one. What *is* to my knowledge unique is not MacDonald's primary experience, but the aesthetic and philosophical use he was able to make of that experience in his fiction. In his Introduction to Greville MacDonald's life of his father, G. K. Chesterton singles out for especial praise one book

> ... that has made a difference to my whole existence, which helped me to see things in a certain way from the start; a vision of things which even so real a revolution as a change of religious allegiance has substantially only crowned and confirmed. Of all the stories I have read ... it remains the most real, the most realistic, in the exact sense of the phrase the most life like. It is called *The Princess and the Goblin (George MacDonald and His Wife* 9).

What, in particular, inspired Chesterton, and gave him such a sense of "realism" was precisely this sense of "two worlds." Elsewhere, in the *Victorian Age in Literature,* he spells it out more specifically:

> ... MacDonald, a Scot of genius as genuine as Carlyle's . . . could write fairy-stories that made all existence a fairy-tale.

> He could give the real sense that everyone had the end of an elfin thread that must at least lead them into Paradise (152).

In short, MacDonald offered a new way of writing in English. Certainly MacDonald's fairy tales resembled the conventional fairy story in their use of magic, and in the introduction of nonhuman beings, but they differed in that their mythological framework was made to serve a very subtle and highly structured literary purpose. Behind the magical beings of MacDonald's universes lie the philosophical and theological principles of a scheme that is as carefully worked out as that of Dante. Indeed, his references to Dante in *At the Back of the North Wind* make it clear that, almost unbelievably, he is inviting just such a comparison. When the little boy, Diamond, actually goes to "the back of the North Wind" we are told that one of the very few who had been there before him "was a great Italian of a noble family, who died more than five hundred years ago." His name was Durante, "and it means Lasting, for his books will last as long as there are enough men in the world worthy of having them" (87). It is quite clear from the descriptions that follow that the back of the North Wind is none other than the Earthly Paradise (*Purgatorio*, cantos xxviii-xxxiii). But it is not, I think, conceit that makes MacDonald deliberately invite comparison with one of the world's supreme allegorists. It is, rather, that he, like Chesterton, is seeking to establish himself within a literary tradition—a tradition not of folklore and primitive ritual, but of complex theological sophistication. Moreover, the comparison is not one of genre, but of content. MacDonald is attempting to open up and articulate areas of human experience that had been more or less dormant ever since the Renaissance. In the face of a predominantly empiricist and scientific culture, concerned to rationalize and, where possible, demythologize the long record of man's awareness of the numinous, MacDonald reasserts the *value* of myth and symbol, not as a primitive relic, nor simply as a literary device, but as a vital and irreplaceable medium of human consciousness. Religious experience is seen not as something to be reduced to psychological or physical terms in order to be articulated, but as itself *a new kind of articulateness*—a symbolic and myth-making activity that taps the very roots of human creativity.

Thus MacDonald's philosophy is inseparable from his theory of symbolism. At its simplest it reassembles the medieval idea of "correspondences" so prevalent also in Dante, but MacDonald's way of applying them is very unmedieval. Greville MacDonald noted a conversation in which his father once tried to explain his ideas on symbolism.

> He would allow that the algebraic symbol, which concerns only the three dimensioned, has no *substantial* relation to the unknown quantity; nor the "tree where it falleth" to the man unredeemed, the comparison being false. But the rose, when it gives some glimmer of the freedom for which a man hungers, does so because of its *substantial* unity with the man, each in degree being a signature of God's immanence. To a spiritual pilgrim the flower no longer seems a mere pretty design on the veil, "the cloak and cloud that shadows me from Thee" for see! she opens her wicket into the land of poetic reality, and he, passing through and looking gratefully back, then knows her for his sister the Rose, of spiritual substance one with himself. So may even a gem, giving from its heart reflections of heavenly glory, awaken like memory in ourselves and send our eyes upwards. So also may we find co-substance between the stairs of a cathedral-spire and our own "secret stair" up to the wider vision—the faculty of defying the "plumb-line of gravity" (*George MacDonald and His Wife* 482).

Clearly this owes much to Coleridge's idea of a symbol—and MacDonald was always quick to acknowledge his debt to Coleridge. For Coleridge a symbol was essentially bifocal; its characteristic quality was that it belonged simultaneously to two different planes of existence, so that it revealed the "Special in the Individual . . . the General in the Especial, or . . . the Universal in the General. Above all . . . the translucence of the Eternal in and through the Temporal" (*The Statesman's Manual* 28-30). In other words, the *defining* quality of a "symbol" in Coleridge's sense was that it brought two separate worlds into relationship with one another. Here, undoubtedly, is one of the roots of MacDonald's two worlds, but there are others no less important. Like MacDonald's, Coleridge's thought is at once Christian and Platonic. But there is a quality shared by MacDonald and Plato that is less evident in

Coleridge: the former were both mystics of a particular kind. Whereas for Coleridge, one feels, the rose could be a symbol of divine purity, for MacDonald, as we have seen, that divine purity, when we finally encounter it, as it were face-to-face, is none other than "our sister the rose": not an abstraction, but a Form more concrete and real than the early abstraction we were anticipating. Similarly, for MacDonald, it is the role of the gem not simply to inspire us, but to awaken within us memories that we have in some sense *always* possessed. We recognize at once the Platonic "recognition" theme running through this, but there is a difference between MacDonald and the earlier Platonists. Whereas for Plato and Dante alike the perception of spiritual truth was a collective process, involving what was common to mankind, for MacDonald, living in and belonging to the world of nineteenth-century individualism, we climb our own "secret stair" to the wider vision. In making this change, MacDonald has, in effect, recognized that a quite fundamental shift of human sensibility has taken place more or less within his own lifetime. The relationship between man and nature had undergone a profound transformation, and this transformation had in turn been mirrored by changes in language. Owen Barfield has observed in this connection what he calls "a sharp divergence in the behaviours of two broad classes of words":

> Of those which refer to nature, or what we now call nature we observe that *the further back we go,* the more they appear to connote sentience or inwardness. Of those on the other hand which refer to human consciousness, the opposite is the case, and their meaning, if I may put it so, becomes more and more outward. Nature, as expressed in words, has moved in the course of time from inwardness to outwardness; consciousness, as expressed in words, has moved from outwardness to inwardness ("The Nature of Meaning" 38).

In an earlier work, entitled *Saving the Appearances,* Barfield had outlined what he saw as the corresponding change in human consciousness that accompanied this historic and irreversible shift of meaning:

> The elimination of original participation involves a contraction of human consciousness from periphery to centre a contradiction from the cosmos of wisdom to something like purely brain activity but by the same token it involves an *awakening*. For we wake, out of universal into self-consciousness. Now a process of awakening can be retrospectively surveyed by the sleeper only after his awakening is complete; for only then is he free enough of his dreams to look back on and interpret them. Thus, the possibility to look back at the history of the world and achieve a full waking picture of his own gradual emergence from original participation, really only arose for man . . . in the nineteenth century (*Saving the Appearances* 182-83).

In the past, myth and symbol had always been the natural vehicles for the expression of collective consciousness and the world of primal participation associated with it—so much that many nineteenth- and even some twentieth-century critics have taken it for granted that that was the only possible referential context for them. MacDonald, on the contrary, two generations before Freud or Jung, showed that myth and symbol could articulate a personal and inner world that differentiates individuals both from one another and from their environment. Nor is that comparison with Jung, of course, accidental. From, as it were, the other side of the fence, the early twentieth-century psychologists were in the process of following the new literary forms evolved in the previous century into a quite new view of the human psyche. The literary is always and of its very nature opposed to the reductionist. For MacDonald, the articulation of truth is in the end inseparable from a discovery of one's own individuality.

Thus Irene, in *The Princess and the Goblin,* has her own "secret stair" by which she comes to her great-great-grandmother in the attic. Lootie, her earthbound nurse, cannot find it, and even Curdie, though he can be made to ascend it, finds nothing for him at the top—only a heap of straw, an old tub, and a withered apple. He has, eventually, to find his own way to the grandmother; even the princess cannot help him there. There are direct autobiographical parallels to these two worlds in MacDonald's own mysticism and his sense of God in nature. Writing to him from Arundel, shortly after his resignation, his wife suddenly steps through cliche into something much more concrete and private when she moves from a description of a "sweet, sunny, breezy Sunday afternoon" to "our one tree . . . whispering most sweetly to me all about you, and Him who cares about both of us" (*George MacDonald and His Wife* 155).

But at another level we find that MacDonald's sense of two worlds affects the very structure of his metaphors themselves. Let us look at another example from *Lilith:*

> I saw no raven, but the librarian—the elderly man, in a rusty black coat, large in the body and long in the tails. I had seen only his back before; now for the first time I saw his face. It was so thin that it showed the shape of the bones under it, suggesting the skulls his last-claimed profession must have made him familiar with. But in truth I had never seen a face so alive, or a look so keen or so friendly as that in his pale blue eyes, which yet had a haze about them as if they had done much weeping.
>
> "I knew you were Mr. Raven," I replied: "but somehow I thought you a bird too!"
>
> "What made you think me a bird?"
>
> "You looked a raven, and I saw you dig worms out of the earth with your beak."
>
> "And then?"
>
> "Toss them in the air."
>
> "And then?"
>
> "They grew butterflies, and flew away."
>
> "Did you ever see a raven do that? I told you I was sexton!"
>
> "Does a sexton toss worms in the air, and turn them into butterflies?
>
> "Yes.
>
> "You saw me do it! —But I am still librarian in your house, for I never was dismissed, and never gave up the office. Now I am Librarian here as well."
>
> "But you have just told me you were sexton here!"
>
> "So I am. It is much the same profession. Except you are a true sexton, books are but dead bodies to you, and a library nothing but a catacomb!" (*Phantastes and Lilith* 210).

The symbolism of this passage, startling as it may seem at first sight, is not all that difficult to work out. The sexton buries men so that they may be raised to a more glorious resurrection: the sacrament of baptism is a ritual enactment of death and rebirth. Even books must be buried and raised to the glory of God; scholarship is otherwise mere meaningless pedantry—performed only as an ego trip for the wormlike academic. Mr. Raven is merely enacting, as a visible and concrete parable, an ancient biblical truth. But what interests me particularly here is not the traditional symbols or the way in which MacDonald is reusing them here, so much as the method by which he has tried to build into an event (a metaphorical event) the sense of two different systems in juxtaposition. The *whole point* of what Mr. Raven has been doing is that it does not make literal sense. We are forced to think round it, to search for some hidden meaning, which is altered itself by the context in the narrative.

I can best illustrate this by putting alongside that passage another quotation from a modern philosopher of language, Douglas Berggren:

> To construe life as a play or a dream is not only to organize or interpret life in different ways, but also to give plays and dreams a significance that they might otherwise not have ... Yet at the same time, if the initial differences between the two referents were not simultaneously preserved, even while the referents are also being transformed into closer alignment, the metaphorical character of the construing process would be lost. The possibility or comprehension of metaphorical construing requires, therefore, a peculiar and rather sophisticated intellectual ability which W. Bedell Standford metaphorically labels "stereoscopic vision": the ability to entertain two points of view at the same time. That is to say, the perspectives prior and subsequent to the transformation of the metaphor's principle and subsidiary subjects must both be cojointly maintained. It is precisely this transformation of both referents, moreover, interacting with their normal meanings, which makes it ultimately impossible to reduce completely the cognitive import of any vital metaphor to any set of univocal, literal, or non-tensional statements. For a special meaning, and in some cases even a new sort of reality, is achieved which cannot survive except at the intersection of the two perspectives which produced it (Berggren 243-244).

There is, Berggren argues, a whole area of human experience which can only be represented by the tensional language of metaphor—stretching us between literally impossible alternatives in order to discover a new meaning, which is neither. It is, in short, this "new sort of reality" only to be found "at the intersection of the two perspectives which produced it" that so interests MacDonald. It provides the central structure for almost every one of his fantasy novels. It has been the fashion in some quarters to decry the passing of the time when it was possible to hold a unified religious "world picture" in which all human knowledge could be integrated into a single, coherent whole, expressive of the greater glory of God. Though this is not the place to argue the point, I believe that such a view of the middle ages (or for that matter, the Renaissance) is simplistic and essentially ahistorical. Suffice it to say that this is not a viewpoint that would have greatly interested MacDonald. For him, (as for Dante), the world existed at the intersection of many perspectives and "languages," no one of which was complete or adequate in itself to describe the full richness of reality—a word to be employed without inverted commas. Allegory, myth, and symbolism are not the media of a unified world picture, but rather, technical literary devices for coming to terms with its essential incompleteness. As we have seen, their origins may lie in his own life and experience, in traditional theology, or in literary tradition, but if we stress too much the autobiographical or traditional aspects of such symbols, we are in danger of missing the very "stereoscopic" quality of MacDonald's writing that makes his metaphors so complex and, in the technical sense, so "modernist."

Works Cited

Barfield, Owen. "The Nature of Meaning," *Seven* 2 (1981): 32-43.
____. *Saving the Appearances*. New York: Harcourt, 1957.
Berggren, Douglas. "The Use and Abuse of Metaphor." *Review of Metaphysics* 16 (1962-63): 237-258.
Chesterton, G. K. *The Victorian Age in Literature*. London: Williams and Norgate, 1913.
Coleridge, S. T. *The Statesman's Manual*. in *Lay Sermons,* Ed. R. J. White. London: Routledge, 1972.
MacDonald, George. *At the Back of the North Wind*. New York:

Airmont, 1966.
———. *Phantastes and Lilith*. Grand Rapids, MI: Eerdmans, 1964.
MacDonald, Greville. *George MacDonald and His Wife*. London: Allen and Unwin, 1924.
Reis, Richard. *George MacDonald*. New York: Twayne, 1972.

The Fairy Tales of George MacDonald and the Evolution of a Genre

By Michael Mendelson

My intention here is to provide an overview of George MacDonald's fairy canon. I will approach this task by first examining the relation between these fairy tales and MacDonald's other literary output, most notably his critical essays and his adult fantasies. Following this general orientation, I will look more closely at narrative elements in three individual tales—"The Light Princess," "The Golden Key," and *The Princess and the Goblin*—that are indicative of MacDonald's fairy tale technique. In the process of this survey, I hope to explore the topology of MacDonald's fairyland and to identify the essential landmarks of the place in a way that will prepare for the more detailed analyses that follow. At the same time, however, I also hope to provide a clear indication of why I believe these tales occupy a distinctive place in the "modernization" of the fairy tale. Consequently, those narrative vignettes I have chosen to highlight are ones in which MacDonald incorporates, transforms, and invigorates the traditional motifs and structures of one of the oldest, most fundamental of all literary forms. I will suggest that these familiar narrative elements are here put to work in the service of a "new mythus," so that the fairy tale becomes a means of symbolic discourse in which MacDonald attempts to expound his own, unique vision.[1] My argument, then, is that the fairy tale as we find it in George MacDonald is an amalgamation of traditional elements and individual themes, and as such it is best approached with an awareness of both the traditions of the genre and the modern ideology that informs these "works of fancy and imagination."

I borrow the term "works of fancy and imagination" from an early collection of MacDonald's fairy fiction (1871) because it helps to distinguish the author's adventures in the realm of the marvelous from his realistic writings.

In any comprehensive edition of MacDonald's works of fancy, his two adult romances would certainly deserve a special place. The first of these adult tales is *Phantastes,* published in 1858 and subtitled "A Fairy Romance for Men and Women." It is filled with traditional fairy tale lore and yet it also initiates a strain of unique, mythopoetic symbolism that is undoubtedly MacDonald's most distinctive literary gift—a gift that will significantly expand the thematic scope of his fairy tales. *Phantastes* also marks the first appearance in MacDonald's work of the *Kunstmarchen,* or artistic fairy tale developed by writers such as Tiecké, Novalis, La Motte-Fouqué (the author of *Undine*), and E. T. A. Hoffmann of "Nutcracker" fame.

Unlike the authentic folk voice that the Grimms tried to recapture, the Romantic authors of the *Kunstmarchen* were fascinated by the mysteries of experience, the dark places of the mind, and the world beyond the finite; as such, they found in the inherent enchantment of the fairy tale a perfect vehicle for exploring our confrontation with the unknown.[2] In the process of this transformation of the traditional *marchen,* the impersonal narrator gives way to a more didactic, ideological voice, a voice that we can hear in all of MacDonald's work. But perhaps nowhere in his fantasies is this voice, with its full prophetic resonance, more robustly intoned than in *Lilith,* MacDonald's last piece of fairy fiction, written at the close of his career in 1895, and probably his magnum opus. This is again a "fairy romance [very much] for men and women," filled with witches, demons, and assorted cosmic phantasmagoria. And while the fairy mythology and narrative innovations of *Lilith* are beyond the scope of this essay, it is important to note that in this seminal work of modern fantasy it is the vocabulary of the fairy tale that provides MacDonald with the narrative language for his "rhetoric of the unreal."[3]

MacDonald's other, less fanciful opus is made up of realistic fiction, a good deal of poetry, some drama, criticism, and translation, along with an extensive series of sermons. Lest our present unfamiliarity with MacDonald as anything besides a fabulist create the wrong impression, it is worth noting that his novels and essayistic sermons earned him a very solid position in the contemporary pantheon of eminent Victorian writers. Of his two dozen realistic novels, the majority are set in rural Scotland, many have strong religious themes, and almost all have been for the most part forgotten. The theological concerns that help make these novels so ponderous came naturally to MacDonald, who took up his pen only after a brief career as a minister, a position he was forced to resign for such heterodox views as believing that animals have souls and that God could love a heathen. Throughout his long literary career, however, his strong religious views inform all of his writing, including his children's fiction—a fact that readers of *At the Back of the North Wind* (1872) are no doubt aware of. We will find this ministerial impulse in evidence in his fairy tales, as well.

Like his canon as a whole, MacDonald's essays fall into two separate groups: his immensely popular "unspoken sermons," and a much smaller number of literary and philosophical essays, two of which are of particular importance to students of his fairy tales.[4] The first of these is a short essay on "The Fantastic Imagination" (1893) that addresses the nature of fairy tales directly. The land of fairy, he maintains, is a strictly imaginative domain: "A little world of its own . . . with its own alternative laws," a world which, though invented, must be harmonious with the moral/ethical laws of the larger, real world. A paramount feature of this literary other world is that, once liberated from its ties to natural/physical law, its potential meanings expand beyond the singularity of the literal: fairyland thus turns out to be a metaphorical, polysemous place where "the truer the art the more things it will mean." Such multiplicity of meanings, MacDonald implies, should curb the tendency to reduce fairy tales to allegory. The particular power of this suggestiveness in fairy tales resides in their ability to wake what MacDonald calls "the forces that lie in the region of the uncomprehended." But unlike the Freudian world in which we live, where the uncomprehended is a realm of libidinal desire and chthonic fear, the unknown for MacDonald—while retaining much of its terror— is enclosed and protected by the divine. For "God sits," the unorthodox preacher maintains, "in that chamber of our being in which the candle of our consciousness goes out in darkness, and sends forth from thence wonderful gifts into the light of understanding. . . ." There is, then, a divine portent implicit in the marvelous events of fairy tales, and the wonder which these events stimulate can lead the imagination toward a kind of understanding that is otherwise ineffable.⁵

This overlapping of the creative and the divine imagination is the subject of MacDonald's more explicitly theological essay, "The Imagination: Its Function and Culture," in which he remarks that "we dare to claim for the true, childlike, humble imagination such an inward oneness with the laws of the universe that it possesses in itself insight into the very nature of things." In this philosophical context, the "kinder und haus" marchen so easily dismissed as narrative toys take on the elevated role of an epistemological tool that can lead the imagination beyond dull facts and the "passing vision" to that which is persistently true and eternal. Indeed, because fairy tales are not chained to the mundane and rational, they have a special license to follow the pattern of the "divine imagination" which uses symbols as its language and provides an archetype for the wonder of the childlike mind. Toward the end of this important essay, MacDonald calls attention to the "spiritual scaffolding" of any work of real vision, a framework that will allow the individual to climb up out of the dark wood and the witch's cave and enter that sanctified space where one's imagination is in harmony with "the highest form of its own operation," i.e. the divine order of things. For MacDonald, the creations of the fantastic imagination offer an unparalleled opportunity to climb the winding stair of consciousness. It is this kind of imaginative ascent that MacDonald's own fairy tales seek to promote.⁶

When we turn to the fairy tales, we find much of MacDonald's mature ideology reflected in these stories. But if MacDonald augments the fairy tale with his own intellectual and theological concerns, he also handles the basic narrative formula of the fairy story with a good deal of reverence. This blend of tradition and personalization is clearly in evidence in MacDonald's first fairy tale, "The Light Princess" (1864), a story based on "Sleeping Beauty" but with a bit of Hoffmann's "Princess Brambilla," a dash of Andersen's comic didacticism, and a good deal of original inventiveness thrown in as well.⁷ This eclecticism is, in itself, a good example of the break that modern, written fairy tales have made with the traditional, oral ones. For as Max Lüthi has repeatedly explained, early storytellers, while willing to transform particular motifs within traditional tales, did not seek to create a personalized tale connected specifically with any identifiable dogma.[8] But after the gentrification of the tales by Perrault and the French romanceurs after the "invention of childhood," and after the Romantic deification of originality, the traditional formulas are continually put to work in the service of a particular author's compelling interests. Like Andersen some decades before him, and unlike the Grimms, MacDonald is no literary archeologist working to uncover the bedrock of the tale; rather, he is interested in how he can adapt shards from earlier material into a new vessel capable of containing the wine of his own message. It is this process of individualizing that I am calling "modernization" and that "The Light Princess" illustrates so well.

The story itself is based on a pun: the "light princess" is both without gravity of body and without gravity or seriousness of mind. As in the case of "Sleeping Beauty," the princess's condition is the result of a witch's curse, though the circumstances surrounding this curse are interestingly modified. In Perrault's version, a king and queen try unsuccessfully for some time to have a child. The same is the case here, but borrowing another introductory motif from Hoffmann, MacDonald makes his king and queen opposites in temperament, with the king as a dour, selfish monarch who blames his lighthearted wife for their lack of an heir. Moreover, in a variation of his own, MacDonald makes the evil witch the king's sister, whose dark disposition is really just an aggravated version of his own peevish self-centeredness. The christening curse, then, while on the one hand a traditional introductory trope, is also (in this instance) an extension of the marital discord (originally expressed in their childlessness) between a somber king and a queen who is good-natured but given to joking. The king's sister (that hidden/neglected part of his heritage who is—according to convention—overlooked at the critical moment) shows up at the christening to condemn the couple with an infant who paradoxically conjoins the polarities of both parents: i.e. an excess of her mother's levity and an extreme case of her father's self-absorption. The king responds to the revelation of the curse by claiming that "she can't be ours!"; but she most emphatically is theirs, and in a graphic, symbolic way that only a fairy tale could render. The critical question, as posed by MacDonald's reworking of the formulaic introduction, is whether romantic love is to prosper in this kingdom in a way it has not with this king, and whether the king's daughter will somehow learn to temper the extremes and harmonize the conflicts of her emotional inheritance.

The light princess is condemned by her curse not only to weightlessness, but also to a prolonged period of childishness—a time analogous to Sleeping Beauty's extended incubation. When the king's army is slaughtered, the princess laughs; when the king storms at her, she claps her hands in glee; and, most tellingly, when she encounters a beggar, she breaks out in "violent hysterics." One of the Chinese Metaphysicians at court is not far off when he says that "she cares for nothing here; there is no relation between her and this world." MacDonald is playing with language here (much after the fashion of his friend Lewis Carroll), since her lack of gravity literally threatens to lift the princess "out of" this world; but in essence the princess's condition *is* one of disconnection with the lives of those around her. As in the case of her aunt, the Witch Makemnoit, this absolute egocentrism threatens to lead her into a kind of emotional hysteria. As she grows up, her giggling turns to a sort of maniacal glee, and we see her "furious," "exploding," even "frantic" with laughter. All this is the dark side of her levity, the result of a life in which all that is unpleasant is suppressed and all compassion is denied. So the difficulty is not simply the prolonged adolescence that besets Sleeping Beauty and Snow White and makes of those stories "parables of puberty" (Reis 77); rather this problem (or better: this additional complication that MacDonald has grafted onto the traditional parable) is the more fundamental, ageless one of the inability to get outside one's self, to empathize with rather than to laugh at one's companions, to feel pity and fear, as well as glee.

Martin Buber describes this general problem as the inability to break the I-It relationship, a pattern of emotional response that trivializes (or makes light of) one's fellows. Without a Thou, rather than an It, in one's life, insists Buber, there *is* no existence (80-85). And in this tale, the inability to keep one's feet on the ground is the narrative sign of just such triviality of character: the princess is disengaged from authentic emotional experience, and so she floats about, disconnected from both the pleasure and pain of life.

As we might expect, the practical conflict facing a fairy tale princess with this condition is, how is she going to respond to the love of the inevitable prince charming? All Sleeping Beauty and Snow White had to do was lie there and wait for him to come—

eventually. But how, asks our author, a princess who has no gravity can fall into anything, much less love, is "a difficulty, perhaps THE difficulty." And so when the prince dutifully arrives, the problem here, in contrast to the traditional tale, is decidedly not one of adolescent sexual reserve. We soon find the princess (who reclaims her physical gravity once she is in water) taking long, sensual swims in the moonlight with her suitor, swims that begin as she climbs into his arms and they jump together from a cliff into the dark, warm water below. These scenes of plunging and swimming are so remarkably sensual that no critic yet has been able to desist from waxing psychoanalytical in response to them (e.g. Reis 77 and Wolff 118). And yet, MacDonald tells us that "whenever the prince ... began to talk to the princess of love, she always turned her head and laughed." Not until she is faced with the possibility of tragedy will the princess's implacable comic mask crack and the possibility first of real tears, and then of real love open up within her.

At this point in the story, MacDonald breaks fully with his narrative precursors and exhibits the imaginative exuberance that C. S. Lewis claimed was his most notable literary quality (Lewis 9). We speed through a series of scenes that illustrate with graphic precision how the princess is threatened by Makemnoit from a secret cave beneath the lake, how the White Snake of Darkness is conjured up and begins to suck the lake dry, and how the selfless prince plugs the leak with his body. The exact significance of this original sequence is itself submerged in a fascinating multiplicity of potential interpretations. What we can assert with some assurance is that the provocative combination of imagistic precision with an uncertainty of semiological reference is a hallmark of traditional tales (*The European Folktale* 70-71, 81-106). And indeed, in his own essay on "The Fantastic Imagination," MacDonald insists that the fairy tale functions not so much "to convey a meaning" as "to wake" one (*A Dish of Orts* 317).[9] So while Robert Lee Wolff is undoubtedly correct when he notes that it is impossible to ignore the Freudian symbolism of these scenes, with the white snake sucking at the inverted breast of a restorative lake, it is also impossible to distill the language of action and imagery that MacDonald employs in this mythopoetic episode into any discursive, didactic concept (Wolff 118).

Suffice it to say, then, that the draining of the lake is an objective correlative for the princess's emotional sterility; as MacDonald puts it, she "felt as if the [evaporating] lake was her soul drying up within her," turning her airy heart "first to mud, then to madness." Having been grounded, so to speak, by her own distress, she is next called to compassion by the martyrdom of the prince, which draws up from within her an untapped wellspring of emotion and tears. Finally outside her own vault of egocentrism, the princess pulls her lover from the lake's hole, sobs (for the first time) over his inert body, and then (also for the first time) falls dramatically to the ground.[10] The heavens respond with a purgative downpour of their own, the lake is refilled, the witch drowned in her vault, the prince revived, and the couple, of course, married. And in the process, the light princess—born of such contrary and incompatible parents, and under a curse of selfishness and triviality—has learned that love, as MacDonald writes, is "a beehive of honey and stings." Like Lewis Carroll's *Alice's Adventures Underground* (also written in 1862), MacDonald's story is a commentary on growth and on arrested growth.[11] But as the comparison should further serve to illustrate, MacDonald, in this—his first fairy story for children—was able to retain the essential ethos of that genre, to infuse it with his own interests and artistry, and so to modernize the fairy tale rather than leave it behind in the creation of an entirely new world of fantasy.

One significant element of this tale, and a factor in the very untraditional development of character that the light princess undergoes, remains to be mentioned: the expanded length of the story. It is about 17,000 words long and runs to 40 pages in Sadler's edition. As such, "The Light Princess" partakes of the modern tendency to protract the narrative scope of the fairy tale, a trend that begins with the almost epic tales of the 17th and 18th-century French writers (some of which are as much as 300 pages long) and is continued in many of the most well-know *kunstmarchen*.[12] The extended length of the modern tales naturally allows for a considerably greater range of thematic development, an innovation that is conspicuous in MacDonald's most mythopoetic fairy tale: "The Golden Key."

In a purely geographical way, this unique fairy tale has enormous breadth, moving as it does through an entire continent of symbolic terrain. At the same time, it traverses a literary route from traditional folk tale to the apocalyptic epic of salvation, so that both "Hansel and Gretel" and Dante's "Paradiso" can be cited as precedents. We begin with Mossy and Tangle, the two principals, at home on the borders of fairyland. But just as in "The Light Princess" where the formulaic opening is redefined, MacDonald here interjects an original, modernizing note. Both children have been contemplating fairy tales just prior to their entry into the other world of fairy; and in consequence, we are led to wonder whether the journey through fairyland is best seen as an epistemological adventure in which the imagination is the actual protagonist and the goal is, as Tangle puts it, to "know" things which are not in our "understanding."[13] Such speculation is fully consistent with the metaphysical nature of the adventures that follow, adventures that begin with a seminal point of doctrine. But in fairy tales, concepts come in iconographic garb; and in this initial episode we have a particularly clear example of philosophy in its fairy form. For just as soon as Mossy leaves his conventional cottage on the frontier of the fairy wood, he encounters a very unconventional rainbow, one that is revealed as a kind of celestial escalator within which beautiful forms ascend in glorious colors toward the blue arch of heaven. This early encounter turns out to be a brief vision granted to what we have heard MacDonald call the "true, humble, childlike imagination," a vision of what, in MacDonald's metaphysics, is the universal law of spiritual evolution. It is the rainbow that provides the concrete figure for this idea of a passage from the mundane to the divine; and, in turn, it is Mossy's initial vision of the highway to heaven that sets the conceptual framework for all that follows. Soon after, Mossy (true to the Wordsworthian tradition) loses "the visionary gleam" but finds the golden key in its place. The motivation of the tale, then, is the fully Romantic effort to reclaim the lost vision, to uncover the special lock and find the way up into the glorious columns of ascending color. Throughout the ensuing search, MacDonald's metaphysics of fairyland are expressed in metaphors of geographical and temporal change; and given the epic scope of the adventure, it is no surprise that the terrain traversed and the time involved are vast.

Mossy and Tangle move, in rapid order, through the Sea of Shadows (a kind of vale of purgatorial beings), to the glimmering cave of the Old Man of the Sea (with its tank of air fish—unusal creatures poised between evolutionary stages), down a winding stair of rock to the cavern of the Old Man of the Earth, and into a volcanic fire where a prophetic infant plays ball with the primal atoms of life. All this time we are moving further down rivers, canals, even under arches and domes, and into caves, caverns and mossy baths. The whole journey—in this phase—is something of a parturition or natal dream in reverse: back up the birth canal to the source in a watery cavern lit with fire.[14] From this seemingly retrograde process, Mossy and Tangle re-emerge (or are reborn) to climb a mountain (like Sinai or Ararat) where the golden key unlocks a final portal and reveals that original covenant of childhood: the rainbow highway that ascends toward heaven and the country that MacDonald, following Plato, calls "the land from whence all shadows fall."[15]

Nor is the temporal dimension of this journey any more truncated. Mossy and Tangle age inexplicably, die and are reborn periodically, and ultimately begin to grow younger as they reach fuller spiritual maturity. This paradoxical progression towards a second, eternal youth is another tenet in the tale's doctrine of spiritual evolution; and by including the Old Men of the Sea, Earth, and Fire in this evolutionary process of regeneration, MacDonald expands the scope of his narrative to millennial proportions. In the development of this expansive mythological canvas, MacDonald constructs what I earlier referred to as a "spiritual scaffolding" that is weighty with ideas such as the value of death, the function of wisdom and imagination in the progress of human evolution, and the intertwined nature of sexual and spiritual identity, ideas that dominate his adult canon as well as his fairy fiction. But "The Golden Key" is the one fairy tale that most fully expresses the spectrum of MacDonald's philosophical concerns, and as such it is the tale most akin to the adult romances. Indeed, we might well raise the question whether this is really a fairy tale at all, since it also borrows so heavily from the narrative formulas of romance and the thematic ambitions of prophetic myth.

And yet, the expansive intellectual component so obvious in "The Golden Key" does have a precedent in what Lüthi calls the universality of folk tales; i.e. the simplicity of the tales allows them to recapitulate the elemental patterns of life: "Whatever in the real world is bound in a complex net of interdependencies and reciprocal ties appears in the folktale in its ultimate isolation and universal interconnectedness" (*European Folktale* 87). The difference in modern tales of universal scope like "The Golden Key" is that whereas the folktale "does not confirm or explain anything" (*Eu-*

ropean Folktale 59), MacDonald provides an identifiable if not strictly allegorical frame of reference through parallels to the Christian dogma of salvation.

Another important point of contact with generic tradition is the centrality of the theme of authenticity. The Opies have written, in connection with "Cinderella," that the story is not so much one of rags to riches, but of "reality made evident" (Opie, 11); i.e. the wonderful events that characterize the happy endings of fairy tales take place when "the situation that exists is utterly accepted," when unfairness is borne without indignation, when loathsomeness is love, or when—like Cinderella, Sleeping Beauty, or the Frog Prince—one is delivered from an inauthentic existence to a true one. Such, indeed, is MacDonald's theme here, only he has transposed the journey towards authenticity into a cosmological realm of mythic proportions in which authenticity is contingent upon the recognition of one's exalted spiritual identity. In other words, MacDonald retains the traditional fairy tale interest in fundamental relationships, but he projects a complicated ideology of his own onto the open, malleable framework of the fairy tale.

The pattern for this hybrid fictional genre—the mythic fairy tale—can be traced back to the Germans, most especially to Goethe and Novalis. Goethe's "Marchen" (1795) and "Klingsohr's Tale" in Novalis's *Heinrich von Ofterdingen* (1800) both attempt the same sort of apocalyptic vision cum biblical saga that is often called "universal geschicte" and that we encounter in "The Golden Key." And interestingly enough, there is a direct reference (and even a footnote—in a fairy tale no less) to Novalis within MacDonald's tale, as though the author was making sure to establish his story's generic lineage. And yet, though MacDonald borrows much of the mythological ambition and the *Stirb und Wende* (or "die and become") theology from his predecessors, his tale remains unquestionably closer to its roots in the fairy tale than did theirs. We learn, as indicated, that Mossy and Tangle live next-door to fairyland and that their separate entrances into the magical wood are both prompted by other fairy tales. We then follow, in fairy tale fashion, the progress of these ever-childlike companions through their series of mythic transformations which involve fairy godmothers, magic animals that often talk, and small cottages or safe havens within the wood and along the way. Instead then of the *gotterdammerung* mood of the German tales, MacDonald maintains the ethos of fairyland throughout. What we have is a set of highly experimental transformations of the core structure of the fairy tale adventure that are radical in both senses of that word: that is, this tale—in its introductory ploy, in its characters and its primary settings, and in many of the motifs it incorporates—is a return to the roots of the genre. At the same time, however, "The Golden Key," through its infusion of an elaborate mythopoetic framework, effects an extreme metamorphosis of the fundamental form. For the student of narrative structure and the evolution of literary forms, this blend of tradition and innovation makes "The Golden Key" as formally imaginative as it is metaphysically provocative.

"The Golden Key" is the last tale in a collection of MacDonald's called *Dealings with the Fairies* (1867). His subsequent fairy tales appeared regularly in children's magazines, including his own *Good Words for the Young*. It was here that his well-known children's novel, *At the Back of the North Wind*, first appeared in serial form (1868-69). After *North Wind*, the most enduring of MacDonald's fairy works for children is undoubtedly *The Princess and the Goblin* (1872). Auden has written of this latter work that it is "the only English children's book in the same class as the Alice books" (Auden v). And certainly, there is something in the schematic simplicity of this novella-length tale that makes it stand out and that helps us understand just how the fairy tale developed in George MacDonald's hands.

The simplified scaffolding of the tale can be divided into three distinct tiers. At the center is the fairy tale princess and her alpine retreat, which is (significantly) half-castle, half-cottage and half-way between the peak and the base of a large mountain. The mountains above the castle are strange, awful, and majestic; while at the base of the mountain, and indeed directly underneath the castle, is a vast honeycomb of subterranean caverns populated by a misshapen race of disgruntled goblins. These malignant beings, having been banished underground, have become grotesque and corrupt, and nourish an overwhelming desire to debase the people of the open air. Their present plot is to kidnap the princess Irene and force her to marry their own debauched prince. But two forces mitigate against this evil design. The first is a young collier named Curdie, who (though a rustic) really lives on the same level as Irene, and who (as a miner) is alert to the dark ways of the goblins. The second bright force—and the representative of the upper, mountain reaches—is a mysterious fairy grandmother who lives in hidden rooms at the top of the palace and whose presence is a beacon for the princess as she struggles to elude the machinations of the goblins. The princess's palace, then, and the pleasant mountain community around it are a middle ground, a strata of "reasonable, harmonious" human life nestled between the sublime grandeur of the mountain and the sky-blue apartment of the ethereal fairy above, and the dank caves of the envious, deformed goblins below (Tanner 53). All this emphasis on the layout and environs of the tale is in some sense traditional, for as Tolkien notes, it is the atmosphere and "coloring" of fairyland that provides the individual tale with its special vibrancy (Tolkien 18-19). On the other hand, MacDonald's descriptions of subterranean caves, mountain cottages, and palace hallways are here dilated much beyond what we would be likely to find in the abbreviated folk tale with its predominant emphasis on plotting. Indeed, MacDonald takes the Romantic tendency toward the pathetic fallacy to its logical end by making this "little world of his own" thoroughly metaphoric in its topography.

Within the vertical universe of this tale, there are two vectors of movement: for while Irene aspires (in a way akin to Mossy and Tangle) to find a direct path that will take her upward to the special rooms of her magical guardian, the goblins plot not only to kidnap her for their own, but also to bring the palace down by flooding it with the brackish waters of their caverns. This kind of conflict between demonic and angelic forces is, of course, standard in fairy tales, where good and bad are absolute commodities, where contrasting extremes are regularly linked, and where, as Lüthi says, the diversity of experience is resolved into a dialectical opposition between the distinct poles of human capability (*Once Upon a Time* 78-79). What is more, fairy tales have a structural tendency to portray these extreme differences in a graphic, even linear way, so that both beauty and distance serve to represent distinctions of character (*European Folktale* 9). In this case, however, the traditional tendencies of the fairy tale structure are once again infused with the writer's own ethos as MacDonald recasts the standard motifs of polar opposites and vertical separation according to his own ideological concerns.

G. K. Chesterton writes of this tale that "there is something not only imaginative but ultimately true about the idea of goblins being below the house and capable of besieging it from the cellars"

(Chesterton 10-11). What may seem particularly true to the modern reader is that the threat is under the house itself, or just below the surface of routine experience. Add to this unsettling proximity the fact that the goblins used to be human, but as a result of their subterranean exile have devolved into an alien species "whose chief business... was to devise trouble for their neighbors" (*The Princess and the Goblin* 13). Taken together, these features make it difficult to see the goblins as anything other than the irrational, sublimated malformations of the unconscious working to undermine (literally) the stability of the ego and to compromise innocence (in the person of the princess Irene). Given the appropriateness of Freudian analogies to so much of MacDonald's imaginative fiction, such a conclusion seems critically just (*see* Tanner 52-53). Nonetheless, the vertical structure of the tale and the fairy tale tradition of a link between opposites forces us to remember that the upper levels of MacDonald's thematic scaffolding (so easily dismissed by psychoanalysis as projections of the superego) invariably have a thematic potency superior to that of the lower demons. So while we may be initially inclined to read the tale as an allegory of ego-integration (the adventures of the ego learning to accommodate threatening instincts), we should also be alert to the fact that a structure for spiritual evolution is as much a part of this tale as it is of "The Golden Key." Indeed, the structural hierarchy of the fairy tale formula, with its room at the top for a mysterious power, offers MacDonald an ideal frame on which to embroider his mystical theology. To ignore this "alternative theology," as Chesteron calls it, is to overlook much of what MacDonald did to transform the fairy tale (Chesterton 12). But whether one focuses on goblins or fairy grandmothers, on the Freudian or the mystical reverberations of the tale, the essential point remains the same: the formal conventions of the fairy tale—which in themselves are thematically neutral—provide George MacDonald with a variable, polysemous medium through which to develop the full range and complexity of his own unique vision. Ultimately, it is MacDonald's ability to enlist the traditional forms and motifs of the fairy tale in the service of this vision that makes this story so successful. When either factor in this harmonious mix—the fairy tale features or the theological struggle—is absent (as is the case in the sequel, *The Princess and Curdie*—1877), the resulting fiction is considerably less compelling.

I do not wish to imply that the adaptation of traditional folk tale patterns and motifs as a vehicle for an individualized ideology is original with George MacDonald. In fact, the history of the literary tale from its appearance in seventeenth-century French salons onward is a clear example of what Northrop Frye would call the "kidnapping" of a genre, or the appropriation of a traditional literary formula for new purposes. One regular feature of the written tales that clearly distinguishes them from their oral predecessors is the "conscious artistry" of the teller, a feature noticeable in the stylistic embellishments of such early figures as Giambattista Basile and Jacob Grimm (Butor 349). Invariably, the display of such artistry has an influence on the ideology of the tale. Another standard feature of the modernized tale is what Jack Zipes calls the "purposeful appropriation" by educated writers of material from oral tales and the conversion of this material into "a type of literary discourse about morals, manners, and values" (Zipes 3). In the process of this appropriation, the function of the tales shifts from the entertainment of the folk to the socialization of children. This didactic component in literary fairy tales is a radical departure from what Lüthi calls the "depthlessness" of traditional folk tales (*European Folktale* 11-23). In a sense, then, all written tales are ideologically committed.

What distinguishes the original fairy tales of writers such as d'Aulnoy, Ruskin, and Andersen is that in the pursuit of their own fictive ideas, they continue to embrace the primary generic ethos so enthusiastically. But no one, I would argue, employs as fully or as effectively as MacDonald the fundamental elements of this very ancient genre: its one-dimensional, stock characters; its conventional locales of wood, castle, cave, and cottage; its paratactic narrative line; and above all, its evocative sense of the fantastic, but the fantastic set within the everyday. Nor does any other modern writer of fairy tales outdo MacDonald in the rendering of that primary fairy tale formula, a formula that pits our deepest fears, our goblins, against our greatest desires, whether these be handsome princes, lost parents, or celestial rainbows (*see* Sale 51). What I have been trying to suggest is that an inspired storyteller like MacDonald can incorporate and transform the conventions of a genre and invigorate them with new life in the process. As such, his tales both maintain and advance the essential dynamic of their genre and so stake out a significant place for themselves in the modern evolution of a very special literary form.

Notes

This essay is a revised form of a paper delivered at the 1985 Children's Literature Association Conference in Ann Arbor. The writer wishes to thank Rebecca Selden, who chaired his session, for her help, and U. C. Knoepflmacher, whose ideas fully inform the present work.

1. The term "new Mythus" is taken from MacDonald's fellow Scot, Thomas Carlyle, who introduces it in *Sartor Resartus*. For a discussion of the influence of this concept, see M. A. Abrams, 123-134.

2. For a brief but helpful introduction to the *kunstmarchen*, see John Trainer.

3. The most extensive analysis of *Lilith* to date is my own "George MacDonald's *Lilith* and the Conventions of Ascent." The quote is taken from Christina Brooke-Rose's fine study of adult fantasy.

4. The literary essays were collected by MacDonald in a volume published late in his career, *A Dish of Orts*. The essay of central interest to readers of the fairy tales, "The Fantastic Imagination," is also available in Glenn Sadler's collection of MacDonald's tales, *The Gifts of the Child Christ*.

5. All the above quotations except the last are from "The Fantastic Imagination." The last one is from "The Imagination: Its Function and Culture."

6. All the quotations in this paragraph are from "The Imagination: Its Function and Culture." The reference to the "winding stair" appears repeatedly in MacDonald's work, most notably in *Lilith*. MacDonald comments on this image directly in Greville MacDonald's biography, p. 482.

7. For the relation between MacDonald's tale and Hoffmann's, *see* Wolff, 118-20.

8. Lüthi's consistent refrain is that "the fairy tale does not confirm or explain; it simply represents" (*European Folktale* 59). For additional comments on the traditional role of the oral storyteller, *see* Lüthi's *European Folktale*, 24-36, 66-80.

9. MacDonald punctuates this notion of the ineluctable tale by attaching the Miltonic motto, "More is meant than meets the ear," to the frame tale surrounding "The Light Princess." Though originally written independently, the story first appeared as an interpolated tale in MacDonald's novel *Adela Cathcart* (1864), a realistic work that includes a number of other tales. In the novel, MacDonald's persona, John Smith,

narrates the tale, which is subtitled "A Fairy Tale Without Fairies" (54). At the end of the tale, one of the listeners summarizes the moral as "no girl is worth anything till she has cried a little" (98).

10. In this connection, it is interesting to note Bruno Bettleheim's contention that the fairy tale is aimed at ego integration "which allows for the satisfaction of id desires" (46).

11. It is fascinating to note that on July 9, 1862, Lewis Carroll actually accompanied MacDonald as he walked to deliver "The Light Princess" to his publisher (*see* Carroll). Undoubtedly, a full comparison between these two contemporaneous tales would yield some interesting results.

12. For a brief examination of the French *contes de fees*, *see* Sale, 52-63. As for elongated *kunstmarchen*, one need only cite Goethe's "Marchen," Novalis's "Klingsohr's Tale," La Motte-Fouqué's *Undine*, Chamisso's *Peter Schlemihl*, and Hoffmann's "The Golden Pot."

13. The self-reflexive movement in "The Golden Key," in which fairy tales seem to be about the nature of fairy-tale thinking, is a feature in several other MacDonald tales, notably "The Carasoyn" and "The Giant's Heart." The distinction between "knowing" and "understanding" is obviously parallel to the Kantian concepts of *vernuft* and *verstand*, roughly translated as "pure reason" and "logical understanding." As an interested reader of German literature, MacDonald was undoubtedly familiar with this distinction.

14. Cf. Wolff, 69-70, 87-91, and esp. 146-47. It is also interesting to note that Tangle's adventures recapitulate the long walk down the rocky stairway leading ultimately to a magic snake that we encountered in "The Light Princess." But whereas Makemnoit's cave is dark and evil, the descent here is into the heart, or core, of things. We see MacDonald, therefore, employing his favorite imagery within different narrative contexts to very different thematic effect.

15. Frank Riga discusses the relationship between the concept of shadows as presented here and in Plato's Allegory of the Cave (*see Republic*, Bk. VII) in his essay, "The Platonic Imagery of George MacDonald and C. S. Lewis: The Allegory of the Cave Transfigured" elsewhere in this book.

Works Cited

Abrams, M. H. *Natural Supernaturalism*. New York: Norton, 1973.
Auden, W. H. "Introduction." in *The Visionary Novels of George MacDonald*. Ed. Anne Freemantle. New York: Noonday Press, 1954.
Bettleheim, Bruno. *The Uses of Enchantment: The Meaning and*

Importance of Fairy Tales. New York: Knopf, 1976.
Brooke-Rose, Christina. *The Rhetoric of the Unreal.* Cambridge: Cambridge UP, 1981.
Buber, Martin. *I and Thou.* Trans. Ronald Gregor Smith. New York: Scribners, 1958.
Butor, Michel. "On Fairy Tales." in *European Literary Theory and Practice.* Ed. Vernon W. Gras. New York: Delta, 1973, 351-56.
Carroll, Lewis. *Diaries.* Ed. Roger Lancelyn Green. Westport, CT: Greenwood, 1974.
Chesterton, G. K. "Introduction." in Greville MacDonald's *George MacDonald and His Wife.*
Frye, Northrop. *The Secular Scripture.* Cambridge, MA: Harvard UP, 1976.
Lewis, C. S. "Introduction." in George MacDonald's *Phantastes and Lilith.*
Lüthi, Max. *The European Folktale: Form and Nature.* Trans. John D. Niles. Philadelphia: Institute for the Study of Human Issues, 1982.
_____. *Once Upon a Time.* Trans. Lee Chadeayne and Paul Gottwald. New York: Frederick Ungar, 1970.
MacDonald, George. *Adela Cathcart.* 1864. London: Routledge, n.d.
_____. *A Dish of Orts: Chiefly Papers on the Imagination and Shakespeare.* 1882. London: Geo. Newnes, Ltd., 1905.
_____. *The Gifts of the Child Christ: Fairytales and Stories for the Childlike.* Ed. Glenn E. Sadler. 2 vols. Grand Rapids, MI: Eerdmans, 1973.
_____. *Phantastes and Lilith.* 1858 and 1895, resp. Grand Rapids, MI: Eerdmans, 1964.
_____. *The Princess and the Goblin.* 1872. New York: Dell, 1986.
MacDonald, Greville. *George MacDonald and His Wife.* New York: Dial, 1924.
Mendelson, Michael. "George MacDonald's *Lilith* and the Conventions of Ascent." *Studies in Scottish Literature* XX (1985): 197-218.
Opie, Iona and Peter. *The Classic Fairy Tales.* New York: Oxford UP, 1974.
Plato. *The Collected Dialogues.* Ed. Edith Hamilton and Huntington Cairnes. Westport, CT: Greenwood, 1974.
Reis, Richard H. *George MacDonald.* New York: Twayne, 1972.
Sadler, Glenn E. (*See* MacDonald, *Gifts,* above).

Sale, Roger. *Fairy Tales and After*. Cambridge, MA: Harvard UP, 1978.
Tanner, Tony. "Mountains and Depths—An Approach to 19th-Century Dualism." *Review of English Literature* 3, 4 (Oct., 1962): 51-61.
Trainer, John. "The Marchen." *The Romantic Period in Germany.* Ed. Siegbert Prawer. London: Institute of Germanic Studies, 1970, 98-120.
Wolff, Robert Lee. *The Golden Key: A Study of the Fiction of George MacDonald*. New Haven: Yale UP, 1961.
Zipes, Jack. *Fairy Tales and the Art of Subversion*. New York: Wildman, 1983.

The Community of the Centre
Structure and Theme in *Phantastes*

By Roderick McGillis

My title derives from chapter 12 of George MacDonald's *Phantastes* (1858). Here MacDonald writes: "The community of the centre of all creation suggests an interradiating connection and dependence of the parts." The sentence is helpful in many ways: we understand MacDonald's notion of multiplicity of dimensions interpenetrating and inter-influencing; we understand that all creation is within a centre and hence all created things are special; at the same time, we understand that individuals are part of a larger entity, a community of the centre. The familiar Romantic paradox of unity in multeity takes yet another expression. A "centre" also suggests inwardness. Something in the centre, something beyond the capability of scientific thought to tabulate or to formulate into an "external law" is at work in the universe bringing creation together. This community of the centre, best articulated in literary fantasy, is a way of knowing that brings humanity together in harmonious variety. This way of knowing is not antirational, but it is imaginative rather than ratiocinative.

Let me explain this point. The passage I began with is from a story that Anodos reads in the library of the Fairy Palace. The story is about "a world that is not like ours," and Anodos cannot recall whether or not the story "was all a poem." The story, as he relates it, is partly in prose and partly in verse. Clearly, this other world is meant to "be full of mysterious revelations of other connexions with the worlds around us." Quite simply, the story warns us that unfulfilled desires breed pestilence. The lives of the people of this planet are long, lonely, and tedious. But this is not the only interesting aspect of the story. How can a revelation be mysterious? What is revealed is uncovered, shown for what it is. Sex is a joy! Yet, as Anodos's overactive libido points up, sex can be joyless, an expression of thoughtless self-gratification. The story teaches Anodos that desire need not be ugly, but that it may be ugly, and certainly it will be so perceived by angelic women, white ladies, and the like.

The story also teaches him about literature. While reading the story, Anodos discovers that he participates in it. In fact, he becomes a character in the action. This happens when he becomes a visitor to the strange land, and it happens again more clearly in the story of Cosmo von Wehrstahl. Reading this second story, Anodos "was Cosmo, and his history was mine." Reader participation, MacDonald says, breeds a "double consciousness" that perceives a "double meaning" in the story, perhaps a personal meaning and a universal meaning. In other words, the story of the strange planet has application to Anodos's particular problem in understanding his desires, and it also applies to the human condition. But the story also draws the reader into a centre, the story. As a detached, analytical reader, Anodos would be outside the centre, at the circumference of the book, but by moving into the story he enters a centre that welcomes all readers who are willing to go beyond the book as formal object and know it from inside. This kind of knowing means having sympathy with the story and understanding how it works. The moral truths apparent in the themes of selfishness and love (evident in both stories read by Anodos in the library) are of less importance than the knowledge that the stories themselves offer. They teach us to know our imaginations. Such knowledge humanizes: to know not only how our minds function, but also to know that literature brings us out of ourselves and into a community of shared images, themes, characters, etc. is to participate in a humane imaginative enterprise. Knowledge gained through story is not irrational or anti-intellectual; it is the result of imaginative sympathy and imaginative understanding. The subjective response and the objective one have validity in relationship.

This is why the revelations are, paradoxically, mysterious. What stories attempt to reveal is beyond the capability of language to articulate. This explains why the story of the strange planet is partly in verse and partly in prose. MacDonald directs our attention to language in its metaphoric role. Literature communicates through image and metaphor, not through concept or abstraction. Yet the quest for the image is endless. MacDonald reminds us throughout his work that what we gain from literature is comforting, but not final. Literature does not realize apocalypse, but it can tell us how to understand apocalypse, not as historic fact but as human possibility. Shelley's *Epipsychidion* comes to mind as a work close to *Phantastes,* not only in incident, but also in mood. It is hopeful, yet sceptical. Shelley's poem presses language to the limits; it attempts to articulate that deep truth which is imageless. But this entails reducing the imageless to the image, and consequently poetry always fails to present deep truth; it must mediate vision. If it didn't, there would be no need for more poems. Anodos must return from his death in Fairy Land in order for this point to be made clear. Once back at his own home, Anodos tells us that in Fairy Land he both found and lost his Shadow. One does not, however, lose one's shadow; one incorporates it. Literature reminds us of dualisms such as shadow and self, and it also reconciles them. But can *we* reconcile them? *Phantastes* closes with the question: "Could I translate the experience of my travels there (in Fairy Land), into common life?"

Fairy Land, or what we might simply call poetry, provides a community of the centre, a place where the imagination is freed from the pressures of desire and convention. This is why Anodos spends so much time reading the "wondrous volumes" in the Fairy Palace Library. In this way, he gains knowledge of himself and of himself in relation to others. The two stories he relates to us illustrate the difference between self-centeredness and the community of the centre. The angel-woman in the first story dies because she will not accept the desire that brings us out of ourselves; and Cosmo in the second story learns that the mirror that encloses the lady must be shattered before true union is possible. The circle he draws when conjuring the lady from the mirror signifies separation, not community. Only by breaking circles of selfhood can we enter centres of community.

The sentence we began with has provided us with a clue to a thematic aspect of the book. It helps us understand the references to mirrors, lakes, reflections, Shadow, globes, circles, and other images of enclosure that abound in the book. All such centres must be shattered in order that a larger community of the centre be revealed. The community of the centre works, then, on at least two levels: the human and the poetic. Anodos is a self-centered young man whose experiences teach him that he is not alone in the universe. His Shadow attempts to keep Anodos from a knowledge of the individuality of others by presenting others as objects, dark fragments of a universe detached from the self. Anodos is at the centre of his world and everything else is outside and useful only as it can gratify his desires. In other words, the Shadow narrows and darkens Anodos's perceptions. Fairy Land (call it poetry or imaginative experience) finally cleanses Anodos's perceptions. He dies. His death gains him entry into the true centre of the universe which is the community of the centre, at once centre and circumference. This ties in with poetry because Anodos's experience is clearly "poetic": he sings many songs; he is a poet. And the true poet, as MacDonald's poem "Of the Son of Man" (1852) makes clear, is "a living lyre" (*Poetical Works,* vol. 2, 269-275); he poeticizes the universe by realizing in life what is searched for in art. Syllables become deeds. However, Anodos returns to this life, and the struggle begins again. The poem, Fairy Land, gives hope—a hope, as Shelley presents it in *Epipsychidion*—that poetry and love build a world divine, if not here, then beyond the grave.

What we are seeing in all this is not merely a theme, but also a structure. *Phantastes* has always been deemed a structureless book, sometimes even a confusing one. The *Athenaeum* review is well-known; it calls *Phantastes* a "Wilderness of wilderment" (580). The *Spectator* reviewer finds himself "in the wildest regions of fairy and fancy" (286), while the *British Quarterly Review* cautions some readers that "a verdict of 'determination of nonsense to the brain'" (296-297) may be the result of reading *Phantastes*. Even a favorable review in *The Globe* indicates a quality of "dreaminess" and "seeming incoherence," although it does not find these defects. An appreciation by E. S. Robertson in 1906 (308-309) accepts the notion of incoherence that MacDonald offers in his epigraph from Novalis finding such mistiness a beauty; after all, shouldn't art aspire to the condition of music?

Even more recent commentators, although differing in their attitude toward incoherence, perceive in *Phantastes* an aimless structure. W. H. Auden implies that *Phantastes*' "allegorical structure" is loose: "there seems no particular reason, one feels, why Anodos should have just the number of adventures he does have." Richard Reis calls the structure "loose" and suggests we are to allegorize the incidents as events in Anodos's childhood, but as Reis admits, "this is not easy to do" (90). He concludes that the "looseness and unevenness of *Phantastes* must be counted as defects" (94). Colin Manlove, in a closely argued chapter on MacDonald in *Modern Fantasy*, says *Phantastes* is "perhaps" MacDonald's "most disconnected" fairy tale (75). More recently, in discussing the circularity of *Phantastes* and *Lilith,* Manlove has described *Phantastes* as "centrifugal " (85). In my reading, it is centripetal and centrifugal. Max Keith Sutton, in a reading that considers Freudian, Jungian, and Kohutian paradigms, refers to "the disorderly nature of the alleged dream which forms the story" (12). And Joseph Sigman, in what is the most complete reading yet of *Phantastes,* finds structure through applying a Jungian paradigm to the book. Consequently, he reads through the episodes from beginning to end to correlate the images with Jung's individuation process. This can appear neat, but why apply a priori structures to a book that provides us with its own structural pattern, a structural pattern that turns out to be poetic rather than psychological? What I mean by this is simply that the structure of the book teaches us to understand what the book means. Structure reflects image and like images it is a way of communicating meaning.

For example, just prior to Anodos's journey to the Fairy Palace he finds his Shadow in a cottage situated in a forest clearing. This cottage, with its cypress tree at one end, is the structural counterpart of the oak tree-cornered cottage Anodos comes upon when he first enters Fairy Land. In the second half of the book, however, there are two more cottages which, structurally, balance the two in the first half: the island cottage with four doors, and the tower that imprisons Anodos. The first of these recalls the oak tree cottage, and the second should remind us that the cypress tree rose at one end of its cottage "like a spire to the building." Two cottages represent hospitality, protection, and nurture; the cypress cottage and the tower represent selfhood, vulnerability, and despair. In every case, the building is a centre, but a polarity exists between a dark, enclosed centre and a bright, expansive centre. The cottage as enclosure in self-centeredness is apparent when Anodos enters the cypress tree cottage. The place has no windows. The woman inside reads, head down, by a reddish light. The place is dim. Negation abides here. Anodos finds his own dark self lurking within.

Opposite to this is the cottage of the old lady who spins in chapter 19. MacDonald's creation of this still centre is as fine an example of what he means by the community of the centre as any in the book. Whereas the notion of permanence in the earlier cottage centred on the book and its doctrine of darkness, here permanence is given a human centre. On a flat island in the sea, Anodos finds a homely cottage, windowless like the earlier one, but differing in essential import. This cottage is an eternal centre in a sea of mutability. Mutability is also apparent in the "few plants of the gumcistus, which drops every night all the blossoms that the day brings forth," that grow near the cottage. Inside sits an old woman who spins by a fire, instead of reading by a lamp. She is old, but beautiful; her eyes are the eyes of a twenty-five-year old. She welcomes Anodos and feeds him like a baby. Later, she sings him an old ballad and then spins; her spinning is musical. (The image is an inversion of the folk tale motif of the spinning witch or wise woman; she becomes for MacDonald a *god*-mother. Compare his *The Princess and the Goblin,* 1872.) Whereas the hag in the earlier cottage reads sophistic philosophy, this lady warms Anodos with poetry. And instead of one door that leads to the narrow closet of the self, this cottage has four doors of tears, of sighs, of dismay, and of the timeless[1] that take Anodos in stages toward an experience of complete integration. Together they reflect wholeness, symbolized by the cottage itself with its maternal and poetic centre. Anodos's experience here does not darken him to others; it reconciles his inner and outer selves. The cottage is a centre from which Anodos explores his past, present, and future; it is a centre of serenity he must learn to internalize if he wishes to get beyond enslavement to his desires and fears. That familiar Romantic paradigm of self-consciousness leading to anti-self-consciousness finds expression in this cottage. Even the sign ∾ that marks the entrance to the cottage through its four doors reflects the idea of an open circle. The circularity of this mark is countered by its open ends that stretch outward. The sign suggests embrace, but not enclosure. Here is the community of the centre: the willingness—indeed, the desire—to embrace others, yet the refusal to bind them to us. This is what the old wise woman does; she willingly succours Anodos, she sacrifices her island for him, and she does this in order not to keep him with her. It is with wisdom that MacDonald chooses a mother for his metaphor of a centre that does not restrict. Mothers remain centres of emotion and understanding for children even while they teach them independence.

Thematically, this incident in the cottage with four doors articulates the community of the centre. Structurally, it balances earlier episodes dealing with the same theme and carries those episodes a stage further. It reminds us that each episode is a centre whose meaning radiates to that larger centre of meaning, the book. Finally, the images—fire, spinning *wheel,* cottage, mother, door—communicate themes and structures: the cottage is a centre of poetry, warmth, selflessness, and natural harmony. What happens in this episode—Anodos learns about himself and experiences love and death—is what happens in the romance as a whole. What should be evident in all this is that the community of the centre as a thematic element provides a way of structuring the book; we need not look elsewhere for help in reading *Phantastes*. The community of the centre is a clue to that structure, both in a thematic sense and in a more strictly "structural" sense. We have already seen the thematic manifestation of this structure in the stories of the strange planet and Cosmo, in the role of the Shadow, and in the incident in the cottage of four doors. But perhaps another example will help prepare us for a move from theme to structure, a move that will illustrate the fact that structure is theme. This is the episode of the country maiden.

The country maiden appears twice in the book, once shortly after Anodos has found his Shadow, and again after he and his dreaded Shadow are locked together in a tower. Incidentally, the first of these appearances occurs one chapter before Anodos lands at the Fairy Palace and three chapters before the middle of the book, while the second appearance occurs one chapter before Anodos's death and three chapters before the end of the book. This sequence ought to suggest that some structural principle is at work, and as we will see later, such a suggestion is absolutely correct.

Before recounting his first meeting with the country maiden, Anodos tells us that the incident "quite cured" him of his fascination for the Shadow. What he does not grasp at the time is the significance of the event beyond its obvious sexual moral. The ultimate significance he could not know at least until he had read the stories in the Fairy Palace Library. Until he reads these, he, and we, can have only partial knowledge of what has happened. But what does happen? The little maiden joins Anodos "One bright noon" as he proceeds on his path through a forest. She is both childlike and womanly, suggesting, as in so many fairy tales, that she is ready to learn the sad truth of what it means to be a woman. She carries a "small globe" which is as bright "as purest crystal." To this she is devoted. In fact, the crystal globe, like Blake's crystal cabinet, keeps the maiden in her child world; Anodos says the maiden "produced on me more the impression of a child, though my understanding told me differently." Anodos and the maiden travel together by day, but separate discreetly at night. But by day the maiden proves a coy mistress, "smiling almost invitingly" at Anodos when he desires to touch the globe. First she tells him he must not touch it, then she changes her mind. When touched the globe emits "a tiny torrent of harmony." The globe is the self-enclosed, artificial and selfish world of childhood. Anodos, influenced by his Shadow, sees the globe as a desirable object, something to gratify his senses; he lusts after it. Clearly his reaction is judged wanting, but so is the girl's.

The maiden and the man satirize each other, as do Blake's states of innocence and experience. Close reading of the passage reveals the complexity of the reactions on the part of the two characters, but without either a reading of the two stories in the Fairy Palace Library or a reading of the maiden's return later in chapter 22, the full implication of the incident is not apparent. We are left, again as in Blake's "Crystal Cabinet," with the notion that the libido casts us out of childhood; it breaks the illusion of a safe, harmonious world. The maiden's wail, "You have broken my globe, my globe is broken," is a complaint against an unregenerate Anodos. What is not yet manifest is that the breaking of the globe constitutes the necessary prelude to the removal of the self as centre to a larger community of the centre.

The two stories that Anodos recounts prepare us for the return of the maiden. The first, as we have seen, illustrates the inchoate existence of life without fulfilled desires, and the second tells us that Cosmo can love completely only by accepting sacrifice, separation, and death. He learns, however, that "good" death is not separation, but completion. For the Lady, the breaking of the mirror is liberation, but also sorrow. We will see what this sorrow can mean when the country maiden returns.

Much later in the book, after his triumphant battle with a Giant, Anodos lapses into pride and finds himself locked in a tower with his Shadow. The country maiden now returns. She proves the regeneration of Anodos. As he lies in his self-prison, Anodos experiences by day the agony of self-hate under the cold glare of the sun, and by night the release of moonlight dreams. During one of his nightly dreams, he wishes he were a child again, "innocent, fearless, without shame or desire." The next day, "about noon," he hears "the voice of a woman singing." The song refreshes and cleanses him; its effect is reminiscent of the bath Irene takes in her great-great-grandmother's bedroom in *The Princess and the Goblin*. It "unmans" (MacDonald's word) him; that is, it returns him to his childhood innocence in order to regenerate him. He is reborn! The song that accomplishes all this ends with two lines that recapitulate our theme:

> From the narrow desert, O man of pride,
> Come into the house, so high and wide.

The tower is a "narrow desert," a centre of self-waste; what lies outside the tower (Fairy Land) is a house that contains many mansions, each a centre of a larger centre.

The song's invitation works mysteriously, and Anodos opens the door. Outside he sees a "beautiful woman" who turns out to be the maiden whose globe he had broken. She tells him her story which sounds remarkably similar to his. Her globe broken, she took the pieces to the Fairy Queen, who merely took them and put them aside, presumably as childish things. Then the Fairy Queen made the maiden "go to sleep in a great hall of white, with black pillars, and many red curtains." Upon waking in the morning, the maiden leaves the house without her globe, no longer feeling the need for it. She has, she says, "something so much better." Sorrow has proved beneficial, providing a necessary fall from innocence. After all, Mr. Vane is right when he says the Little Ones in *Lilith* are incomplete. They know nothing of sorrow and therefore they cannot be fully human. The fairy maiden is now a poet whose songs are deeds that deliver people. She now lives by her songs which manifest her relationship with others; with "room to roam" she has found that there is "only one home/For all the world to win."

The community of the centre waits for Anodos. By merely opening the door to his tower, he leaves it behind, and soon—by offering himself in a gesture of self-sacrifice—he attains the community. Lying dead in the bosom of the earth, Anodos enjoys participating in "the whole earth, and each of her many births." He has gone one better than the maiden. She sings of relationship; he experiences relationship. Anodos enters flowers, floats above the earth, and feels a limitless power of understanding and sympathy. This is possible, however, "in the realms of lofty Death." He returns to earth; he dies into moral life to continue his "more limited" bodily life. Here he can only hope to translate his experiences in Fairy Land into action, to further a day when a true community will exist.

What the book deals with, then, is what Keats calls "Identity." *Phantastes*, as its many references to Novalis, Wordsworth, Shelley, Coleridge, Schiller, Heine, and other of their contemporaries suggests, is a "Romantic" statement. It deals with the struggle to attain consciousness and to overcome self-consciousness. It reconciles opposites. It tries to intellectualize the imagination, to reassociate sensibility. A famous passage in Shelley's *Defence of Poetry* provides a gloss on MacDonald's book:

> The great secret of morals is love; or a going out of our nature, and an identification of ourselves with the beautiful which exists in thought, action, or person, not our own. A man, to be greatly good, must imagine intensely and comprehensively; he must put himself in the place of another and of many others; the pains and pleasures of his species must become his own. The great instrument of moral good is the imagination; and poetry administers to the effect by acting upon the cause. Poetry enlarges the circumference of the imagination by replenishing it with thoughts of ever new delight, which have the power of attracting and assimilating to their own nature all other thoughts, and which form new intervals and interstices whose voice forever craves fresh food (Shelley 487-488).

The mention of "circumference" reminds us of our theme. This widening of our vision is not mere emotionalism. Rather it is a way of knowing. As MacDonald writes in his essay, "The Imagination," we can know a flower in two ways: the way of the botanist who tears it to shreds, and the way of the poet who understands what the flower is by understanding imagery.[2] And we can only know this by understanding the different imagery possible in flowers and weeds, and knowing further that these images are products of our imaginations. The garden of flower fairies offers Anodos a lesson in selfishness, possession, and class that is merely an expression of what he already knows but only now has the strength to imagine.

Since the book is so clearly structured around this theme of a centre, it is reasonable to look more closely at the structure itself to see whether it communicates to us in this imaginative way. As we have seen, most readers look for an order and a progression of incidents unfolding logically from beginning to end, and most readers are disappointed when they discover a looseness about MacDonald's plotting.[3] This looseness, however, will only appear if we read the book in a conventional manner, something we inevitably do on a first reading. Once we have the whole book in our minds a different structure begins to take shape, a structure based on the notion of a centre. M. H. Abrams has taught us to read Romantic works as spiral journeys beginning where they end, but ending on a higher level of consciousness. This is brilliant and instructive. I should, however, like to adjust this pattern by shifting attention not to beginning and ending, but to the centre. The structure I suggest is apparent in such Romantic texts as *The Rime of the Ancient Mariner, The Prelude, La Belle Dame Sans Merci,* and *Heinrich von Ofterdingen*. MacDonald undoubtedly got his structure from Novalis's unfinished romance where it is both clearer and more complex than in *Phantastes*. The idea of the community of the centre is, of course, pervasive in Romantic works.

Phantastes has twenty-five chapters. Chapter 13, the central chapter in the book, contains the story of Cosmo von Wehrstahl. Cosmo's name is a clue to the theme of centre and circumference. In this central chapter Anodos, who claims he *is* Cosmo, learns the true nature of love as a going out of ourselves. Cosmo dies with a smile on his face; he has attained his desire: relationship and community. This central chapter looks backwards and forwards. The book both moves towards this centre and away from it, expressing the idea that the revelation presented here is not final. Romanticism constantly reminds us that we move towards revelation and back from it. Revelations constitute good moments, eternal centres amid the flux of events in time and space. This central chapter in *Phantastes* tells us we move toward death, but before we die, we ought to strive for constant rebirth within the mutable world. At the end of *Phantastes,* Anodos returns a new man, but he faces the task of maintaining his newness until he achieves the "great good" which is evident in the smile on Cosmo's dead lips.

However, the importance of the centre is clearer still. Chapters 10 through 16, the middle seven chapters, leaving nine on either side, take place in the Fairy Palace. The first three chapters of this group (10 to 12) recount Anodos's arrival at the Palace and his exploration of it. The centre chapter takes place in the Palace Library. The final three chapters (14 to 16) tell of the dancing statues and the veiled maiden. The Palace is an ideal. In it Anodos is fed and refreshed. He is instructed through literature and art, but he departs because he has not yet achieved the permanence of the image. He shares Cosmo's experiences, but he wants the marble lady to share his experiences. His selfish desire cannot end happily. He brings the lady to life through the power of song, but he drops poetry for sexuality and loses her. But the Fairy Palace has served its purpose; in it the dance continues. In art we find relaxation, relationship, and freedom from false desires. By reducing art to sensual life, we profane it.

The art/life complex also divides on either side of this centre. Chapters 1 to 9 deal with, among other things, Anodo's attitude toward women. He idealizes them. For example, the lady which he perceives in a block of alabaster is "more near the face that had been born with me in my soul, than anything I had seen before in nature or art." His interest is in females that represent art (marble lady), fairyland (the tiny fairy in chapter 1), or childhood (the country maiden). When he falls willing victim to the Alder-Maiden, he mistakes his ideal for a natural woman, a femme fatale who incorporates throughout Romantic poetry the notion of nature as object as separate from us and as desirable. Anodos succumbs to the actual, to the fiction that the natural world has an existence separate from him. His stay in the Fairy Palace ought to tell him that all things exist together as products of the human imagination. Ideals remain ideals and only wither when we touch them. This is the problem raised by all Romantic literature. If ideals are to benefit us they must be actualized. And any actualization can only reduce them much as criticism inevitably reduces art.

The second part of the book, after Anodos leaves the Fairy Palace, not only confronts Anodos with his past (in the episode in the Old Woman's cottage with the four doors), but also with his desire for an ideal woman. He learns that the marble lady is, in fact, a lady of flesh and blood complete with a lover. He learns to accept this and love the lady anyway. He meets the country maiden, now a full-grown woman dedicated to her art. He is welcomed back home by his sisters. He must accept the female for what she is, another human being with worries and responsibilities just like him. Both male and female must strive to achieve an ideal, not to reduce an ideal to their level. And perhaps they can work together strengthening each other. Sir Percivale and the lady would seem to substantiate this.

What this examination hopes to illustrate is that the structure of *Phantastes* is not accidental. In directing our attention both toward the central chapter and chapters and out toward the beginning and ending, the structure reflects a prominent theme: the community of the centre. Each episode in this episodic book not only repeats ideas but also clarifies them. Anodos's adventures lead him towards a centre where he is alone and not alone. He must learn to tell the difference between being alone and sharing his existence with others. The book, by directing us inward and outward at the same time, reminds us that at the centre we can find the cosmos. At the centre we might well be at the circumference. At the very least, by moving toward this centre, Anodos "enlarges the circumference of his imagination."

Notes

1. What lies beyond each door roughly corresponds to Blake's four levels of existence: Ulro, Generation, Beulah, Eden. The first door, of tears, takes Anodos to his childhood, a time of lost innocence, separation, guilt, and fear. For him it is agony. The second door, of sighs, picks up the theme of separation, but when Anodos plucks up courage to enter the door leading to the bedroom of the white lady and her lover, Sir Percivale, he accepts a world of generative sexuality. The door of dismay, which comes next, leads to reconciliation: Anodos becomes reconciled with his past, his ancestors, and with death. We have also moved from the country (vale) of tears to the city, a premonition of Jerusalem. Logically, the fourth door will take us that extra level to Eden (in Blake's sense), but MacDonald is, of course, not Blake, and what he gives us is a fleeting and tantalizing glimpse of the timeless. Max Keith Sutton, in his article "The Psychology of the Self in MacDonald's *Phantastes*," examines the lady in this cottage as a "therapist" who allows Anodos "to face once more the key figures from his past" (14).

2. In this same essay, MacDonald writes: "science may pull the snowdrop to shreds, but cannot find out the idea of suffering hope and pale confident submission, for the sake of which that darling of the spring looks out of heaven" (*A Dish of Orts* 10). Keith Wilson cites a similar passage in MacDonald's sermon "The Truth" from *Unspoken Sermons: Third Series* (1889) in his analysis of the imaginative act that perceives "a natural object's 'truth'" (142).

3. An exception is John Docherty, who notices a "threefold organisation" in *Phantastes* (26). Docherty's discussion of the structure of *Phantastes* is remarkably close to mine; I might point out that my paper was written long before Docherty's fine article appeared.

Works Cited

Abrams, M. H. *Natural Supernaturalism*. Oxford: Oxford UP, 1971.
Athenaeum. Review of *Phantastes*. November 6, 1858, 580.
Auden, W. H. "Introduction." in *The Visionary Novels of George MacDonald*. Ed. Anne Freemantle. New York: The Noonday Press, 1954. Reprinted in W. H. Auden. *Forewords and Afterwords*. New York: Vintage Books, 1973, 268-273.
British Quarterly Review. Review of *Phantastes*. Vol. 29, 1859, 296-297.
Docherty, John. "A Note on the Structure and Conclusion of *Phantastes*." *North Wind: Journal of the George MacDonald Society* 7 (1988): 25-30.
The Globe. Review of *Phantastes*. December 30, 1858.
MacDonald, George. *A Dish of Orts*. London: Sampson, Low, Marston, 1895.
———. *Phantastes*. London: Smith, Elder, 1858.
———. *Poetical Works*. Vol. 1. London: Chatto and Windus, 1893.
Manlove, C. N. *Modern Fantasy*. Cambridge: Cambridge UP, 1975.
———. *The Impulse of Fantasy Literature*. Kent, OH: Kent State UP, 1983.
Reis, Richard. *George MacDonald*. New York: Twayne, 1972.
Robertson, E. S. "A Literary Causerie: *Phantastes*." *Academy* 70 (1906): 308-309.
Shelley's Poetry and Prose. Ed. Donald H. Reiman and Sharon Powers. New York: Norton, 1977.

Sigman, Joseph. "Death's Ecstasies: Transformation and Rebirth in George MacDonald's *Phantastes.*" *English Studies in Canada* 2 (1976): 203-226.

Spectator. Review of *Phantastes.* December 4, 1858, 1286.

Sutton, Max Keith. "The Psychology of the Self in MacDonald's *Phantastes.*" *Seven* 5 (1984): 9-25.

Wilson, Keith. "The Quest for 'The Truth': A Reading of George MacDonald's *Phantastes.*" *Etudes Anglaises* 34 (1981): 140-152.

The Goddess in the Belfry
Grandmothers and WiseWomen in George MacDonald's Books for Children

By Nancy Willard

C. S. Lewis gives credit to George MacDonald for baptizing his imagination, and I should like to start this paper with the event which baptized mine. I was sitting with my aunt during morning prayer at Saint Joseph's Episcopal Church, and, much impressed with the priest's vestments, I whispered,

"Auntie Joan, when I grow up I want to be a priest."
"Girls can't be priests," said Auntie Joan.
"Then I'll be a priestess," I said.
"There are no priestesses in the Episcopal church," said Auntie Joan.

The look she gave me let me know that a priestess was altogether different than a priest. It was something dangerous, possibly wicked. Years later, when I came across the definition for priestess in the dictionary, I understood my aunt's concern. But before I give it to you, let me give you Webster's definition of a priest. A priest is "one whose office it is to perform religious rites, and especially to make sacrificial offerings." A priestess, on the other hand, is defined as "a girl or a woman who officiates in sacred rites, especially of a pagan religion." No wonder Auntie Joan thought I was on the road to hell. And I think what first attracted me to George MacDonald was his blend of pagan and Christian mysteries in a single figure.

Like the great goddesses of the major religions, past and present, she goes by various names. In *The Lost Princess*, she is called the "Wise Woman," the "goddess-child." In *The Golden Key*, she is "the lady" and "Grandmother," and though the child Tangle calls her "my grandmother" and the fish she keeps call her Mother, the lady herself does not claim to be the grandmother or the mother of any particular creature. In *The Princess and the Goblin,* she is called Irene, the great-great-grandmother of the young princess of the same name. In *The Princess and Curdie,* MacDonald says she is as large and strong as a Titaness and he names her the Mother of Light. Curdie calls her the Lady of the Silver Moon, and the miners believe she is Old Mother Wotherwop, a witch who strikes men blind and poisons wells and kills cattle. "What does it matter how many names if the person is one?" she asks Curdie. "That which is inside is the same all the time.... It is one thing the shape I choose to put on, and quite another the shape that foolish talk and nursery tale may please to put upon me" (54, 55).

For purposes of this paper, I shall call her the goddess, for I believe that MacDonald found her among the goddesses served by those pagan priestesses which the dictionary writers must have had in mind. Her names shed some light on her ancestry. As Irene, she is one of the three goddesses of Greek mythology who control the seasons. Irene brings peace, Dike justice, and Eumenia order. Though MacDonald's goddess bears only the name of the peacemaker, she could just as well answer to the names of her sisters. In *The Lost Princess* she brings order out of the chaos that the ill-behaved princess Rosamond has caused in the royal palace, and in *The Princess and Curdie* she brings order to the corrupt kingdom of Gwyntystorm and brings to justice those who plotted against the king. When MacDonald calls her a Titaness, is he thinking of Rhea, the titaness worshiped in ancient Greece as Magna Mater, the great mother? When he shows her as the Lady of the Silver Moon and houses her in a high tower of the palace where she spins by the light of the moon hanging in her chamber, is she a descendant of Diana, virgin goddess of the moon, caretaker of the woods and the wild creatures in it. Or perhaps she is Frau Berchte, the goddess of distaff and spindle, whose name in Old High German means luminous, and of whom Jacob Grimm writes: "In snow-white garments she shows herself by night in princely houses, she rocks or dandles the babies, while their nurses sleep: she acts the old *grandmother* or *ancestress* of the family" (280).

We shall never know the temples of those lost goddesses, but I am sure that the homes MacDonald chooses for his goddess are very like those the ancients themselves would have chosen. Here is the lady's cottage in *The Golden Key,* as the young girl Tangle first sees it:

> There was a bright fire in the middle of the floor, upon which stood a pot without a lid, full of water that boiled and bubbled furiously. The air-fish swam straight to the pot and into the boiling water, where it lay quiet (*Gifts* 157).

In MacDonald's description, earth, air, fire and water are as vividly present as Tangle and the lady herself. The cottage is moss-green, as if it grew out of the earth, and Tangle's room for the night is an arbor, "cool and green, with a bed of purple heath growing in it," upon which shines "a large wrapper made of feathered skins of the wise fishes, shining gorgeous in the firelight" (*Gifts* 161). A fish flies into the cooking pot so that the lady may eat it. But to be eaten by the goddess is not to be destroyed; it is to be sacrificed and changed from water to air, flesh to spirit: an aeranth, a "lovely little creature in human shape, with large white wings" (*Gifts* 167, 160). The fish is a sign for Tangle who will soon set out on her own quest. "Even the fishes, you see," says the lady, "have to go into the pot, and then out into the dark" (*Gifts* 163). The end of the story will find Tangle and her companion Mossy in a cave, searching for a door "till it grew so dark that they could see nothing, and gave it up" (*Gifts* 176). But like the fish, they climb out of the darkness into the air where "beautiful beings of all ages climbed along with them" (*Gifts* 177).

From the outside, the lady's cottage gives no clue to the inside. It is "round, like a snow-hut or a wigwam . . . The fact was, it had no windows; and though it was full of doors, they all opened from the inside, and could not even be seen from the outside" (*Gifts* 162). How could her house be otherwise? The goddess does not open her doors to everyone. "No one ever gets into my house who does not knock at the door, and ask to come in," says the Wise Woman to Rosamond, in *The Lost Princess* (*Gifts* 213). And no one can can find the door who does not see it with trust in and obedience to the one whose house it opens. When she arrives at the Wise Woman's cottage, Rosamond, fearful and rebellious, finds no door at all.

> But the old woman ... had told her that she must knock at the door: how was she to do that when there was no door? But ... if she could not do all that she was told, she could, at least, do a part of it: if she could not knock at the door, she could at least knock—say on the wall.... A loud noise was the result, and she found she was knocking on the very door itself (*Gifts* 215-217).

Like the lady in *The Golden Key,* the Wise Woman lives in a cottage green with moss. She too has a fire and a bed of heather, for she would never allow her guest "to sleep upon any thing that had no life in it" (*Gifts* 218). But where the lady had a tank of water in which the enchanted fish flashed among green plants and flowers of all colors, the wise woman has a well, "just big enough to wash in..." (*Gifts* 224). Beside the well lies a towel, a comb, and a brush. Before we can be cleansed in a magic well, we must learn to wash in an ordinary one. Before we can be purified by an enchanted fire, we must know how to care for the fire which warms us. The goddess' first command is obedience. To Rosamond she says,

> You must keep the cottage tidy while I am out. When I come back, I must see the fire bright, the hearth swept, and the kettle boiling ... and the heather in blossom—which last comes of sprinkling it with water.... But on no account leave the house till I come back ... or you will grievously repent it.... Dangers lie all around this cottage of mine: but inside, it is the safest place—in fact the only quite safe place in all the country (*Gifts* 220).

To those who obey the goddess, her house, whether cottage or tower, is home. In *The Princess and the Goblin,* when the goddess tells the young princess Irene she must go downstairs to the room from which she came, the child says, "I'm so glad, grandmother, you didn't say—*go home*—for this is my home. Mayn't I call this my home?" (132). Whether great-great-grandmother's house looks like a home depends on the spiritual state of her visitor. Instead of the spinning wheel and the roof of stars, and the light like the moon hanging from the roof, and the fire of roses, Curdie sees, on his first visit, a garret, a tub, a heap of musty straw, a withered apple, and a ray of sunlight coming through a hole in the roof (191). "Seeing is not believing," explains great-great-grandmother to the astonished princess, "it is only seeing" (193).

But all those homes which the goddess occupies have this in common: fire and water for the cleansing of those who seek her. The first cleansing is the mother's care for her child. When Tangle and Rosamond arrive, the dirt of the world is washed away. They are given new clothes, and fed with bread and that nourishment which only a mother can give, milk. In *The Lost Princess,* when the child Agnes is put into a chamber which acts like a mirror for her ugly spirit, she is beyond the reach of bread, yet the wise woman mothers her still:

> The moment she was asleep, the Wise Woman came, lifted her out, and laid her in her bosom; fed her with a wonderful milk, which she received without knowing it; nursed her all the night long, and, just ere she woke, laid her back in the blue sphere again (*Gifts* 236).

For those less in need of spiritual correction, the bath not only cleans, it restores whoever receives it to a more perfect condition than before. Like baptism it requires the consent of the one that undergoes it. "You will not be afraid of anything I do with you—will you?" asks the lady before she lays Tangle into the tank with the feathered fishes, who clean her (*Gifts* 159). She is quite literally immersed in creation: earth (the green plants and flowers of all colors), air (the feathered fishes), and water, and she is ready to stand before the fourth element, fire. A novice in the lady's order, she is dressed in a green robe like the lady's; Tangle is now one of the family.

Irene's great-great-grandmother also asks that the young princess go willingly when she carries her to the tub which shows no bottom but only "stars shining miles away as it seemed in a great blue gulf" (196). To her small initiate, she says, "Do not be afraid, my child." And when the princess says, "No, grandmother," she is immersed in perfect peace, the rightful gift of the goddess Irene (196). The young princess, too, is dried by the fire. Her great-great-grandmother draws the child's nightgown through the flames and brings it forth "white as snow" and smelling of all the roses in the world. The girl is not merely clean, she is renewed. "When she stood up on the floor, she felt as if she had been made over again" (197).

After the cleansing, both Irene and Tangle are put to sleep, that state of oblivion so like death by which we pass back and forth between dreams and the ordinary world of our senses.

Water cleans and heals, but it is fire that purifies. The fire which Tangle walks through when she leaves the lady's cottage scorches her to the bone but does not "touch her strength"; tempered by the fire she walks among molten metals trickling from rocks in the country of the Old Man of the Fire. "But the heat never came near her," MacDonald assures us (*Gifts* 173). For holding his hands in the rosefire of the princess Irene's great-great-grandmother, Curdie, in *The Princess and Curdie,* receives the gift of knowing the spiritual condition of a man by shaking hands with him. When what men do makes them less than human, she explains, "the change always comes first... in the inside hands, to which the outside ones are but the gloves." Curdie will "know at once the hand of a man who is growing into a beast, nay ... feel the foot of the beast he is growing ... " (70). In the Wise Woman's cottage, fire mends the mirror Rosamond smashes to pieces, and it might mend Rosamond herself, were she strong enough to bear it.

When MacDonald calls the goddess "Mother of Light," he reminds us that at the heart of Mother Earth, under its rivers and living creatures, burns the destroyer and transformer, fire. In *The Princess and Curdie,* when Curdie and his father meet her in the darkness of the mine, Curdie beholds "the whole creation ... gathered in one centre of harmony and loveliness in the person of the ancient lady who stood before him in the very summer of beauty and strength" (49). The sacrifice of the feathered fish which Tangle witnesses is a nursery version of the sacrifice of the princess Irene's father witnessed by Curdie. The goddess gives him, not to the peace of air and the forgetfulness of water, but to the tempering fire of roses. "She stooped over the table-altar, put her mighty arms under living sacrifice, lifted the king, as if he were but a little child, to her bosom, walked with him up the floor, and laid him in his bed. . . . All was safe; all was well" (202-203).

Though the picture of the goddess as priestess accepting a sacrifice is pagan, the steps which lead her followers to that altar are not. Even my auntie Joan could have found no quarrel with confession, repentance, trial, and judgment as the way to salvation. To the goddess, what does it mean to be saved? In *The Princess and Curdie,* when the boy confesses to the sin of complacency, she tells him, "There is only one way I care for. Do better, and grow better, and be better" (31). MacDonald himself explains what this means: "There is this difference between the growth of some human beings and that of others: in the one case it is a continuous dying, in the other a continuous resurrection . . . The boy should enclose . . . the old child at the heart of him . . ." (17, 18). Taught by the goddess, the king says, "Now . . . I am compelled to believe many things I could not and do not yet understand . . ." (167). Put differently unless we become as little children, we cannot enter the kingdom of heaven.

The stumbling block to grace is self-love. To correct it, the Wise Woman has in her house a number of "mood-chambers" worthy of Hieronymus Bosch. "Its mood will come upon you," she tells Rosamond, "and you will have to deal with it" (*Gifts* 261). Rosamond cannot be a real princess, she reminds her, until she is a princess over herself. Provoked to anger, Rosamond learns to turn the other cheek and repent of her willfulness. In *The Princess and Curdie,* the great-great-grandmother, disguised as a chambermaid, exhorts the king's household with all the moral fervor of John the Baptist. "Repent ye: for the kingdom of heaven is at hand" (Matthew 3:2) becomes "The messenger . . . sent me to you again . . . to tell you to repent" (175). Lest anyone take Curdie for a Christ figure sending the goddess to preach the Gospel, MacDonald identifies him with the messenger, thus linking him to the Baptist rather than to Christ: "Behold, I send my messenger before thy face, which shall prepare thy way before thee" (Luke 7:27). And as promised, judgment falls on Gwyntystorm (going-to-storm). The goddess' white birds are the avenging angels; the enemy is "pursued and buffeted by the white-winged army of heaven" (213).

Jehovah was not the first deity to take a humbler form that He might serve His people. Pillar of fire, faithful servant, can MacDonald's Christian-pagan lady do less? "The king rose and kneeled on one knee before her. All kneeled in like homage. . . . But she made them all sit down . . . Then in ruby crown and royal purple she served them all" (217).

Works Cited

Grimm, Jacob. *Teutonic Mythology.* Trans. James Steven
    Stallybrass. London: W. Swann Sonnenchein and Allen, 1888.
MacDonald, George. *The Gifts of the Child Christ.* Vol. 1. Ed. Glenn
    Edward Sadler. Grand Rapids, MI: Eerdmans, 1973.
_____. *The Princess and Curdie.* Harmondsworth, Middlesex:
    Penguin, 1973.
_____. *The Princess and the Goblin.* Philadelphia: David McKay,
    1920.

Social Conscience and Class Relations in MacDonald's "Cross Purposes"

By A. Waller Hastings

"Cross Purposes" has been largely neglected by critics who have grouped it, correctly I believe, with George MacDonald's lesser works. Those critics who have dealt with this fairy tale have tended to conclude, with Wolff, that it is "on the whole a failure" (Wolff 1961, 128). Despite its minor status, however, the tale merits closer attention as one of MacDonald's earliest fairy tales for children[1] and as an important early indication of some of MacDonald's later themes.

"Cross Purposes" bears a particular resemblance to MacDonald's acknowledged masterpiece, "The Golden Key," written five years later. Both feature a pair of children from different social classes who move through a symbolic landscape. Mossy in "The Golden Key" and Richard in "Cross Purposes" share a devotion to a maternal figure (Richard's mother and Mossy's great-aunt), and both prefer reading to other, more social games. The girls in both stories clearly belong to a higher class than the boys, although Tangle in "The Golden Key" is made more sympathetic than Alice in the earlier story. The children in both stories learn to love each other through a shared quest for passage out of fairyland. In "Cross Purposes," they return to their everyday world; in "The Golden Key," they move to a celestial home in "the country whence the shadows fell" (MacDonald 226). "Cross Purposes" thus seems an early attempt at the visionary fairy tale perfected in "The Golden Key." Significantly, however, issues of social class that are muted in the later text are rendered much more explicitly in "Cross Purposes."

Jack Zipes has argued that Victorian fairy tales were an important arena for social commentary: "It was through the fairy tale that a discourse about conditions in England took place" (*Victorian Fairy Tales* xi). Victorian children's writers used the fairy tale to "raise social consciousness about the disparities among the different social classes and the problems faced by the oppressed due to the industrial revolution" (*Victorian Fairy Tales* xix). The fairy tales were aimed at both middle-class children and the adults who bought or read the stories to those children.

The association of sometimes radical political ideas with fairy tales has a long history. Many of the traditional tales that began making their way into English middle-class nurseries during the eighteenth century depict victories for peasant or working-class heroes. Such folktales contain an important subtext: those who prove themselves worthy may marry the prince or princess and succeed to a kingdom, transcending the limitations of their native class. This implicit commentary on social-class divisions was made explicit by Hans Christian Andersen, whose literary fairy tales for children were first translated into English in 1843. As in the traditional fairy tale, his characters often begin in the peasantry but rise in class. Many of his tales, furthermore, have contemporary social settings and realistically depict the suffering of rural peasants and urban poor. The subversive component of Andersen's work was somewhat modified by his own feelings of inadequacy. If his protagonists rise, they typically do so only by accepting and accommodating themselves to the social system, as Andersen himself did.

Overt fantasies of class mobility occur less frequently in the writings of English fairy tale writers, but the acute social conscience that Andersen brought to such tales as "The Little Match Girl," "The Candles," and "The Story Old Johanna Told" manifests itself in many English literary fairy tales. For instance, Ruskin's *The King of the Golden River*, which attempted to follow the traditional pattern of the Grimms' tales, can be seen as a parable about capitalist society. The black brothers of Ruskin's fairy tale, ironically characterized as "very good farmers" who "killed everything that did not pay for its eating," are thinly disguised caricatures of laissez-faire industrialists, who

> worked their servants without any wages, till they would not work any more, and then quarreled with them, and turned them

out of doors without paying them. It would have been very odd, if with such a farm, and such a system of farming, they hadn't got very rich; and very rich they *did* get. They generally contrived to keep their corn by them till it was very dear, and yet it was never known that they had given so much as penny or a crust in charity... (Zipes, *Victorian Fairy Tales* 16).

The brothers' farm fails because they have pursued wealth as their prime commandment, refusing hospitality to South West Wind. Similarly, they fail to effect the conversion of the golden river because they fail tests of brotherhood by refusing water to the three thirsty figures, avatars of the King of the Golden River, whom they encounter while climbing the mountain. Gluck succeeds because he is willing to share of himself, even if it means giving up the quest; his actions assert a larger brotherhood than simple blood relationship.[2]

The social discourse of the nursery is more clearly evident in the expositions of the plight of the poor in fairy tales from the 1860s. Figures such as Tom in Kingsley's *Water Babies* and the apple woman in Ingelow's *Mopsa the Fairy* suffer in the real world and find relief through their escape to their respective fairylands. The realistic portions of *At the Back of the North Wind* fall into the same category; the book's depiction of the life of the working poor relates it to many adult novels of the period that similarly seek to raise middle-class consciousness. The impact of such depictions in children's literature was potentially incendiary, as Wolff (1961) points out:

> Novels of social indignation were seldom, like *At the Back of the North Wind,* books ostensibly for children, tricked out in lavishly gilt-stamped cloth, with a little girl on the front cover looking out of a window in the moon (158).

The little crossing guard Nanny's fear that old Sal may beat her is reminiscent of Andersen's match girl, who dares not return home without selling all of her matches and so perishes in the snow. While the realistic portions of *At the Back of the North Wind* contain most of the social analysis, social reform remains an important component of the fantasy as well, as we see North Wind punishing those who have abused others, in particular abusers of children.

MacDonald's unique contribution to the social discourse of the Victorian fairy tale, however, was in his combination of social critique with visionary narrative. Like William Blake before him, MacDonald did not regard the visionary and socio-political realms as either separate or inimical, and rooted his fantasies in social reality. Even his most transcendent Christian fantasies (he refused to let them be called allegories) have a strong component of social critique and imaginative exploration of a Christian Socialist utopia.

Stephen Prickett has written that MacDonald's world is an inconsistent meeting place of two realities, one material and one spiritual, neither of which by itself can explain experience (187). To date, most critics of MacDonald have focused on the spiritual realms, giving less attention to the social aspect of his work. MacDonald's fairy tales, says Colin Manlove, are centrally about God, not man (98). But this is a God who works in a social and material world; MacDonald's theology, like that of F. D. Maurice, is intimately connected to his sociology. MacDonald's fairy tales constitute a critique from a Christian Socialist perspective upon the society in which they were created.

Like other Victorian writers, MacDonald rejects a society based purely on material considerations, on the Mammon worship that values the advantageous marriage or the striving for ever-greater wealth. The British economy at midcentury seemed to many Englishmen to have secured the promise of the traditional fairy tale, of class mobility and undreamed-of wealth for those who prove themselves worthy. The great children's literature of Victorian England emerged against the background of what historian George Kitson Clark has called the "High Noon" of Victorianism, the third quarter of the nineteenth century, during which England found itself in an era of relative peace, contentment, and well-being (31). At first the social criticisms implicit in so many mid-Victorian fairy tales seem incongruous in such a period, but prosperity can disguise very real social discontinuities, as it does in our own society. Surface serenity tends to promote smug self-satisfaction, against which socially conscious children's writers reacted just as did their adult counterparts. This was the period, remember, in which Charles Dickens, whose own work was strongly influenced by his childhood reading of fairy tales[3], produced his darkest novels, castigating the smug middle-class with its sins of Podsnappery.

MacDonald's own experience with his parishioners at Arundel led him to conclude that wealth retarded spiritual development, a belief he expressed in one of his sermons: "One may readily conclude how poorly God thinks of riches when we see the sort of people he sends them to" (quoted in Raeper 86-87). In place of capitalist philistinism, he tried, along with other socially conscious Victorian fantasists, to offer a society formed on sympathy and cooperation. But how to do so in the fairy tale mode, which shares with the society that is being rejected a reliance on material rewards to validate the individual?

In MacDonald's fairy tales, characters succeed only by caring for other people and opening up to those others' emotional concerns and physical needs. Success is measured more often in the difficult passage through life to a Christian redemption than in traditional fairy-tale terms. Emphasizing the Christian Socialist principle of cooperation over competition, MacDonald eschews the traditional fairy tale tension between siblings, in which only one may succeed in the quest. The road to salvation and a proper life is typically a shared one in his tales, usually shared between male and female protagonists.[4] This is the pattern MacDonald established in an explicitly class-conscious context in "Cross Purposes."

As the fairy tale begins, the Queen of Fairyland dispatches two of her subjects, a fairy (Peaseblossom) and a goblin (Toadstool), to bring a human boy and girl to her court. Social class in Fairyland seems related to gender. The "graceful" Peaseblossom, who has "pretty ways of doing things," is a member of the court and the daughter of the prime minister (*Complete Fairy Tales* 187); she is dispatched to bring back Alice, the squire's daughter. The dirty, raucous Toadstool, on the other hand, is clearly *not* an aristocrat. If he has any function at the court, it is that of court jester. He is less evil perhaps than the goblins of *The Princess and the Goblin* (although they too have humorous qualities), but his underground lifestyle associates him both with them and with the miners of the Princess books. The boy, Richard, is as far below Alice on the real-world social scale as Toadstool is below Peaseblossom in Fairyland society:

> He was so poor that he did not find himself generally welcome; so he hardly went anywhere, but read books at home, and waited upon his mother. His manners, therefore, were shy,

and sufficiently awkward to give an unfavourable impression to those who looked at outsides. Alice would have despised him; but he never came near enough for that (191).

Class and gender differences between Richard and Alice are emphasized in the narrator's comments on the distance between them in their everyday world and in their situations immediately before being lured into Fairyland.

Alice is lying in bed when Peaseblossom appears to entice her; Richard, on the other hand, is on an errand to the marketplace to get an umbrella for his mother, using pennies he has saved. The two children appear to be about the same age, but the peasant boy, Richard, must work and run errands, while the squire's daughter, Alice, has leisure to relax in her bedroom.

The alliance of class status and gender that occurs here tends to impose on the adventures of Richard and Alice a more traditional folktale pattern which Zipes has characterized, "The male acts, the female waits" (*Subversion* 25). This link between female gender and higher class status seems to be a clear defect in the tale's social vision, since it simultaneously asserts a new relationship between classes and appears to endorse the existing relationship between the sexes. A more active Alice would diffuse the class message, but the passive Alice that MacDonald created instead suggests that women are not to be included in the reformed social vision. This is at variance with such later MacDonald masterpieces as "The Day Boy and the Night Girl," where the relationship between social class and gender is reversed and the lower-class Nycteris is a far more active heroine than Alice. In "The Golden Key," Tangle's superior class status does not prevent her from taking a very active role in the quest. But Alice, like a traditional fairy tale heroine, relies on the hero to effect her escape. Except for the mutual guidance the children provide each other through a dark passageway, every move of the escape is initiated and carried out by Richard.

Richard and Alice reappear in "The Golden Key" as Mossy and Tangle. While Mossy's class status is less clearly established than Richard's, he appears to be of a lower class than the merchant's daughter, Tangle, who has servants to wait on her. Like Richard, Mossy is concerned initially, though briefly, with financial need. He first thinks of the golden key in terms of monetary worth, but is told by his great-aunt, "Better never to find it than to sell it"

(*Complete Fairy Tales* 210).[5] "The Golden Key" challenges the material basis of laissez-faire capitalism as well as the similarly material rewards of the traditional fairy tale. Success for Mossy and Tangle does not consist in simply finding the physical key — Mossy does so within the first few pages of the story — nor in an advantageous marriage — they are symbolically "wed" in Grandmother's house before the quest really gets underway. Rather, their quest is complete only when they have won through a partially shared life to a reunion with each other and with the spiritual ideal. It is the process that counts, the narrow path and difficult climb that both must follow to reach the shadow-sea and their cooperation in crossing that sea.[6]

Process is what counts for Alice and Richard, as well, a fact that is accentuated by their return to their previous lives at the end of their sojourn in Fairyland. Each must overcome character deficiencies related to their class status: Alice her unjustified snobbery and Richard his diffidence. When Alice and Richard first meet in Fairyland, she wonders "how ever the poor widow's son could have found his way into Fairyland" and feels his presence there to be "an invasion of privilege" (196). Hers is the smug assumption of class differences as part of the natural order. MacDonald's project in "Cross Purposes" is to disrupt such assumptions by providing a vision of an *un*natural order in which class is irrelevant to individual value.

In the early part of their sojourn in Fairyland, Alice constantly abuses Richard, stressing his innate class inferiority. When he drives away their captors, she refuses to sit beside him, thinking of her father's probable reaction were he to see the two talking together. As Richard leads her out of Fairyland, Alice follows "not of her own will, she gave him to understand, but because she could do no better" (200). Alice's class prejudice begins to weaken after Richard, recognizing that she becomes cross whenever he speaks to her, resolves to remain quiet. The unbearable silence soon causes her to take Richard's arm, preferring contact even with a lower-class human being to her lonely terror. But even as she becomes dependent on him, Alice's attitudes toward Richard are dominated by social class feelings:

"It is very strange," she said to herself; "for he is quite a poor boy, I am sure of that. His arms stick out beyond his jacket like the ribs of his mother's umbrella. And to think of me wandering about Fairyland with *him*!" (201-202).

Her fears increasing as they enter a pitch-dark passageway, Alice addresses her companion as "dear Richard," at which he instantly and improbably falls in love with her. Alice surprises herself by falling in love with Richard as well.

In a traditional fairy tale, this mutual love achieved through a sequence of shared adventures would most likely end in a marriage between the two, a public recognition of the inherent equality of the extremes of village society. But in "Cross Purposes," such a conclusion is denied; the stirrings of love contribute to the children's escape from Fairyland but have no residual effect when they return to the "real" world. In Fairyland, love for another causes one's eyes to project a light that reveals only the loved one — suggesting the role of imagination in romantic love, where the image of the loved one depends on the mental state of the lover. In love with Alice, Richard can guide her steps, even though he cannot see his own path. Alice can see him but not herself. So, through cooperation made possible by love, they make their way through the darkness.

They emerge from the dark passage into the home of a crooked old man who acts as a surrogate for the outside society in trying to separate the children. Richard apologizes for intruding and the old man replies, "Oh, certainly, certainly, my dear young people. Use your freedom. But such young people have no business to be out alone. It is against the rules" (204).

He seats Richard and Alice on opposite sides of the hearth, placing himself and the cat between them. When the two children try to hold each other's hands for reassurance, the cat becomes a steep hill between them, swelling until they cannot even see each other. The obstacle disappears only when Richard refuses to acquiesce in the separation and stabs the hill/cat with his pocketknife. The old man emerges as a representation of the restrictive, class-based society; like Alice's father, he disapproves of their companionship. His twisted language allows him to evoke "freedom" while simultaneously imposing restrictive rules of behavior on the children. His apparent hospitality, under cover of which he forces the lovers apart, suggests the disguise of manners by which the social world enforces its repressive standards.

The children become separated again and see each other atop high towers divided by a wide chasm, a visual representation of the social gulf that exists between them in the mortal world. The chasm proves to be an optical illusion; however, they are close enough to reach out to each other across the space, and the floor is only a couple of feet beneath them. The optical illusion suggests that the social forces separating the couple are also illusory and can be overcome through love and faith. To MacDonald, who would have extended Christian brotherhood even to the animal world, this affirmation of human relationship is surely part of the message of the story. Coupled with the narrator's earlier comment that Richard makes an unfavorable impression on "those who looked at outsides," this scene calls for a more penetrating social vision that transcends class divisions. The children's ability to see each other in the darkness only after they have begun to love suggests one component of this new vision. The other is faith in themselves or in a higher providence; it is faith that allows Richard to jump from his tower and effect a reunion with Alice. MacDonald seems to say that only when we can see each other through the eyes of love and faith, not blinded by social constraints, can we achieve our maximum human potential.

While the children have learned to look at each other in a different way in Fairyland, it makes little difference once they return to the everyday world of the village. Unlike traditional tales, "Cross Purposes" ends without a marriage or a material reward for the protagonists. There *is* a marriage of sorts at the end, however. Toadstool and Peaseblossom are punished for their failure to bring the children to the Queen of Fairyland by being compelled to live together for seven years. The depiction of marriage as torture rather than reward subverts the traditional fairy-tale ending and forces the reader back to a consideration of process, since the ending holds out little other incentive to emulate Richard and Alice. The obstacles that were overcome in Fairyland seem to reassert themselves in the outside world, as the children return to their previous situations. Whatever has been gained in Fairyland fails to transform either child's social reality.

While "The Golden Key" ends with an affirmation of faith and the promise of a better world, "Cross Purposes" concludes a bitter attack on social customs with a return to the status quo. Richard and Alice end their quest, not with a transcendent reunion, but with a reversion to their old roles. Less has changed for them even than in the folk tales of fairy captives who find years have passed in the outside world during their visit to Fairyland, since Richard and Alice arrive back in the mortal world at exactly the instant they left it. They *may* have learned through their experiences in Fairyland. Alice, one hopes, will no longer sneer at the poor, and Richard has shown his innate strength. But while the two children no longer wish to be separated, the class distinctions that operate in this world intervene to force them back into roles that their experience has seemingly prepared them to transcend. The negative vision of the ending only serves to accentuate the sharp condemnation of the class-bound values of the "real world."

The absence of even a symbolic reward at the end of "Cross Purposes" seems to limit the tale's effectiveness, although it becomes more comprehensible when seen in the context of MacDonald's Christian Socialism. While MacDonald's social conscience is clearly reflected in his depiction of social ills, his vision of a better society depends on internal transformation rather than radical social reform. The social views of F. D. Maurice, like those of Kingsley (who was also influenced by Maurice), emphasized *individual* reform rather than social activism. In the Christian Socialist scheme of things, it is sufficient that Alice has learned to value the least of her brethren, not that she try to improve their lot. Maurice sought to instill in the working class a sense of themselves as spiritual beings through moral education; political and economic measures would not be necessary, if only people realized the universal spiritual kingdom of Christ (Norman 6-8). MacDonald's tale follows this Maurician logic, seeking greater goodwill rather than overt social reform. But it is difficult to see what effect this internal transformation was to have in the real world.

The inadequacy of individual transformation to deal with ingrained social attitudes that affect and are modulated by an outside world accounts, I think, for the unsatisfactory nature of the ending of "Cross Purposes." The problem of individual goodwill versus societal constraints is finessed much better in "The Golden Key" precisely *because* class issues are muted. The later story focuses almost exclusively on the individual characters, whose quest does not bring them into contact with ordinary society and who never return to the "real" world in which social constraints act. There is in the later story a concord between the process and the desired end that is never established in "Cross Purposes." Nevertheless, the insistence in the earlier fairy tale on class consciousness may suggest ways of understanding MacDonald's later work.

Notes

1. While "Cross Purposes" was once thought to be an inferior imitation of *Alice in Wonderland,* Wolff's discovery of its 1862 publication in *Beeton's Magazine* ("An 1862 'Alice'") establishes a claim for the originality of the story as well as for its role as a marker of MacDonald's later creative concerns.

2. Both of the wicked brothers fail even the test of blood. Hans mocks his brother Schwartz in jail and Schwartz gets his revenge by denying water to the image of Hans (actually the king of the golden river). Their abuse of Gluck, of course, reveals both brothers to be ignorant of the true meaning of brotherhood.

3. For an analysis of the way Dickens's imagination was shaped by fairy tales, *see* Michael Kotzin, *Dickens and the Fairy Tale* (Bowling Green, OH: Bowling Green U Popular P, (1972), and Harry Stone, *Dickens and the Invisible World* (Bloomington, IN: Indiana UP, 1979).

4. Zipes discusses the phenomenon of dual heroes in *Fairy Tales and the Art of Subversion:*

> ... there are always male and female protagonists, who learn to follow their deep inclinations, respect each other's needs and talents, and share each other's visions. Together they overcome sinister forces which want to deprive them of possible happiness and the realization of an ideal community (*Subversion* 105).

However, the split between male and female co-protagonists is less universal in MacDonald's fairy tales than this statement suggests. The joint ventures that feature so prominently in the *Princess* books and some of the shorter tales are present only marginally in *At the Back of the North Wind,* where Diamond never really achieves an alliance with the little crossing sweeper Nanny (North Wind, while a female principle, remains an agent of magical change rather than a partner to Diamond), and in such tales as "The Light Princess" and "Little Daylight," where the princesses serve as rewards to the princes rather than true partners. "The Shadows" features just one hero, Ralph Rinkelmann.

5. The great-aunt's warning is reminiscent of the advice given by the King of the Golden River to Gluck, that it would not be good for the river to turn into real gold. Mossy, unlike Gluck, gives no further thought to the

commercial possibilities of the golden key, but still dreams of finding it for its intrinsic properties.

6. Cynthia Marshall discusses the way in which the meaning of the fairy tale develops only through the process of the quest, not through its end. Marshall's account helps to explain why the finding of the key itself is handled so simply and minimizes the troubling status of "Mossy's privileged ownership" of the key. *See* her "Reading 'The Golden Key': Narrative Strategies of Parable" elsewhere in this volume.

Works Cited

Kitson Clark, G. S. R. *The Making of Victorian England*. Cambridge, MA: Harvard UP, 1962.

Kotzin, Michael. *Dickens and the Fairy Tale*. Bowling Green, OH: Bowling Green U Popular P, 1972.

MacDonald, George. *The Complete Fairy Tales of George MacDonald*. New York: Schocken, 1977.

Manlove, C. N. "George MacDonald's Fairy Tales: Their Roots in MacDonald's Thought." *Studies in Scottish Literature* 8 (1970): 97-108.

Norman, Edward. *The Victorian Christian Socialists*. Cambridge: Cambridge UP, 1987.

Prickett, Stephen. *Victorian Fantasy*. Hassocks: Harvester, 1979.

Raeper, William. *George MacDonald*. Tring: Lion, 1987.

Stone, Harry. *Dickens and the Invisible World*. Bloomington, IN: Indiana UP, 1979.

Wolff, Robert Lee. "An 1862 Alice: 'Cross Purposes'; or, *Which Dreamed It?*" *Harvard Library Bulletin* 23 (1975): 199-202.

_____. *The Golden Key: A Study of the Fiction of George MacDonald*. New Haven: Yale UP, 1961.

Zipes, Jack. *Fairy Tales and the Art of Subversion: The Classical Genre for Children and the Process of Civilization*. New York: Wildman, 1987.

_____, Ed. *Victorian Fairy Tales*. New York: Methuen, 1987.

The Golden Key
Milton and MacDonald
By Celia Catlett Anderson

The influence of the German Romantics on George MacDonald is generally acknowledged, but not as much attention has been given to the pervasive influence of John Milton. That MacDonald admired Milton above virtually all other English poets is quite clear from MacDonald's comments in *England's Antiphon* (194-211). Furthermore, one of MacDonald's central ideas, "that good is the one power and that evil exists only because *for a time* it subserves, cannot help subserve the good" (*Sermons* 204-05) echoes *Paradise Lost* and also the Lady's words in *Comus* on "the Supreme good t'whom all things ill/Are but as slavish officers" (ll. 217-18). Miltonic ideas surface in many of MacDonald's works. One in which the influence is demonstrable is *The Golden Key*. There are strong links between Milton's masque *Comus* and MacDonald's fairy tale. Internal evidence suggests that in writing *The Golden Key* MacDonald derived inspiration, title, and some of his imagery from Milton's masque.

When, in the opening scene of the masque, the Attendant Spirit announces,

> Yet some there be that by due steps aspire/ To lay their just hands on that Golden Key/ That opes the palace of Eternity (lines 12-14),

we have a capsule statement of the theme of MacDonald's fairy tale. The similarities between the two works are not, however, a simple matter of plot. *Comus* centers on the ordeal of the Lady, a young virgin accosted in a dark forest by an evil sorcerer, finally freed from his spell by the agency of the river goddess Sabrina, and then conducted safely home with her brothers. In *The Golden Key,* Mossy, the hero, runs into a forest to seek a sapphire-studded golden key at the end of the rainbow, and, finding it and a house in the woods occupied by a magical Grandmother, meets a girl named Tangle and goes with her on a lifelong pilgrimage to find the lock which the key opens. Ultimately, the two discover the matching five sapphires in a keyhole in one of the columns of the rainbow, and they climb the rainbow's winding stairway to "the land whence the shadows fall" (*Golden Key* 78). This is obviously not simply another version of *Comus.* Instead, MacDonald's story is, in part, an expansion of some themes contained in Milton's drama. The most important of these are the primacy of the search for salvation, the perils and rewards of metamorphosis, the acceptance of natural sensuality, and a symbolic recognition of the value of the subconscious.

Some of these themes are expressed in similar imagery in the two works, and these similarities present the clearest evidence of Milton's influence on MacDonald's story. One image, the golden key to heaven, is, of course, commonplace. The key is usually in the hands of Saint Peter, a convention Milton follows in *Lycidas.* In both *Comus* and *The Golden Key,* however, the key is held by a lay individual, not by a priestly symbol of ecclesiastical power, an interesting, Protestant-minded variation that suits both Milton's and MacDonald's views on salvation. In *Comus,* the key, once mentioned, is not referred to again, although the "Palace of Eternity" (line 14) that it opens is the reward promised in the epilogue. In the masque, Virtue, aided by heaven, allows ascent to paradise, leading one to assume that the Golden Key is also a gift of Virtue.

MacDonald, using a fairy tale convention, makes the key a magic talisman that Mossy carries with him until his quest is completed. The key earns him the respect of the ageless Grandmother who lives in the cottage deep in the forest; it allows him to recognize (without fear) that the Old Man of the Sea is death; finally, it "opes the Palace of Eternity." MacDonald's extended use of the key as symbol makes its meaning more ambiguous than that of Milton's key. Robert Lee Wolff, in his Freudian reading of MacDonald, first says that the key is the phallus (and the fact that it and the keyhole are set with five sapphires, possibly representing the five senses, does suggest a physiological if not a strictly phallic interpretation). But Wolff goes on to note that although MacDonald's use of "essential sexual symbols" is interesting here and elsewhere, the key may also "stand for the poetic imagination, for warmth and kindness, for religious faith, for love" (*The Golden Key: A Study of the Fiction of George MacDonald* 138). This broader interpretation of the key's symbolism serves the complexities of the story better than one that restricts its symbolic value to sexuality.

When Mossy first finds the key, he wonders,

> Where was the lock to which the key belonged? It must be somewhere, for how could anybody be so silly as to make a key for which there was no lock? Where should he go to look for it? He gazed about him, up into the air, down to the earth, but saw no keyhole in the clouds, in the grass, or in the trees (*Golden Key* 9-10).

The passage implies that the key, though given in this world, is meant for something beyond the physical. As Richard Neuse argues, in *Comus* Milton defines virtue as the spiritual integrity springing from the right use of the senses. This meaning also applies to MacDonald's five-gemmed golden key.

A second symbol, only glimpsed in *Comus,* but used overtly by MacDonald, is the rainbow. In Milton's poem the rainbow is referred to three times. First, when the Attendant Spirit descends from heaven, he does so in the colors of the rainbow: "I must put off/These my sky robes spun out of *Iris'* Woof" (lines 82-83), the spirit tells the audience before disguising himself as a shepherd. Later, Comus, speaking falsely to the Lady (but more wisely than he knows), describes her brothers:

> Their port was more than human, as they stood;
> I took it for a faery vision
> Of some gay creatures of the element
> That in the colours of the Rainbow live
> And play i' th' plighted clouds. I was awe-struck,
> And as I past, I worshipt; if those you seek,
> It were a journey like the path to Heav'n
> To help you find them (Lines 297-304).

In the epilogue, it is "*Iris* there with humid bow" (line 992) who "drenches with *Elysian* dew" (line 996) the flowers in the garden of Adonis. Milton has combined the classical notion of Iris as messenger of the gods with the biblical use of the rainbow as a symbol of God's covenant with humans. The closing lines of *Comus,* "if Virtue feeble were,/ Heav'n itself would stoop to her" (1022-23), therefore may also refer to the rainbow.

In *The Golden Key,* MacDonald uses the metaphor of the rainbow as a path to heaven with childlike literalness. When Mossy first encounters the rainbow in the forest, "in each of the colours, which was as large as the columns of a church, he could see beautiful forms slowly ascending as if by the steps of a winding stair" (*Golden Key* 5-6). And the climax of the book is Mossy's and Tangle's entrance into the rainbow: "They climbed out of the earth; and, still climbing, rose above it. They were in the rainbow....They knew that they were going up to the country whence the shadows fall" (77-78). This is close in spirit to the epilogue of *Comus* with its ascent through the paradisical gardens and its final promise that Virtue "can teach ye how to climb/Higher than the sphery chime" (lines 1020-21). MacDonald's use of the rainbow may well have been influenced by Milton's handling of the same symbol in *Comus.* The greater explicitness in *The Golden Key* may result from the difference in genre, or from MacDonald's combination not only of Christian and classical mythology but also of the Norse myth in which Bifrost is the rainbow bridge leading to Asgard, the home of the gods.

Iris's "humid bow," with its dewy grace, brings us to a central metaphor that both writers use: water as a means of salvation. Of course, the shared Christian symbolism of water as grace, the agent of baptism, can scarcely be used as an argument for the influence of Milton on MacDonald. But there is a shared psychological symbolism for water in both the masque and the fairy tale. In both the symbol is complex, and my argument for parallels will focus on the ways in which Milton and MacDonald use water in connection with the subconscious, with sensuality, and with metamorphosis.

In Milton's *Comus,* Sabrina, as river goddess, is the personification of water as a healing force. An understanding of the nature of her curative powers is therefore important. Neuse holds that "By entrusting herself to the waters it would seem that Sabrina comes to symbolize spirit at the other end of the scale from the attendant spirit.... As river goddess she represents ... the 'lower', unconscious life of Nature" (56). He adds that it is "the clash of sensual nature and chaste austerity" (57) which brings about the Lady's paralysis and that

> Sabrina's liberation of the Lady thus involves what is most profoundly natural in her, in that it is drawn up and presented to consciousness.... Sabrina becomes a symbolic expression of man's lower nature, seen truly in a new light, transformed, namely as no longer in conflict with spirit and reason, but as harmoniously responsive to them (58).

MacDonald, who wrote in one of his essays, "God sits in that chamber of our being in which the candle of our consciousness goes out in darkness" (*A Dish of Orts* 24-25), might well be sympathetic to Neuse's reading of *Comus*.

A symbolic use of water, similar to Milton's in *Comus*, is present in *The Golden Key*. Compare, for instance, Sabrina's metamorphosis with Tangle's cleansing in "Grandmother's" fish tank. When Sabrina, fleeing dishonor, flings herself into the Severn,

> The Water Nymphs that in the bottom play'd,
> Held up their pearled wrists and took her in,
> Bearing her straight to aged *Nereus'* Hall,
> Who piteous of her woes, rear'd her lank head,
> And gave her to his daughters to imbathe
> In nectar'd lavers strew'd with Asphodel,
> And through the porch and inlet of each sense
> Dropt in Ambrosial Oils till she reviv'd
> And underwent a quick immortal change,
> Made Goddess of the River (*Comus*, lines 833-43).

When Tangle escapes entrapment by a magic tree, and, her face stained with tears and dirt, reaches Grandmother's cottage in the forest, the girl learns that three years have elapsed and she is now thirteen. Tangle is stripped of her nightgown and thrown into

> a deep tank, the sides of which were filled with green plants, which had flowers of all colours.... It was filled with beautiful clear water, in which swam a multitude of such fishes as the one that had led her to the cottage.... the fishes came crowding about her. Two or three of them got under her head and kept it up. The rest of them rubbed themselves all over her, and with their wet feathers washed her quite clean (*Golden Key* 20-21).

Although the ordeal with the tree parallels the Lady's confinement by Comus, the bath among the fish, an eerily sensual rite of passage into womanhood, suggests similarities between Tangle and Sabrina.

Tangle's later metamorphosis is literally in "Nereus' Hall." In the Old Man of the Sea's subaqueous home, Tangle is led to

> a great basin hollowed out of a rock.... Large green leaves and white flowers of various plants crowded up and over it, draping and covering it almost entirely.... No sooner was she undressed and lying in the bath, than she began to feel as if the water were sinking into her, and she were receiving all the good of sleep without undergoing its forgetfulness (*Golden Key* 52-54).

This particular passage concerns Tangle's death (she later realizes she has not breathed since leaving the basin), but, as in Milton's description of Sabrina's drowning, the sensory images are strong and suggest the healing powers of the senses, while the submersion suggests the power of the subconscious. MacDonald uses water as symbol elsewhere in this way. Water, as Wolff notes, is of major importance in *Phantastes,* where "the delicious uterine water-experiences symbolize the change" of the hero's state from "harshness" to the "refreshing and beautiful and comfortable" (70).

The realm of the unconscious or subconscious is important in both *Comus* and *The Golden Key*. Milton and MacDonald use both submersion in water and passage through a forest to represent the deep recesses of the human spirit, where body and soul are in touch with each other. In the masque, Milton divides the evil aspects of our "lower" nature from the acceptable ones: Comus, son of Bacchus and Circe, and his animal-headed "rout of monsters" must be rejected by the Lady because they deny reason and promote surrender to depraved sensuality; Sabrina and her water nymphs, on the other hand, may be accepted as beneficient primal forces whose sensuality is healing. Milton understood the benign nature of these water nymphs who, like their Grecian antecedents, saved men from destruction. The Attendant Spirit's prayer catalogs the names of Tethys, Leucothea, and Thetis (lines 870-76), all good "mermaids" found in Greek literature. In medieval thought, however, mermaids were an emblem of *luxuria* and agents of damnation, and a writer less sensitive and aware than Milton might well have put Sabrina and Comus's companions on the same moral level. Even Comus's role is somewhat legitimized. If the Lady is to reach maturity, she must be tested by traveling through the forest where he rules. She can then safely join the "rout" of country dancers at Ludlow-Castle during the finale of the masque, where Comus is present in spirit as the ritually accepted lord of misrule.

A casual reading of *The Golden Key* might suggest that MacDonald has left out Comus and the Bacchus-Circe elements, but I believe that they, along with Sabrina, are subsumed in the figure of the old lady. Grandmother, one of the many lovely crones who are MacDonald's trademark, lives, as Circe does, in the center of a pathless forest. She is, as is Comus, the warder of strange interbred creatures, hers half-fish, half-owl, and, as in Sabrina's case, she lives surrounded by green plants, flowers, and fish. Ruling from her moss-covered hut which opens only from the inside and only at night—"the red light of the fire flowing from it like a river through the darkness" (*Golden Key* 29-30), the Grandmother represents the primal forces in our nature which must be met if we are to make a successful pilgrimage through life. She is, with her green dress, her eyes containing stars, moon, and sun, Nature herself and MacDonald finds no evil in her.

What evil there is in the story seems to emanate from fear of the forest. It is not Comus but a humanoid tree that captures and detains Tangle "as the last of the light was disappearing" (*Golden Key* 13-14) and it is a fearless, luminous "air-fish" that rescues her. The forest, as John Arthos points out in his study of *Comus,* "comes close to us, not as locality but as a fear of the mind" (*On a Mask Presented at Ludlow-Castle by John Milton* 28). In *The Golden Key,* the connection between fear and misperception is shown clearly in the scene in which Tangle is driven from her room. She sees "an ape making faces at her out of the mirror" (12), symbolically a misjudgment of her own nature. Then, further played upon by the fairies, who know she has been reading the story of the three bears, Tangle imagines she hears the bears coming up the stairs, climbs out her window, and runs to the forest. MacDonald informs us that "this was the very best way she could have gone; for nothing is ever so mischievous in its own place as it is out of it" (13). Tangle flees this "rout of monsters" and must, like the Lady in *Comus,* confront nature rather than continue to fear it. In both instances the girls, having escaped intrapment (by tree and by Comus) and having met nature (Grandmother and Sabrina), grow beyond a paralyzing fear of evil.

It is curious, as Lee Jacobus has pointed out in his article "Milton's *Comus* as Children's Literature," that in one sense *Comus* is a children's story, more so perhaps than *The Golden Key* is. Milton concentrates on a rite of passage for the Lady and her brothers; all three are adolescents and still part of the father's household. The action of the play centers on a trial that brings maturity: "Heav'n hath timely tri'd their youth" (*Comus* line 970). MacDonald, on the other hand, summarily treats the transition from childhood to puberty. Tangle's flight, capture by the tree, the simple announcement that three years have passed, and her bath in the air-fish's tank are all we are told of her maturation. Mossy simply appears in outgrown clothes. If, as Wolff holds, their subsequent wandering through the forest is symbolic of their transition to adulthood, this too is treated briefly. More than half of *The Golden Key* deals with Mossy's and Tangle's pilgrimage through adulthood and beyond death. In contrast, all of *Comus* concerns an adventure of young people.

At the center of both stories, however, is a metamorphosis of character connected with the spiritual evolution that informs all nature. As Milton presents it, in rather medieval terms, there is descent and ascent on the great chain of being. Those who "taste through fond intemperate thirst" (line 67) from Comus' cup have their human countenance changed "Into some brutish form of Wolf, or Bear,/Or Ounce, or Tiger, Hog, or bearded Goat" (lines 70-71) which, according to Karl Wentersdorf, are all animals with medieval or classical precedents as emblems of lechery. As the Elder Brother phrases it, unchastity causes the soul to grow "clotted by contagion" (line 467) and "quite lose/The divine property of her first being" (lines 468-69). However, when the soul has "saintly chastity" (line 453), angels serve it,

> Till oft converse with heav'nly habitants
> Begin to cast a beam on th' outward shape,
> The unpolluted temple of the mind,
> And turns it by degrees to the soul's essence,
> Till all be made immortal (*Comus* lines 459-63).

The Elder Brother is close to the words of the Attendant Spirit—"love virtue, she alone is free,/She can teach ye how to climb" (lines 1019-20)— but the change to a higher state does not come straightforwardly in *Comus*. The Elder Brother is voicing a Neoplatonic dualism which seems to be rejected by the action of the masque. Milton condemns mindless sensuality, but also condemns spirituality that does not account for our bodies as well as our souls. Sabrina symbolizes the necessary descent into nature that must precede the ascent toward heaven.

MacDonald holds a similar theory, and a comparison of his view of spiritual ascent and descent with that of Milton can aid in deciphering the often dreamlike images in *The Golden Key*. Like the sister and brothers in *Comus*, Mossy and Tangle are among those "that by due steps aspire" to open "the Palace of Eternity"; however, the "due steps" again do not lead straightforwardly to the rainbow's stairs. The two wander in a forest, in a valley of shadows (a Platonic image made palpable in *The Golden Key*), and into the underworld. There, separated from Mossy, Tangle descends first below water, to the home of the Old Man of the Sea, then down into the bowels of the earth, where she moves through scorching heat until she "fell exhausted into a cool mossy cave" (*Golden Key* 59). She finds the Old Man of the Fire, a child who, reminiscent of the Son playing before God the Father at creation, is "playing with balls of various colours and sizes" which must have "an infinite meaning in the change and sequence" (*Golden Key* 60). This passage (as MacDonald tells us in a rare footnote) owes something to Novalis, as undoubtedly the whole of Tangle's journey through water, earth, and fire does. Novalis (the Latin name of Friedrich von Hardenburg, 1772-1801) was a major influence on MacDonald, whose first literary work (1851) was the translation of twelve of Novalis' spiritual songs. Novalis held, as did other German Romantics, a

"Neptunist" theory that water was the primal substance, "the white blood of the mother" (quoted in Wolff 70), that the elements were always recombining and evolving, and, further, as Wolff describes the theory, that "the order of creation ascended from minerals through plants through animals to man, each evolving upward into the next category, and man himself destined to evolve toward God" (37). These theories, another expression of the idea of the great chain of being, are similar to those held by the mystic Jakob Boehme (1575-1624), who seems to have been a minor influence on Milton. The common source of this tradition may mean that if Milton's use of metamorphosis influenced MacDonald, it was in this case more reinforcement that primary inspiration.

The most interesting symbols of metamorphosis in *The Golden Key*, and ones that seem close in spirit to Milton's ideas, are MacDonald's air-fish that become "aeranths." Sent by the Old Man of the Sea, these strange creatures, "made like a fish, but covered, instead of scales, with feathers of all colours" (*Golden Key* 13), serve the same purpose as Milton's Attendant Spirit (with his "robes spun out of *Iris'* woof"), which is to guide through the forest those who by "their tender age might suffer peril" (*Comus* line 40). An air-fish leads both Tangle and Mossy to the cottage. Then these hybrid creatures, which swim through the air "as a fish does through the water" *(Golden Key* 13) and which have fish-bodies and the head of an owl, undergo a curious metamorphosing ritual. They swim into a boiling pot and, after being eaten, emerge in spirit from the pot, "a lovely creature in human shape, with large white wings" (26). In this state they are called aeranths, a word that seems to be of MacDonald's own making. It is apparently a combination of the Greek *aer* (air) and *anth,* either from *anthos* (flower) or from *anthro* (man), or possibly a play on both. The aeranths also remind one that the Greeks personified the soul (Psyche) with butterfly wings. These air-fish/aeranths confer upon the person who eats them the ability to understand animal speech. After Tangle has eaten the fish, she understands what the sounds of the forest mean; "she could tell what the insects in the cottage were saying to each other too. She even had a suspicion that the trees and flowers . . . were holding midnight communications with each other" (*Golden Key* 26). She can, in other words, hear things "that no gross ear can hear" (*Comus* line 468), in a way which indicates a union with nature as well as a spiritualization of the mind. Perhaps there is also a sacramental reading here, as the fish is a traditional symbol for Christ.

In both stories there is a melding of the spiritual and the physical, and, although some differences have been shown between Milton's and MacDonald's use of metamorphosis, of the personification of natural forces, and of symbols like the key, the rainbow, water, and the forest, nevertheless, it should be clear that both writers see the evolution of man toward God as a complex and nature-bound process, not as a dualistic denial of the body in favor of the soul. If *The Golden Key* is based in part on *Comus,* then MacDonald's story is in one sense an interpretation of Milton's masque that anticipates much modern commentary. From the reverse perspective, a careful reading of the masque can enrich our understanding of the fairy tale. MacDonald obviously admired Milton, and I believe he paid homage to him by drawing on *Comus* in writing *The Golden Key.*

Works Cited

Arthos, John. *On a Mask Presented at Ludlow-Castle by John Milton.* Ann Arbor, MI.: U of Michigan P, 1954.
Jacobus, Lee. "Milton's *Comus* as Children's Literature." *Children's Literature* 2 (1973): 67-72.
MacDonald, George. *A Dish of Orts.* London: Sampson, Low, Marston, 1893.
_____. *England's Antiphon.* London: Macmillan, 1871.
_____. *The Golden Key.* New York: Farrar, Straus and Giroux, 1967.
_____. *Unspoken Sermons.* Second Series. London: Longmans, Green, 1886.
Milton, John. *Comus* in *John Milton: Complete Poems and Major Prose.* Ed. Merrit Y. Hughes. Indianapolis, IN: Bobbs-Merrill, 1977.
Neuse, Richard. "Metamorphosis and Symbolic Action in *Comus.*" *ELH* 34 (March 1967): 49-64.
Reis, Richard H. *George MacDonald.* New York: Twayne, 1972.
Wentersdorf, Karl P. "The 'Rout of Monsters' in *Comus.*" *The Milton Quarterly* 12 (Dec. 1978): 119-25.
Wolff, Robert Lee. *The Golden Key: A Study of the Fiction of George MacDonald.* New Haven: Yale UP, 1961.

Reading "The Golden Key"
Narrative Strategies of Parable

By Cynthia Marshall

"The Golden Key" is regularly recognized as George MacDonald's masterpiece in the fairy tale mode. The work may not be, however, without its problems for modern readers, who may question the integrity of the tale's structure. "The Golden Key" seems, for example, repeatedly to be on the verge of concluding. It opens with the boy Mossy's desire to find the golden key at the end of the rainbow; he shortly discovers the key, and "the quest seems accomplished, the story over" (Wolff 135). Mossy must, however, discover the key's purpose, so his quest is renewed. Meanwhile the girl Tangle has also entered the enchanted forest of the tale; when Mossy and Tangle are drawn together, a romantic resolution seems imminent, but once again there is a fresh beginning. And so throughout the pilgrimage to "the country whence the shadows fall" (226): each time the characters, separately or together, reach a goal—the "lofty precipice" (225) from which they first glimpse the shadow lake, the high country beyond the shadows, the Old Man of the Sea, the Old Man of the Earth, the Old Man of the Fire—the proffered reward is renewal of the quest. The plot may be read as an allegory of human life which reaches fulfillment only in heaven; nevertheless the paratactic structure betokens formal looseness.

Pilgrimage plots are by nature, of course, structurally slack, since the number of possible episodes is seemingly infinite, and the connection between them often tenuous. And I would be content to ascribe the perceived formal weakness in "The Golden Key" to the pilgrimage pattern, were it not for another, larger question: the reason for the disparity in the assigned paths of Mossy and Tangle.

Roughly a third of the tale traces the separate journeys of the characters to the same destination. Each must visit the Old Man of the Sea, but Tangle must also find her way to two other Old Men; her travels involve a descent into the earth and a difficult passage across the desert. Mossy, by contrast, leaves the Old Man of the Sea and walks directly across the water to the foot of the rainbow, where he finds Tangle waiting for him. "Why," one wonders with Robert Lee Wolff, "has [Mossy] this advantage over Tangle, except that he is a man?" (144-45). The simple answer is that "he has an instrument which she has not" (145), but one might then question why Mossy has the golden key at all. Why must Tangle endure so much more than Mossy? And why, upon reaching the great hall at the doorway to paradise, must she wait seven years for Mossy's arrival before she achieves entry? By assigning different paths to the two pilgrims and by focusing on Tangle's difficulties, MacDonald calls into question the apparent premise from which the story proceeds—i.e., there was a boy who found a golden key. The key itself resonates with symbolism, as do the sea of shadows, the rainbow, and the three Old Men. But is the inequality of Tangle and Mossy also symbolic? If so, can we be content to suppose, with Wolff, that "MacDonald is saying that woman's lot is suffering" (147)? Can we, on the other hand, suppose that Tangle finds adequate recompense for her lengthy journey in her allowed vision of the Old Man of the Fire—"the oldest man of all" (235)—or in her seven-year rest at the gate of paradise?

These perceived difficulties arise partially from a feminist response to the tale, but they involve wider issues of readership and textual meaning. My chief concern is whether Mossy's having the key and Tangle's not having it can be called thematically meaningful. In what follows I will address this concern by examining "The Golden Key" in relation to Matthew 20:1-16, an apparent source of the tale's theology. The biblical parable of the hired laborers is, like "The Golden Key," a figuration of heaven and the difficulties of getting there. Embedded in a gospel context of warnings about the dangers of material wealth and the rewards of renunciation, the parable purports to illustrate the paradox that the "first shall be last; and the last shall be first" (Matt. 19:30). This particular parable is thematically reminiscent of "The Golden Key," but my goal is not source study per se: rather, I propose consideration of the narrative strategies of parable, attending in particular to the assumptions readers make about textual significance. In this way I hope to illuminate how MacDonald's symbolic structure mystifies, and occasionally alienates, readers.

Frank Kermode cites the parable of the hired laborers as an example of Matthew's "habitual rhetoric... of excess" (*Guide* 391). It illustrates, then repeats, the message that closes the preceding chapter: the "first shall be last; and the last shall be first." And in spite of its legalistic patina, its precise, objective vocabulary, its workaday situation, the parable is, both in its placement within the gospel and in its internal rhetoric, excessive. But the excess is camouflaged by the ordinary, mechanistic tone of the householder's arrangements. I quote the parable from the King James Version:

> For the kingdom of heaven is like unto a man that is an householder, which went out early in the morning to hire labourers into his vineyard. And when he had agreed with the labourers for a penny a day, he sent them into his vineyard. And he went out about the third hour, and saw others standing idle in the marketplace, And said unto them; Go ye also into the vineyard, and whatsoever is right I will give you. And they went their way. Again he went out about the sixth and ninth hour, and did likewise. And about the eleventh hour he went out, and found others standing idle, and saith unto them, Why stand ye here all the day idle? They say unto him, Because no man hath hired us. He saith unto them, Go ye also into the vineyard; and whatsoever is right, that shall ye receive. So when even was come, the lord of the vineyard saith unto his steward, Call the labourers, and give them their hire, beginning from the last unto the first. And when they came that were hired about the eleventh hour, they received every man a penny. But when the first came, they supposed that they should have received more; and they likewise received every man a penny. And when they had received it, they murmured against the goodman of the house, Saying, These last have wrought but one hour, and thou hast made them equal unto us, which have borne the burden and heat of the day. But he answered one of them, and said, Friend, I do thee no wrong: didst not thou agree with me for a penny? Take that thine is, and go thy way: I will give unto this last, even as unto thee. Is it not lawful for me to do what I will with mine own? Is thine eye evil,

because I am good? So the last shall be first, and the first last: for many be called, but few chosen (Matt. 20:1-16).

The parable teaches how heavenly reward transcends earthly notions of worthiness; it was understood in the early Church to refer to Gentiles who would receive salvation alongside Jews who had long "labored" in the faith (Jerusalem Bible). Upon the inauguration of eternity, temporal concerns will dissolve. By analogy, Tangle's difficulties should become irrelevant once the tale's conclusion is reached: individual paths to salvation are unimportant; what matters is reaching the heavenly goal. But such an interpretation would, of course, depend upon our glossing "The Golden Key" with the theological tenets of the parable; moreover, the tale itself leads one to identify and empathize with Tangle, and hence to expect some sort of explanation for her fate.

Expectations play a part in the parable of the hired laborers as well: the tone, recounting terms for employment, hours worked, and disputes over payment, is determinedly legalistic, concerned with lawfulness in absolute manifestations of right and wrong, good and evil. The legal emphasis is surprising, given the conceptual basis in paradox, which runs counter to our ordinary notions of justice. But the parable's apparent immersion in human notions of legal behavior—established wages and so forth—leads readers to expect a logical conclusion. We join the early morning employees in anticipating reasonable callibration of labor, only to be told that no equation is possible between human notions of justice and divine ways: "is thine eye evil, because I am good?" The revealed message is the one Job heard from the whirlwind—that all things are lawful for the creator, who reserves the right to do as he chooses with "[his] own."

Unlike parables such as that of the sower or the marriage feast which place the lord in a position of overriding authority from the start, the parable of the hired laborers entices readers into supposing that orderly, even equitable employee-employer relations will adhere. Each time the householder hires additional laborers, a sense of orderly dealings is confirmed, and because the time of day is mentioned in each case, one might assume it to be a meaningful factor. The parable uses narrative repetition—four sets of laborers instead of the two (early and late) minimally necessary and four intervals of employment—to create certain expectations, which are subsequently dashed. This reversal of expectations is crucial to the parable's effect: there must be an unanticipated leap from the ordinary world of mercantile arrangements to the transcendent principles of divine reward. The point is not, in fact, even the one stated: the last are not "first," since all are paid equally. The stated theme itself conceals the further message of God's allowed injustice (from a human perspective), his utter immeasurability by human standards.

In offering an example of how "the last shall be first," the tale fulfills one of the definitions of parable, from classical Greek *parabole,* a "comparison" or "illustration" or "analogy" (Kermode, *Secrecy* 23). To say this, however, is only to observe that the tale fulfills its own stated terms, since the theme is stated explicitly. One might similarly observe that Mossy gains easier access to paradise because he holds the golden key. Discovering *what* the golden key is, however, or determining *why* the last shall be first, involves the more complex level of parabolic meaning, the sense in which "parable" is equated with the Hebrew *mashal,* a "riddle" or "dark saying" (Kermode, *Secrecy* 23). Kermode comments on the veiled content of parables:

> To divine the true, the latent sense, you need to be of the elect, of the institution. Outsiders must content themselves with the manifest, and pay a supreme penalty for doing so. Only those who already know the mysteries—what the stories really mean—can discover what the stories really mean (*Secrecy* 23).

The paradoxical "manifest" meaning of Matthew's parable—"the last shall be first"—suggests an inverted justice which might well leave the reader disturbed about divine logic and, by implication, divine benevolence. The "latent sense," which I have alluded to above and which is summarily contained in the challenge, "Is it not lawful for me to do what I will with mine own?," depends upon the reader's *prior* recognition of God's omnipotence, of the inscrutability of divine ways. The last are not first (or equal as the case may be) for any particular reason, other than to demonstrate the purely earthly relativity of time and its measurements, to show, in terms of the parable, the lordliness of the lord. So the riddling meaning, that divine justice is mysterious, is revealed only to those who "already know the mysteries." As the biblical Christ himself explained, when asked why he spoke in parables:

> Because it is given unto you to know the mysteries of the kingdom of heaven, but to them it is not given. For whosoever hath, to him shall be given, and he shall have more abundance: but whosoever hath not, from him shall be taken away even that he hath (Matt. 13:11-12).

It is this requirement of prior understanding that distinguishes parable from allegory, which also involves multiple levels of significance, but does not presuppose the reader's membership in an enlightened group. We should, I think, take serious note of Louis MacNeice's remark that "in the realm of parable writing, no one went further than MacDonald in the whole of the nineteenth century" (95), for his fictions are characterized by a closed, almost smug quality—by an assumption that the reader acknowledges the shared import of his symbolic utterances. Approaching "The Golden Key" as parable, one quickly determines the manifest reason why Mossy receives preferential treatment: because he has the golden key and Tangle does not. But what of the "latent," the true, riddling meaning? A gender-conscious modern reader may answer the riddle by acknowledging the phallic symbolism of Mossy's key. A reader familiar with MacDonald's biography may ascribe Mossy's good fortune to something akin to the Calvinist doctrine of pre-election, a cornerstone of the Scottish Presbyterian church of MacDonald's boyhood.[1] From the perspective of German and English romantic traditions, one might suppose the key to be symbolic of imagination, which opens the doors to perception and understanding. In the case of biblical parable, the "latent" meaning is actually self-evident, since the entire biblical text is founded upon the basic assumption of the reader's acknowledgment of God. Lacking that orthodoxy, how might we discrimate between the possible meanings of MacDonald's parable? Is there a key that unlocks the meaning of "The Golden Key"?

MacDonald himself was tantalizingly resistant to the notion of stable meaning. He claimed that "a genuine work of art must mean many things; the truer its art, the more things it will mean" ("Fantastic Imagination" 317). Moreover, "Everyone who feels the story will read its meaning after his own nature and development" (316);

should the reader's meaning differ from the author's, MacDonald complacently allowed that "your meaning may be superior to mine" (317). Despite the appealing generosity of those remarks, there is a coy touch of gamesmanship evident, since the concept of "meaning" presupposes a source for that meaning. As E. D. Hirsch writes, "verbal meaning is, by definition, that aspect of a speaker's 'intention' which, under linguistic conventions, may be shared by others" (218). In ostensibly cutting "meanings" loose from the mooring of authorial intention, MacDonald practices a game familiar to deconstructionist critics. Those who appeal to MacDonald's "mysticism" play along with him. A perfect example is Auden's directive on reading "The Golden Key": "'You must throw yourself in,'" he writes, quoting the Old Man of the Sea, "'There is no other way'" (85). Immersing oneself in a stream (here a subterranean stream) of narrative entails abandoning the stable footing of an interpretive stance. According to the self-validating logic of parable, "only those who already know" what the story really means—those who have thrown themselves in—"can discover what the stor[y] really mean[s]." In the case of biblical parable, the discovered "real meaning" can be shared and articulated; it meets Hirsch's criteria of being "both unchanging and inter-personal, [so that] it may be reproduced by the mental acts of different persons" (219). This is not the case with "The Golden Key." As I noted above, the central symbol of the story invites interpretations ranging from the phallus to pre-election to religious faith to poetic inspiration. By juxtaposing sexual, Christian, and romantic symbolism, MacDonald complicates and perhaps altogether subverts the act of interpretation. Can any "meaning"—sharable and unchanging—be derived by throwing oneself into the story? Or has MacDonald abdicated completely the position of authorial responsibility? To what might we then attribute the high marks the story receives from many readers?

The answer, I think, is that the story provides its own gloss, the key to its "latent meaning," through a kind of narrative self-referentiality. We, as readers searching the significance of the story, are embarked on a quest similar to that of the characters in the fiction. This leads us to assume a meaning in the process of search itself. The revelation is gradual. While the significance of the original object of the search, the key, is ambiguous or simply unapparent to readers, that of the ultimate goal, the "country from whence the shadows fall," is more explicit: the country is the source of the shadows; it is in some way higher since shadows "fall" from it; and since it produces shadows, it is a land of substance and solidity. The "meaning" of the country as what is usually in our culture called heaven is available even without acquaintance with the Platonic myth of the cave, from which it probably derives. There is a process, in other words, of increasing clarity, a gradual unfolding of meaning as the story progresses. The actual golden key, laden with symbolic import but resistant to precise translation, is a figure for the interpretive dilemma. Discovering the "key" to the story, the interpretive clue or code that will open its meaning, is a preliminary step; the process of search continues even after the key is found.

This drawing of the reader into the process of the story is achieved largely through a rhetoric of excess such as that noted in Matthew's parable of the hired laborers. The rhetorical device of *amplificatio* was familiar to educated writers through the nineteenth century. Erasmus describes the effect of *copia* thus:

> Nature herself especially rejoices in variety; in such a great throng of things she has left nothing anywhere not painted with some wonderful artifice of variety. And just as the eye is held more by a varying scene, in the same way the mind always eagerly examines whatsoever it sees as new (16).

Application of the technique creates two observable results: a temporal delay in the stream of narrative plot and a verbal dilation of scope or significance. Actually these two senses were originally one: to prolong or delay or defer meant also to expand or enlarge or amplify; both meanings were encompassed by the verb "dilate" (OED).[2] MacDonald, by delaying the fulfillment of the quest, dilates or expands the tale's verbal texture and its significance. MacDonald's parable is far more "copious" than Matthew's, but in each case, the *delayed* fulfillment avails the narrative *dilation* that draws the reader into the story's scope.

"The Golden Key" is usually read as a profoundly teleological narrative. As Stephen Prickett puts it, Mossy and Tangle are "pilgrims through life whose reason is only to be found in their destination" (189). The pilgrimage pattern produces a linear, goal-directed, narrative sequence; MacDonald uses delay to restrain the course towards fulfillment. We might imagine the narrative as a flowing stream; each frustration in the children's progress acts like a dam, restricting the flow of water toward the ultimate goal and simultaneously creating a deep pool above the dam. The passages dense with imagistic and visionary detail correspond to the pools; a purely linear narrative sequence would omit passages such as that describing Tangle's day of listening to the forest animals speak (and quarrel) (220-21). Her journey through the center of the earth—"she was in the secret of the earth and all its ways" (224)—is likewise the result of her delay in reaching her destination, as is the marvelous vision of the Old Man of the Fire, "a little naked child, ... playing with balls of various colors and sizes":

> Tangle felt that there was something in her knowledge which was not in her understanding. For she knew there must be an infinite meaning in the change and sequence and invidiual forms of the figures into which the child arranged the balls, as well as in the varied harmonies of their colours, but what it all meant she could not tell.... For seven years she had stood there watching the naked child with his coloured balls, and it seemed to her like seven hours ... (234-35).

Tangle is, to be sure, the tale's visionary subject. Mossy's privileged ownership of the golden key, which seems so unfair an advantage when one focuses on the *telos* of the plot, declines in importance if the focus shifts to the tale's imagistic texture. It is possible, in other words, to view Mossy with his key as the enabling figure, allowing Tangle to achieve the visions that might be understood as the goal and purpose of the story.

Mossy's relatively simple passage to the rainbow corresponds to the relatively simple understandings of the tale afforded by various interpretive "keys." Glossing the story with Freudian or biographical or religious schemes will produce coherent interpretations and allow the reader to reach his or his destination of a stable meaning. But is Mossy's way—walking on the surface of the water, unaware of "how a shining fish under the waters directed his steps" (238)—necessarily preferable to Tangle's journey through the interior and the visions afforded there? By focusing primarily on Tangle's adventures, MacDonald implies the importance of the difficult, prolonged way. By proliferating symbolic resonances, he launches the reader on a difficult way of her or his own.

An assumption that reaching the "country whence the shadows fall" is the all-important goal can lead to dismay over Tangle's unequal struggle and to a sense that the story fails to reach an appropriate climax. Wolff even confesses a disappointed sense of "letdown" (147) when Mossy and Tangle are reunited. By analogy, the parable of the hired laborers can seem illogical to those who adopt the position of the early morning laborers and their expectations of payment. In each case, readers' expectations must be overturned to reveal true meaning.

Matthew's parable depends upon a prior recognition of the condition of reading—it assumes an audience of the faithful who will seek revelations about the Christian God. To a certain extent MacDonald seems to make similar assumptions. His charge to the reader to take whatever meaning he or she finds in a story betrays a confidence that "meaning" exists; he wrote that a fairytale "cannot help having some meaning; if it have proportion and harmony it has vitality, and vitality is truth" ("Fantastic Imagination" 316). His notion of meaning, however, is loose even to the point of diffusion ("Everyone . . . who feels the story, will read its meaning after his own nature and development" [316]). Because MacDonald cannot presuppose an audience of initiates already familiar with the latent meaning he will reveal, the tale suffers a degree of mystification. The quest for meaning, then, is never fully satisfied in the tale. But to the extent that MacDonald defers attention from the plot and directs it toward imagery and description, the experience of reading—the copious narrative—takes precedence. Indeed, "The Golden Key" privileges process and vision over goal and achievement. Mossy and Tangle never actually reach their final destination: the tale closes with MacDonald's speculation that "by this time I think they must have got there" (240), but in our last glimpse of them they are "still climbing" (240) through the rainbow's arch.

Notes

1. MacDonald overtly rejected his Calvinist heritage, even going so far as to propose that animals might be saved and that the heathen could repent after death (Greville MacDonald 177-80). However, certain of his fictional works suggest an ongoing struggle to throw off the mantle of Calvinism's rigid duality of good and evil. *See* my article "Allegory,

Orthodoxy, Ambivalence: MacDonald's 'The Day Boy and the Night Girl,'" *Children's Literature* 16 (1988): 67-70.

2. *See* Patricia Parker (519-35) for an extensive discussion of the *dilatio* concept.

Works Cited

Auden, W. H. "Afterword." in George MacDonald. *The Golden Key*. Illus. Maurice Sendak. New York: Farrar, Straus, and Giroux, 1967.

Erasmus, Desiderius, of Rotterdam. *On Copia of Words and Ideas. (De Utraque Verborum ac Rerum Copia.)* Trans. Donald B. King and H. David Rix. Milwaukee, WI: Marquette UP, 1963.

Hirsch, E. D., Jr. *Validity in Interpretation*. New Haven: Yale UP, 1967.

Kermode, Frank. *The Genesis of Secrecy: On the Interpretation of Narrative*. Cambridge, MA: Harvard UP, 1979.

_____. "Matthew." in *The Literary Guide to the Bible*. Ed. Robert Alter and Frank Kermode. Cambridge, MA: Harvard UP (Belknap), 1987.

MacDonald, George. "The Fantastic Imagination." *A Dish of Orts: Chiefly Papers on the Imagination and Shakespeare*. London: Edwin Dalton, 1908.

_____. "The Golden Key." in *The Complete Fairy Tales of George MacDonald*. New York: Schocken, 1977.

MacDonald, Greville. *George MacDonald and His Wife*. London: Allen and Unwin, 1924, reprinted New York: Johnson, 1971.

MacNeice, Louis. *Varieties of Parable*. Cambridge: Cambridge UP, 1965.

Parker, Patricia. "Dilation and Delay: Renaissance Matrices." *Poetics Today* 5, 3 (1984): 519-35.

Prickett, Stephen. *Victorian Fantasy*. Bloomington, IN: Indiana UP, 1979.

Wolff, Robert Lee. *The Golden Key: A Study of the Fiction of George MacDonald*. New Haven: Yale UP, 1961.

The Platonic Imagery of George MacDonald and C. S. Lewis
The Allegory of the Cave Transfigured

By Frank Riga

C. S. Lewis never concealed his indebtedness to George MacDonald, calling him his master and claiming he probably never wrote a book without quoting or referring to him. Even a less-than-thorough reading of the two writers reveals this indebtedness on almost every level, and in book after book, the twentieth century fantasist, scholar, and Christian apologist took his inspiration, and often his substance, from his nineteenth century Scottish predecessor.[1]

Biographically, moreover, one of the principal turning points in Lewis's religious history came when, on March 4, 1916, almost by accident, he purchased and read the Everyman edition of MacDonald's *Phantastes*. Though there is a steady mention of MacDonald in his letters after March, it is not until his conversion, in the Trinity term of 1929, that Lewis became an avid devotee of MacDonald, searching out and reading everything he wrote, including the three-decker Victorian novels that most readers consider less than stimulating. Lewis suggests the reason for this devotion in his letter to Arthur Greeves of October 10, 1929: MacDonald "seems to know everything and I find my own experience in [*Diary of an Old Soul*] constanty . . . " (*They Stand Together* 313). Though Lewis is here speaking specifically of the *Diary,* he continued to discover his own experience in MacDonald, and that, I think, as much as any explicit, literary influence, accounts for the similarity of their work.

In his letters to Greeves, Lewis details his enthusiasm for MacDonald, and any full and careful study of the similarity between Lewis and MacDonald might easily take its point of departure from them. I will not attempt so ambitious a task, but a letter of June 22, 1930, does suggest what I will attempt. In that letter, Lewis discusses a novel he is writing, now lost, which he called *Moving Image*. Describing it, he says, "it is to be almost a Platonic dialogue in a fantastic setting with story intermixed. If you take *The Symposium, Phantastes, Tristram Shandy* and stir them up all together you will about have the recipe" (364). The reference to *Tristram Shandy* is intriguing, but what I wish to investigate is the connection Lewis makes between his work and that of MacDonald and Plato. As a student of philosophy, Lewis knew Plato's work, and his path to conversion led through Berkeleianism and Absolute Idealism. MacDonald's Christianity is also heavily marked by Platonic and neoplatonic elements. Since both MacDonald and Lewis were thoroughgoing supernaturalists, who believed in the reality of both the material world and the spiritual world, the Platonic cast of mind was perhaps natural to them. And in working out the relationship between the two worlds, often in "fantasy that hovers between the allegorical and the mythopoeic" (Lewis, *George MacDonald* 14), Lewis and MacDonald quite naturally used Platonic imagery. Yet as "mere Christians," who believed in the truth of Christian doctrine, their Platonism had to be impure in order to accommodate the essential goodness of the flesh and its ultimate purification and resurrection.

In the following discussion, I will argue that MacDonald and Lewis not only use Platonic imagery—and in particular the cave imagery of *The Republic* —to suggest Plato's scheme of things, but that they also transform that imagery to express a hypostatic union of the world of flesh and the world of spirit. They both had Platonic impulses, and thus interpreted their experience in the light of them, but they were also Christians, and thus understood their light in both material and spiritual terms.[2]

Plato's Allegory of the Cave is well-known, and I wish only to highlight some of the salient features of the imagery and their implications. The allegory rests on commonplace metaphoric uses of light as intellectual comprehension. Common phrases in the language, now dead metaphors, attest to this usage: "to enlighten," "to illuminate," "to throw light on," "to have a bright idea," "to be in the dark," and the almost indispensable, "to see," are only a few examples. An old popular song bemoans, "I'm beginning to see the light," and in biblical imagery, Christ is "the light of the world."

In Plato's cave, there are two sources of light: the fire built by the guardians, and the sun, the source of all light. The guardians use the artificial light, the cave's fire, to control other men; only a few men, the philosophers, arrive at the source of light, the sun. Yet the light in the cave *is* light and makes possible the shadows that the enchained men take for reality. Because the cave's light and shadows reveal part of the truth, some men argue that the cave's light is the only light there is. The source of light, the sun, cannot be brought into the cave, and so in order to see it, the prisoner must get free and leave the cave. The cave, then, cannot be transformed and thus it must be transcended. The cave, in other words, cannot be part of the higher world of truth. This is one of the principal differences between Plato, on the one hand, and Lewis and MacDonald, on the other. For them, the Incarnation of Christ has transformed the world, since, as one of the creeds has it, the Incarnation worked "not by conversion of the Godhead into flesh, but by taking of the Manhood into God." Christ's assumption of a body saves and sanctifies the world of flesh since he has not "fallen" into flesh, but has raised it up. At the end of time, then, the transformed cave, and the glorified flesh that dwells within it, will be part of transcendent reality. This belief has radical implications for MacDonald's and Lewis's Platonic impulses.

The shadows in the Platonic cave, though they resemble real things, are really shadows of images, and though the images themselves resemble real things more fully than the shadows, their truth can only be judged when they are compared to the reality they imitate. To those bound in the cave—the unenlightened—the shadows are true and constitute the only reality they know. The shadows give meaning to their lives. The guardians who control the images that cast the shadows, reward or punish those bound in the cave, and the guardians, for whatever reason, have an interest in maintaining the deception. The prisoners, because they know no better, love their world and thus the confinement and deception that constitute it. They will fight to maintain it and will hate anyone who, claiming to have seen the light, attempts to undermine it. Moreover, since leaving the cave and journeying to the sun is both difficult and painful, the prisoners who attempt it must either be courageous and self-driven or they must be compelled to undertake the journey. Once they have achieved the vision of the sun, however, they no longer wish to dwell in the cave, since it no longer has any attraction for them. Yet, with their knowledge of the truth they are the very ones who should be the guardians, Plato's philosopher-kings. MacDonald and Lewis do place their enlightened characters in positions of influence. In their novels and stories, the protagonists, once illuminated, work in the world to make the vision of truth prevail, sometimes as kings and sometimes as ordinary citizens.

Because Plato's allegory derives from commonplace metaphoric uses of light and shadow, many similar images in MacDonald and Lewis may be merely a function of such usages. The difficulty of determining the degree of Platonism in what might be called Platonic imitations is illustrated in one of MacDonald's stories, "The Shadows" (*Gifts of the Child Christ*). The story deals with the adventures of Ralph Rinkelmann, who, during an illness, becomes the king of the fairies and is taken on two dream journeys by the shadows in his room. These are the shadows of his own kingdom, and during his first journey, he hears how they have helped men avoid their worst natures. On his second journey, he learns of shadows not in his domain that poison human life. If the good shadows are illusions that help men, the evil shadows are preoccupations that sour them. The two kinds of shadows are associated with two ways of responding to reality and suggest two different habits of mind. Rinkelmann's dealings with both sharpen his understanding of life, and yet, it is clear that the work of the good shadows is preferable to that of the bad. After his first journey, he concludes that it was more than likely "that he had seen a true vision; for instead of making common things look commonplace, as a false vision would have done, it had made common things disclose the wonderful that was in them" (*Gifts* 114). So while the story deals with a shadowed room from which the confined protagonist journeys to greater knowledge, his return does not lead to dissatisfaction as does the return to Plato's cave. No matter how the shadows are interpreted, whether as illusion or fairies, their function is to enhance, not dismiss, material reality. The imagery of the story, then, suggests something of a Platonic journey, but the conclusion is non-Platonic. It is precisely differences such as this that, as I will show later, transform the Platonism of both MacDonald and Lewis.

But other of their narratives coincide more fully with Plato's allegory, and the recurring pattern suggests that both MacDonald and Lewis share a Platonic cast of mind. In one of MacDonald's best known fairy tales, "The Golden Key," the protagonist, Mossy, finds the key of the title early in the story and, with his friend, Tangle, then searches for the keyhole for which the key was made.

In undertaking their quest, Mossy and Tangle analogically make the journey of life. Though the episode is brief, Mossy and Tangle do most of their aging crossing a plain, the surface of which "was everywhere crowded with shadows" (*Gifts* 165). The shifting forms of the shadows suggest many moving and beautiful images of life, and some of the shadows even suggest more pleasing things than either of the children know how to describe. After years on the plain, narrated as one passing day, and after both are old, "They felt the gathering darkness, and something strangely solemn besides, and the beauty of the shadows ceased to delight them" (166). But even earlier, at the midpoint of their journey across the plain, their love of the shadowed beauty was marked by another element: "they were each longing after the country whence the shadows fall" (166).

Underlying the often complex movement of the narrative, then, is a substructure of Platonic imagery. The quest parallels the journey of Plato's unchained prisoner who seeks the reality beyond the shadows and images of the cave. Unlike the freed prisoner, however, Mossy and Tangle do not discover the intelligible world of perfect form through philosophic meditation; instead they live an ordinary human life, loving the things of this world and yet dimly knowing these prefigure something more pleasing than either can describe. The Platonic journey thus becomes the journey of the soul, which only through death can enter "the country whence the shadows fall." The Platonic imagery of "The Golden Key" finds its proper context in MacDonald's religious intention, since, for him, the pagan vision must be completed by revelation.

C. S. Lewis's Platonic impulses also manifest themselves in several of his books, and in his first published novel, *Out of the Silent Planet* (1938), the introductory section ends with a Platonic cave image transposed to outer space. While on a walking tour, Elwin Ransom, the Oxford philologist, is abducted by Devine, one of his former schoolfellows, and Weston, the great physicist, and is taken to Malacandra, or Mars, aboard their spaceship. On their journey to Malacandra, Ransom alters his notion of space, changing it from the cold, dark vacuity of modern imagining to something filled with life and light, the plenitude of an older imagining. So when the spaceship approaches Malacandra, Ransom is lost in thought.

> They were falling out of the heaven, into a world. Nothing in all his adventures bit so deeply into Ransom's mind as this. He wondered how he could ever have thought of planets, even of the Earth, as islands of life and reality floating in a deadly void. Now, with a certainty which never after deserted him, he saw the planets—the "earths" he called them in his thought—as mere holes or gaps in the living heaven—excluded and rejected wastes of heavy matter and murky air, formed not by addition to, but by subtraction from, the surrounding brightness. And yet, he thought, beyond the solar system the brightness ends. Is that the real void, the real death? Unless...he groped for the idea... unless visible light is also a hole or gap, a mere diminution of something else. Something that is to bright unchanging heaven as heaven is to the dark, heavy earths. . . . Things do not always happen as a man would expect. The moment of his arrival in an unknown world found Ransom wholly absorbed in a philosophical speculation (40).

The parallel to the Allegory of the Cave seems almost too patent to be coincidental. The earth, like the shadows on the cave wall, is "formed not by addition to, but by subtraction from, the surrounding brightness." The surrounding brightness itself, like the cave's fire, may only be "a hole or gap, a mere diminution of something else." And that final brightness, like the sun that the unchained prisoner sees, may be "to bright unchanging heaven as heaven is to the dark, heavy earths. . . . " This powerful parallel is reinforced by the circumstance that, like the unchained prisoner who is "reluctantly dragged up a steep and rugged ascent . . . into the presence of the sun himself" (*Dialogues* 381), Ransom is abducted and forced to take his journey. The purpose of Ransom's journey, like that of the unchained prisoner, is to have him achieve a larger and fuller vision of truth. That Ransom should arrive at an unknown world "wholly absorbed in a philosophical speculation" simply enunciates the theme of his education, a theme that will recur throughout his adventures on Malacandra.

One of the primary objectives of that education is the transformation of Ransom's understanding of reality, a transformation that is at odds with the modern sensibility. His sensibility, like that of all cave dwellers, was shaped by the images shadowed forth by the guardians and poets, and in his case, especially the poets. Soon after his abduction, Ransom learns he is to be surrendered to the sorns, and in his fear, he tries to image the reality of this "extra-terrestrial Otherness":

> His mind, like so many minds of his generation, was richly furnished with bogies. He had read his H.G. Wells and others. His universe was peopled with horrors such as ancient and mediaeval mythology could hardly rival. No insect-like, vermiculate or crustacean Abominable, no twitching feelers, rasping wings, slimy coils, curling tentacles, no monstrous union of superhuman intelligence and insatiable cruelty seemed to him anything but likely on an alien world (35).

The last descriptive phrases here—the "monstrous union of superhuman intelligence and insatiable cruelty"—are a precise description of Wells's invading Martians in *The War of the Worlds*. Both this allusion and the mention of Wells's name prepare the reader for Ransom's adventures on Malacandra, which is Mars, and explain his terror of the sorns, to whom he would be given. But as he lives among the *hrossa,* one of the three rational creatures on Malacandra, he begins to revise his initial view, and instead of cruel monsters, he finds peaceful and rational creatures living in a pre-lapsarian state of nature.

When Ransom finally does meet a sorn face to face, the event is arranged to remind the reader of the movement of Ransom's education. To reach Meldilorn, the capital of Malacandra, he must traverse the mountains and seek the help of Augray, a sorn. A light guides him to Augray's habitat and he "came at last to what seemed a cavern mouth." The light is firelight.

> He came to the mouth of the cave and then, unsteadily, round the fire and into the interior, and stood still blinking in the light. When at last he could see, he discerned a smooth chamber of green rock, very lofty. There were two things in it. One of them,

dancing on the wall and roof, was the huge, angular shadow of
a *sorn*; the other crouched beneath it, was the *sorn* himself (90).

Again we have the images of Plato's allegory, but now they are juxtaposed so the shadow and the reality within the cave reveal their true relationship. After overcoming his initial fear, Ransom continues revising his understanding of sorns. The sorns, in fact, are the intellectuals of Malacandra, but their intelligence is not joined to "insatiable cruelty." If he had once thought of them as "ogres" and "goblins," he soon learns that "Titans" or "Angels" would have been better words (101). His life among the Malacandrians, then, has widened his sympathies, and he has been able to escape the confinement within his own consciousness by comparing it "with thought that floats on a different blood" (103).

Ransom, however, is a good man who, though shaped by the opinions and images of his own world, is always disposed to learn the good and do it. Devine, with his lust for wealth and power, and especially Weston, with his almost maniacal ambition to perpetuate man's physical and intellectual existence throughout space, are more compelling instances of the modern consciousness. They are driven by both the lowest and the highest aspirations of modernity, and yet both men, *sub specie,* are parochial, egotistical, and pernicious. Neither has learned anything from his experience on Malacandra. Weston is "bent," that is, he has so distorted the law of the love of kindred that it has become folly. With nothing left but greed, Devine is "broken." Weston is more dangerous, since "a bent *hnau* [a rational creature] can do more evil than a broken one" (139). Once his own education is complete, Ransom, unlike the unchained prisoner of Plato's cave, returns to the earth willingly, and as one who enjoys the pleasures of the flesh, his first act is to order a pint of bitter. But on earth, he has been entrusted with the mission to counteract "the force or forces behind 'Weston'" that pose, not merely planetary and temporal dangers, but ones that are cosmic and eternal (153). The first steps in accomplishing that mission are educational, to change men's understanding of reality:

> What we need for the moment is not so much a body of belief as a body of people familiarized with certain ideas. If we could even effect in one percent of our readers a change-over from the

conception of space to the conception of Heaven, we should have made a beginning (154).

Such a change in the conception of reality, of course, leads to a change in the response to it: the dark, cold vacuity of space draws a different response than the life-filled plenitude of Heaven. Like Plato's philosopher, then, Ransom must persuade others of his larger vision of truth, but unlike Plato's philosopher, he will embrace the claims and peculiarities of the flesh in his vision.

The educational purpose of Ransom's journey, which coincides with that of Plato's allegory, repeats itself in another image used by both MacDonald and Lewis that has Platonic implications, the image of a painting or a picture. Like the images in the cave used to cast the shadows, pictures and other artistic representations attempt to approximate reality and do not merely provide a shadowed outline of it. Plato relegates pictures to the region of imitation, and like the material world itself, to learn about pictures may be a way to pass beyond them, but ultimately they cannot impart truth because they are not part of intelligible, and thus transcendent, reality. In MacDonald and Lewis, however, pictures are not merely adumbrations of reality; they are approaches or entrances to its fullest manifestations. On the terrestrial level, the use of pictures provides the characters with a way to participate in a fuller human life because such a life will be perfected in the transcendent world; and on the transcendental level, their use attempts to show the connection between terrestrial life and its incarnational transcendence.

Both MacDonald and Lewis use pictures as an entrance to a fuller human life. In MacDonald's "The Wise Woman, or The Lost Princess: A Double Story," Rosamund, the princess, and Agnes, the shepherd-child, enact the prince and the pauper story by exchanging roles. The exchange of roles occurs when, wandering in a great hall magically attached to the Wise Woman's cottage, each of the girls, at different times, sees a picture that seems to represent her heart's desire. As they gaze at the pictures, they step over the frames and find themselves in the reality the paintings have depicted. That reality, however, is not what they imagined, and the events that follow painfully correct their false understanding.

Similarly, Lewis, in *The Voyage of the Dawn Treader,* effects the transfer of the children from England to Narnia by means of a picture. While visiting their priggish cousin, Clarence Eustace Scrubb, Edmund and Lucy Pevensie discover a painting of a Narnian ship in the attic. As they gaze at the picture, the three children are drawn into it and find themselves in the reality it depicts. The passage mechanism, from image to reality, is not the only similarity of Lewis's novel to MacDonald's tale. Eustace, who in his own way is as nasty and selfish as Rosamund and Agnes, also undergoes a transforming education in the strange land. But Eustace is more like the unchained prisoner from Plato's cave: he not only finds his educational journey painful, but he is also unwilling to begin it. In all three cases, however, the children are taught how their willful selfishness unfits them for living a human life. As Lewis reminds us in several places, to transcend human life you must first know and live it. The use of pictures in these narratives, then, allows the children a way to develop decent human responses and to act on them.

A purer Platonic application of the picture imagery is seen in the way MacDonald uses it to suggest the afterlife. In his novel *At the Back of the North Wind,* his use of such imagery illustrates the transcendence of the world and human life. North Wind takes Diamond, the child protagonist, on a journey to the country at her back. Diamond is seriously ill at the time, and to get there, he must pass through North Wind. When he recovers, he returns to earth. While in the country:

> He could not say he was very happy there, for he had neither his father nor mother with him, but he felt so still and quiet and patient and contented, that, as far as the mere feeling went, it was something better than mere happiness. Nothing went wrong at the back of the north wind. Neither was anything quite right, he thought. Only everything was going to be right some day (90-91).

That Diamond should reach this country when he is seriously ill and near death indicates that it has something to do with an afterlife. The country itself is not heaven, but a sort of antechamber to heaven, suggesting that even here truth and reality are not complete. As the medial place of development, with earth on one side and heaven on the other, the existence of the country evokes the three-tiered structure of the Platonic allegory, i.e., from shadow to image to reality. Yet Diamond first gets there without dying, and his earnest wish, throughout the novel, is to return. So at the end of the novel, when it is obvious that he is about to die, North Wind asks him if he would be afraid to pass through her again. He answers that he would do it gladly if he could "only get another peep of the country" at her back (278). She then tells him he has never seen it yet, that, in fact, he has seen "only a picture of it. The real country at my real back is ever so much more beautiful than that. You shall see it one day—perhaps before very long" (278). The picture adumbrates reality, and since the reality is a place in the afterlife, it can only be enjoyed after death. Again, as in "The Golden Key," MacDonald uses a Platonic image for a reality that can only be understood by reference to religious belief.

In *Lilith*, the last of his adult fantasies, MacDonald again tries to convey a sense of the afterlife and its relationship to earthly life. Many of the themes discussed earlier also appear in *Lilith*. The children in the novel, for example, cannot grow into a full human life because they cannot cry, the natural response to fear, pain, and sadness. When the Shadow passes over them, they feel fear for the first time, indicating that, if they are to transcend the human condition, they must first get that far. The images of light and dark pervade the novel, and the deepest pit of darkness is Lilith's own mind. She must emerge from her own confining consciousness and join with God, the Law of Liberty. But in his image of the afterlife, MacDonald gives a most precise formulation of the interconnection of the terrestrial and the transcendent world. All of the characters in the novel move toward sleep, or death, to be purified and transformed in order to enter the afterlife. As Vane, the protagonist, describes his new condition, "I walked on the new earth, under the new heaven, and found them the same as the old, save that now they opened their minds to me, and I saw into them" (414). The new heaven and earth are the same as, and yet different from, the old. He arrives in his new condition on a summer-day that was "more like itself, that is, more ideal, than ever man that had not died found summer-day in any world" (414). And somewhat later, he adds:

> I know not whence came the stone that fashioned [the gate], but among them I saw the prototypes of all the gems I had loved on earth—far more beautiful than they, for these were living stones—such in which I saw, not the intent alone, but the intender

too; not the idea alone, but the imbodier present, the operant outsender: nothing in this kingdom was dead; nothing was mere; nothing only a thing (418).

If nothing was "only a thing," of course, it had to be at least that much. The words in this passage are only an imperfect way of speaking about the ineffable, but the fleshy life, or the copy, is assumed by the archetype (or in MacDonald's word, the prototype). Like the unbound prisoner who sees the sun and outer reality, Vane describes his new condition by reference to his former, but the objects of that earlier condition, e.g., the stones, unlike the shadows or images in the cave, are not illusions, but rather defective realities.

In *The Last Battle,* Lewis uses Platonic imagery in a similar way to define the relationship of Narnia to the true Narnia or, in the anagogical equation, the relationship of mortal life to eternal life. But here, unlike all of the instances examined so far, the parallel to Plato is stated explicitly. As the final novel in the Narnia Chronicles, *The Last Battle* deals, not only with the last war, but with the apocalyptic end of the Narnia to which the earth children have come as saviors and kings. As in "The Golden Key," *At the Back of the North Wind,* and *Lilith,* the children involved in the story die and pass on to the afterlife. They enter the eternal world, and as they move "further up and further in," they soon discover that this new country is at once familiar and different. Old landmarks they knew in Narnia are all about them, and yet these landmarks somehow seem more real than the reality they knew. Digory explains the phenomenon to Peter:

> When Aslan said you could never go back to Narnia, he meant the Narnia you were thinking of. But that was not the real Narnia. That had a beginning and an end. It was only a shadow or a copy of the real Narnia, which has always been here and will always be here: just as our own world, England and all, is only a shadow or copy of something in Aslan's real world. You need not mourn over Narnia, Lucy. All of the old Narnia that mattered, all the dear creatures, have been drawn into the real Narnia through the Door. And of course it is different as a real thing is from a shadow or as waking life is from a dream (169-70).

The shadow imagery in this passage, of course, reminds us of the Allegory of the Cave, and if the children's Narnia is only a "copy," an image of a real thing, its truth can now be judged by comparing it to the real Narnia. Since a shadow or a copy is an imperfect representation of things richer and more real, old Narnia is merely the ectype of the true Narnia, the archetype. Digory adds, after giving the above explanation, "it's all in Plato, all in Plato," and then, underlining the educational motif, he further adds in mild consternation, "bless me, what *do* they teach them at these schools!" (170).

The mode of transcendence here, like that in *Lilith,* is not exactly Platonic, since "All of the old Narnia that mattered, all the dear creatures, have been drawn into the real Narnia through the Door," implying, as Lewis maintains or implies in all his novels and religious writings, that man's afterlife, no matter how transfigured, somehow retains its materiality. Lewis's transcendence is incarnate while Plato's is discarnate. Speaking of the resurrection of the body in his essay, "Transposition," Lewis says:

> May we not, by a reasonable analogy, suppose . . . that there is no experience of the spirit so transcendent and supernatural, no vision of Deity Himself so close and so far beyond all images and emotions, that to it also there cannot be an appropriate correspondence on the sensory level? Not by a new sense but by the incredible flooding of those very sensations we now have with a meaning, a transvaluation, of which we have here no faintest guess? (*Weight of Glory* 29).

Lewis here speculates on the consubstantiality of earth and heaven, since from the Christian perspective, man is incarnate spirit, and if incarnate, the spirit and its ultimate habitation must accommodate the substance of the flesh. The true Narnia stands in relationship to the copy as Christ's deity stands to his humanity: that is, the Incarnation worked "not by conversion of the Godhead into flesh, but by taking of the Manhood into God." As a result, earth and flesh are not made inessential excrescences, but are glorified; instead of returning to the nothing from which they were made, they are impelled to become more like the principle that made them.

If Plato's allegory implies that the cave cannot be transformed but must instead be transcended, then MacDonald's and Lewis's use of similar imagery suggests that the cave, not only can be transformed, but will be transformed and, in a sense, already has been transformed in the Incarnation. As my discussion of the picture image of "The Wise Woman" and *The Voyage of the Dawn Treader* suggests, both MacDonald and Lewis demonstrate that the experience of life, rightly understood, not only prepares man for the afterlife, but also teaches him how to behave in this life. For them, man's education in the cave, guided by intimations of immortality, imposes duties, and yet these duties are not merely onerous obligations, but also the proper joys of man's sojourn on earth. In "The History of Photogen and Nycteris," MacDonald gives, from the viewpoint of this essay, his most complete critique of the Allegory of the Cave. The tale shows at once, through the imagery of light and dark, that the cave must be transcended, but also that the transcendence occurs by transformation. Photogen and Nycteris learn that to separate the day from the night perverts reality and that the two must be brought together in a marriage—a marriage of love that prefigures the marriage of heaven and earth.

"The History of Photogen and Nycteris" begins as an experiment in behavior modification, carried on by the witch, Watho, who, though she "desired to know everything, . . . cared for nothing in itself—only for knowing it" (*Gifts* 63). Though she was not "naturally cruel," she "had a wolf in her mind" that made her cruel. So possessed by her desire to know and her wolfish cruelty, she obtains two newborn children, a boy and a girl, for her experiment. The Day Boy, Photogen, is never allowed to experience darkness, and the Night Girl, Nycteris, is never allowed to experience any light except for that of the lamp that dimly illuminates her chambers. Though both children are reared by Watho in her castle, they, like the day and night associated with them, are never allowed to meet and, by the very terms of the experiment, cannot meet.

The dark cave, illuminated by artificial light, then, is the world in which Nycteris grows up. The chambers in which she is lodged were modeled on the tomb of an Egyptian king, and in them, she desires something more or different, and the only way she can express it to herself is "that she wanted more room" (69). Feeling this confinement, she would pour over "the coloured bas-reliefs on the walls."

These were intended to represent various of the powers of
Nature under allegorical similitudes, and as nothing can be made
that does not belong to the general scheme, she could not fail at
least to imagine a flicker of relationship between some of them,
and thus a shadow of the reality of things found its way to her
(69).

Later, when she first meets Photogen after escaping from her
chamber and mistakes him for a creature like herself, a female,
Nycteris surmises, "she must, of course, like herself, have got out
of a cave, in which Watho and Falca [the servant] had been keeping
her" (84). But even confined in her dark, cavelike rooms, she is
transfixed by the lamp and its light, "giving her the feeling as if her
eyes could go in and into its whiteness," since the light was
"somehow also associated with the idea of space and room" (69).

This striking similarity to Plato's allegory completes itself in
Nycteris's escape from her chambers. When her lamp accidentally
breaks and the light goes out, she wants to follow it *out,* and groping
about her chamber, she accidentally pushes against a door and
"tumbled out of the cavern" (71). Still in the dark, she spies a firefly
that has wandered into the castle from the garden. She follows it,
"and, because all light is one, any light may serve to guide to more
light. If she was mistaken in thinking it the spirit of her lamp, it was
of the same spirit as her lamp . . . " (72). The firefly leads her into
a bright summer night, lit by the moon which she at first believes
is her lamp. She soon realizes the moon is not her lamp and thinks,
rather, that "it is the mother of all the lamps" (73). She also realizes
that "her goalers" had made her a "prisoner" and had kept her in
ignorance: "Life was a mighty bliss, and they had scraped hers to
the bare bone!" (74). She now concludes the moon is the sun she
had read about in books, and she associates the moon she had read
about with her chambers, "the cave and the lamp that hung there"
(74). She has, of course, one more journey to make before she
discovers the sun, and when she does, like the unchained prisoner
of Plato's cave, she is blinded by its brilliance. She fears it, thinks
of it as death, and wants the softer moonlight. She must grow
accustomed to the sight of the upper world, and as she does, she
passes through a series of experiences similar to Plato's unchained
prisoner. Plato's comment also becomes a precise gloss on
Nycteris's development:

At first he will see the shadows best, next the reflections of men and other objects in the water, and then the objects themselves; then he will gaze upon the light of the moon and the stars and the spangled heaven; and he will see the sky and the stars by night better than the sun or the light of the sun by day (*Dialogues* 381-82).

While meeting the needs of his narrative, MacDonald manages to present Nycteris's movement from darkness to light as an almost perfect parallel to Plato's allegory. Along with the light and the dark, the cave and the images on the wall, the confinement and the difficult ascent, the confused identification of the light and the blinding brilliance of the sun, he conveys that the guardians manage the whole circumstance for their own purposes. The confined prisoner escapes her bondage and finds a larger, truer world, and knowing the truth, she can judge the cave and its shadows. In making her judgment, she concludes that she has been a prisoner, closed off from the "mighty bliss" of her life. Were this the end of MacDonald's story, he would merely seem to be recapitulating Plato, showing "in a figure how far our nature is enlightened or unenlightened" (*Dialogues* 380). But with the story of Nycteris, he tells the story of Photogen, the Day Boy who was never to experience the night. His narrative is the inverse of hers and moves him from the light to the discovery of the dark. If the light were Plato's truth, then why should MacDonald make Photogen learn of the dark which, no matter how it participates in the truth, always remains an imperfect representation of it? The answer to this question of course reveals that MacDonald's Platonism is impure, not because he misunderstands or distorts it, but because his vision of life embraces the flesh and the material world in a way that a pure Platonism would not allow.

Photogen discovers darkness through his pride. While he is hunting, an unknown animal, perhaps a leopard or a young lion, runs from him. He asks his attendant what kind of animal it was, and adds, "what a coward it must be" to run away. His attendant responds that the sun makes such creatures uncomfortable, but "as soon as the sun is down, he will be brave enough" (78). This determines Photogen to wait for sundown and to face the beast, to test its courage and his own. But with darkness comes fear, and "the terror and the darkness rushed together, and he knew them for one"

(79). As the narrator comments, "he was but a spark of the sun, in himself nothing" (79). Driven by fear, he runs away in panic and, his courage gone, he realizes that "he had only had courage, not been courageous" (79). To emphasize this fall from what he had "thought himself" and the pride that motivated it, the narrator quotes Milton's description of Satan: "How fallen, how changed." To be courageous, Photogen, like all children, must learn not to be afraid of the dark, but he can only do that in the natural world of day and night, and not in one where the corresponding halves of reality are artificially separated. In Photogen's fall from light, MacDonald's critique of Plato's allegory becomes clear. In Plato, the cave is only an illusion of true reality, and as it cannot be transformed, it must be transcended. In order to participate in true reality, the unbound prisoner must leave the cave entirely. Plato's dualism, then, forces individuals to discard the common reality they experience in order to attain the intelligible reality they can know. Plato has, in effect, separated the knowledge of experience from the knowledge of contemplation, judging the one false and the other true. MacDonald seems to imply the unhealthy nature of this dichotomy in his portrait of Watho, who "cared for nothing in itself—only for knowing it" (63). In the history of Photogen, however, MacDonald insists that a man is not fully human unless he can learn to live in the cave's darkness, since darkness is not evil or false in itself, but one of the constituent elements of reality.

Yet MacDonald does not merely insist on what life teaches us daily—that the world must be endured. It must also be loved. So once Nycteris and Photogen are freed from their confinement in half-complete worlds, they grow in courage, sympathy, and love; they mature in the great virtues necessary to human life. As Nycteris tells Photogen:

> And you must learn to be strong in the dark as well as in the day, else you will always be only half brave. I have begun already—not to fight your sun, but to try to get at peace with him, and understand what he really is, and what he means with me—whether to hurt me or to make the best of me. You must do the same with my darkness (97).

They have each discovered the condition of the other, and as light is the corresponding half to darkness, so the male is the corresponding half to the female. Separated, male and female are less than human, since each is only half of human reality, but joined, they are not only a whole, but a whole that is greater than the sum of its parts. Still in the dark, Photogen tells Nycteris: "I could not see your lovely eyes but for the light that is in them: that lets me see straight into heaven through them. They are windows into the very heaven beyond the sky. I believe they are the very place where the stars are made" (97). This is love, albeit romantic love, but as in Plato, such human love leads to heavenly love. The cure for the alienation of the halves is marriage since each is necessary to the other: "She has got to teach me to be a brave man in the dark, and I have got to look after her until she can bear the heat of the sun, and he helps her to see instead of blinding her" (101). Within a year of their marriage, Nycteris has come to love the day best and Photogen the night: she because "the day was greater than the night, and the sun more lordly than the moon," and he because the night was "the mother and home of Nycteris" (101). This traditional notion of marriage associates the male principle, or day, with rule and dominance and the female principle, or night, with generation and nurture. These are mythic equivalences and indicate the conventional roles of men and women. MacDonald's marriage of Photogen and Nycteris argues for the joining of day and night, light and dark, spirit and flesh, male and female into a natural wholeness, one manifested in our common experience of earthly love.

But what has become of heaven, the world beyond the cave? Nycteris gives the answer in the last words of the story: "But who knows ... that when we go out, we shall not go into a day as much greater than your day as your day is greater than my night" (101). This passage has a strong echo of the passage already quoted from Lewis's *Out of the Silent Planet,* where Ransom speculates that the possible brightness beyond the solar system may be "to bright unchanging heaven as heaven is to the dark, heavy earths ... " As pointed out earlier, this passage from Lewis parallels the imagistic regress of Plato's allegory, where the light outside the cave is to the fire within as the fire is to the shadows. "The country whence the shadows fall" of MacDonald's "The Golden Key" implies the same world picture. And as I have argued previously, Lewis believed that man is incarnate spirit, and for both him and MacDonald, this belief requires that man must learn to live properly in the flesh of this world so that it can be transfigured in the next. Unlike the liberated prisoner of Plato's cave, who discards each new level of experience as he moves closer to the transcendent world of intelligible forms, Rosamond and Agnes, Eustace Scrubb and Ransom, Mossy and Tangle, Photogen and Nycteris, and all of the Pevensie children must first attempt the good life on earth, hoping for a better hereafter. But the afterlife, as Mr. Vane and Digory Kirk explain, is more of the same, yet better and different, "different as a real thing is from a shadow or as waking life is from a dream." This is the Kingdom come, in which the wound of isolation and the wound of alienation are healed; in which the world of flesh and the world of sprit, divorced by sin, are married in love. If Plato's transcendent world remains discarnate, that is not good enough for MacDonald and Lewis. For them, the flesh, too, has claims. So it is appropriate to end this discussion with marriage, since the work of MacDonald and Lewis is finally a comedy, a comedy at once human and divine.

Notes

1. My discussion of the Allegory of the Cave is indebted to Allan Bloom's Commentary to his translation of *The Republic* (New York: Basic Books, 1968), pp. 401-410. It is also indebted to my colleagues, Dr. Herbert J. Nelson and Dr. Stanley Vodraska, both of the Canisius College Department of Philosophy. In educating me, they may well have proved not all men are capable of metaphysical argument.

2. Although this essay is restricted to the Allegory of the Cave in its consideration of Plato, one other Platonic theme that appears in the work of the two writers should be mentioned because of its bearing on the question of epistemology. Both propose a theory of knowledge that has parallels to the theory of reminiscence set forth in Plato's *Phaedo*. As Cebes says there:

> Your favorite doctrine, Socrates, that knowledge is simply recollection, if true, also necessarily implies a previous time in which we have learned that which we now recollect. But this would be impossible unless our soul had been in some place before existing in the form of man; here then is another proof of the soul's immortality (*Dialogues* 67).

The discussion of reminiscence is much longer, but this quotation is sufficient to suggest the eternal, and thus absolute, quality of knowledge that, when remembered, will have an effect on the way human life is lived.

In other words, truth exists in a pure form some place uneffected by time and change, and in some way, man has access to it. For Plato, pre-existence and memory account for man's knowledge of truth. For MacDonald and Lewis, the imagination and reason participate in this eternal realm. One of the best single statements of this position in MacDonald comes in his essay, "The Imagination":

> Such embodiments of truth are not the results of man's intention, or of the operation of his conscious nature. His feeling is that they are given to him; that from the vast unknown, where time and space are not, they suddenly appear in luminous writing upon the wall of his consciousness. Can it be correct, then, to say that he created them? Nothing less so, as it seems to us. But can we not say that they are the creation of the unconscious portions of his nature? ... From that unknown region we grant they come, but not by its own blind working.... God sits in that chamber of our being in which the candle of our consciousness goes out in darkness, and sends forth from thence wonderful gifts into the light of that understanding which is His candle. Our hope lies in no most perfect mechanism even of the spirit, but in the wisdom wherein we live and move and have our being. Thence we hope for endless forms of beauty informed of truth. If the dark portion of our own being were the origins of our imaginations, we might well fear the apparitions of such monsters as would be generated in the sickness of a decay which could never feel—only declare—a slow return towards primal chaos. But the Maker is our Light (*Dish of Orts* 23-25).

In language that echoes Plato's Cave imagery, MacDonald here argues the imagination participates in the transcendent world of God by way of the unconscious, and through it, God sends His revelations of beauty and truth, and of Himself. Like the imagination, moreover, dreams are also a doorway between time and eternity. MacDonald's concept of dreams is biblical, and in the Bible, dreams are a medium of truth. In *At the Back of the North Wind,* the chapter entitled, "Diamond's Dream," fills out Plato's theory by suggesting that Diamond, in his dream, has had a vision of his former existence in the transcendent world. In Lewis, a similar idea is proposed to Greeves in a letter of August 31, 1930. Discussing the similarity of themes and characters between his poem, *Dymer*, and MacDonald's novels, he says:

For we don't individually invent these things, perhaps. Look how the "empty castle" theme is present in *Phantastes, Wilfrid, & Dymer.* No doubt it passed into *Dymer* from *Phantastes:* but then, from it, in *Dymer,* I passed on to the mysterious bedfellow without any guidance from MacDonald—and only *now* find that he has got that bit of the story too, only in another book. Don't you get the feeling of something waiting there and slowly being recovered in fragments by different human minds according to their abilities, and partially spoiled in each writer by the admixture of his own mere individual invention? (*They Stand Together* 388).

He does not give the full machinery nor does he imply pre-existence, but the pattern is similar. Man, in some way, gathers in that which already exists "there." Lewis's defense of the validity of reason, moreover, rests on a similar concept. In *Surprised by Joy,* when he found that materialism did not allow for an adequate theory of knowledge, he concluded "that mind was no late-come epiphenomenon; that the whole universe was, in the last resort, mental; that our logic was participation in a cosmic *Logos*" (209). The whole argument in *The Abolition of Man* is based on a similar position.

Ultimately, the implications of a theory of reminiscence do not allow for moral relativism, a solely naturalistic intelligence, or a soul that dies with the body. Moral ideas, reason, and imagination are connected to the transcendent world, and man has access to it. The Incarnation, of course, adds another dimension to these implications.

Works Cited

Lewis, C. S. *The Allegory of Love: A Study of Medieval Tradition.* London: Oxford, 1936.
_____. *The Last Battle.* New York: Collier, 1970 (1956).
_____. *Out of the Silent Planet.* New York: Macmillan, 1965 (1938).
_____. *Reflections on the Psalms.* New York: Harcourt, 1958.
_____. *Surprised by Joy: The Shape of My Early Life.* New York: Harcourt, 1955.
_____. *They Stand Together: The Letters of C. S. Lewis to Arthur Greeves (1914-1963).* Ed. Walter Hooper. New York: Macmillan, 1979.

_____. *The Voyage of The Dawn Treader.* New York: Collier, 1970 (1952).
_____. *The Weight of Glory and Other Addresses.* Grand Rapids, MI: Eerdmans, 1965 (1949).
_____, ed. *George MacDonald: An Anthology.* London: Geoffrey Bles, 1946.
MacDonald, George. *At the Back of the North Wind.* New York: Airmont, 1966 (1871).
_____. *A Dish of Orts, Chiefly Papers on the Imagination and on Shakespeare.* Illus. Cyrus Cuneo and G. H. Evison. London: Edwin Dalton, 1908. Norwood Editions, 1977.
_____. *The Gifts of the Child Christ: Fairytales and Stories for the Childlike.* Vol. I. Ed. Glenn E. Sadler. Grand Rapids, MI: Eerdmans, 1973.
_____. *Phantastes and Lilith.* Intro. C. S. Lewis. Grand Rapids, MI: Eerdmans, 1964.
Plato. *The Dialogues of Plato: A Selection.* Trans. Benjamin Jowett. New York: Liveright, 1927 (1893).

Diamond and Kilmeny
MacDonald, Hogg, and the Scottish Folk Tradition

By William Raeper

It could be argued that George MacDonald's *At the Back of the North Wind* is more of a vision than a tale. For, what the reader takes away from the book is surely not a story or a sequence of events, but feelings—feelings about North Wind as an attractive and haunting form of death, or puzzlement as to the meaning of Diamond's and Nannie's suggestive and inexplicable dreams. The book strikes a continuing note of wonder in the imaginations of children, inviting them to respond to it, and it is this, perhaps more than anything else, which has kept MacDonald's book on household shelves for more than a century.

At the Back of the North Wind stands apart from MacDonald's other works for children in that it is set squarely in Victorian London and not, like the others, in a remote magical realm of bygone years. The world of cabdrivers and gentility, social problems and piety is pleasingly evoked. It is true, too, that Diamond, the book's focus, shares many features of the Victorian child hero—his saintliness in helping others, his cardboard priggery, and finally even his death. What saves Diamond, however, from a descent into complete and utter sickliness is that he becomes a fairy child—a Scottish brownie, in fact—going about the streets of London doing good. The reader does not have to accept Diamond as fact, but can enjoy him as fantasy. The book has a double story, superimposing two worlds, or perhaps two visions of the same world, on top of each other, and it is to MacDonald's credit that he uses the fairy to illuminate the mundane so successfully.

On a close inspection, the book does reveal a complex of learning and levels which are highly arresting as the reader perceives MacDonald translating his theological and imaginative ideas into language fit for children. Herodotus and his Hyperboreans are cited on the first page, for instance, and more than a passing reference is made to Durante (Dante), renamed by MacDonald to point up the universal value of his visionary poetry. Herodotus and Dante may seem weighty names to bandy about in front of children, but there is another, younger figure to complete the trio of pioneers who have recounted something of the back of the north wind, and this is a peasant girl called Kilmeny. Kilmeny, who shows many of the same changeling qualities as Diamond, could almost be seen as a Tangle to Diamond's Mossy, or as an Irene to his Curdie, the other half of a fairy pair.

Kilmeny was the subject of a poem in James Hogg's *The Queen's Wake* (1813). The setting of *The Queen's Wake,* an uneven collection of poems, is a competition of poets at a celebration in the honor of Mary, Queen of Scots. Though Hogg did not, in the end, award the laurel to the poet who sang *Kilmeny,* history has certainly singled out this short poem as one of the greatest lyrics in Scottish literature. Generations of Scottish schoolchildren have had to learn it, and MacDonald, too, must have known it from boyhood. Briefly, it tells of Kilmeny, a young girl, who falls asleep in a wood and is taken by a spirit to "the land of thought." She remains there for seven years before returning home once more, but only for a short spell. "For Kilmeny was pure as pure could be." She is a magical virgin, a Beatrice, too good for mortal life and fit only for the highest reaches of heaven. MacDonald placed her and Dante side by side when he came to write *At the Back of the North Wind*:

> I will tell you something of what two very different people have reported, both of whom knew more about it, I believe, than Herodotus. One of them speaks from his own experience, for he visited the country: the other from the testimony of a young peasant girl who came back from it for a month's visit to her friends. The former was a great Italian of noble family, who died more than five hundred years ago . . . Durante was an elderly man, and Diamond was a little boy, and so their experience must be a little different (113-114).

Then MacDonald goes on to quote some of Hogg's poem. In fact, Hogg's lyric appears to have provided a few of the salient features of the country at the back of the north wind. Though MacDonald claimed, "I have now come to the most difficult part of my story. And why? Because I do not know enough about it," he did, in fact, describe the back of the north wind in evocative detail, drawing on Hogg's description of the land that Kilmeny is taken off to:

> A land of love, and a land of light,
> Withouten sun, or moon, or night:
> Where the river swa'd a living stream,
> And the light a pure celestial beam:
> The land of vision it would seem,
> A still, an everlasting dream (*Selected Poems* 34).

Life as a dream is, of course, MacDonald's perpetual theme, taken from medieval literature and the writings of the German Romantics, but there are some closer parallels between the back of the north wind and the "land of thought" that Kilmeny wakes up in. There is no sun, for example, but "plenty of a certain still, rayless light" (*North Wind* 115). While Kilmeny is surrounded by spirits, similar to those who appear in MacDonald's "Parable of the Singer" in his long poem, *Within and Without,* the people at the back of the north wind are isolated though kind individuals who communicate without speaking. More important is the river. The river at the back of the north wind is a holy source of life, bubbling and singing. It is this river's song that Diamond continues to babble in his apparently nonsensical ballads throughout the rest of the book: "He insisted that if it did not sing tunes in people's ears, it sung tunes in their heads" (116). The river Kilmeny is laid in also has a song, and its waters bless her with eternal life, just as Diamond's trip to the back of the north wind "saints" him with another order of life which he must bring back to bless and improve the everyday world:

> Then deep in the stream her body they laid,
> That her youth and beauty might never fade;
> And they smiled on heaven when they saw her lie
> In the stream of life that wandered bye.
> And she heard a song, she heard it sung,

> She kend not where; but sae sweetly it rung,
> It fell on her ear like a dream on the morn:
> "O! blest be the day Kilmeny was born!"
> *(Selected Poems 36).*

There is a certain kind of Platonism mixed in with Diamond's and Kilmeny's experiences, as well as an inadequacy in describing the otherworldly scenes. For the country at the back of the north wind is only a picture of the true country where Diamond is destined at the end of the book, surely heaven, while Kilmeny's lofty "land of thought" (also heavenly) has a Greek ring to it. Both Kilmeny and Diamond eventually return to earth in different ways.

From this point on in MacDonald's book it becomes clear that it is not North Wind herself, but going to the back of her which is most important, for she is hardly in evidence for over two hundred pages after Diamond's return. Diamond journeys home, a saint and a fairy, to do the will of God in the London streets before finally departing this life because he is too good for it. Kilmeny, however, fulfills no such pious purpose. As in the traditional Scottish ballads, she vanishes (for seven years—Diamond is only gone for seven days, but in both cases a traditional note sounds) only to reappear briefly before returning once more to the spirit land. Paradoxically and similarly, Diamond is too good to live, while Kilmeny is too good to die. Yet Kilmeny and Diamond share more than just a surface similarity. Both spring from a shared consciousness—a Scottish consciousness—and this aspect of MacDonald's shaping as a writer has often been passed over. Even in MacDonald's long series of Scottish novels, critics have tended to look at the romantic or theological aspects of his fiction rather than at their distinctive Scottish flavor. At the same time, any examination of his fantasy writing has either scrutinized its German roots or else veered in the direction of Freud or Jung when looking for a theory. In effect, MacDonald's Scottishness has been overlooked and, for a Scottish writer who was so emphatically Scottish in his dress, speech and character, this is an uncomfortable blind spot when assessments are made of him as a writer.[1]

MacDonald was a farmer's boy from the northeast of Scotland, while Hogg was a shepherd from the border country of Ettrick. Though the two areas are separated by geography, they are not too widely separated by tradition. Both are lowland, both are steeped in ballads and folktales, and both are rural. In fact, the Huntly burn in the ballad of Thomas the Rhymer, which runs through the borders close to Hogg's home, is the same Huntly of MacDonald's birthplace, for the Gordons took the name with them when they moved from the Borders to Aberdeenshire after being granted lands there by Robert the Bruce.

In the countryside where Hogg and MacDonald grew up, the world of the ballad was the world of everyday life. Hogg claimed that his grandfather had seen fairies and that he had witches in his ancestry. MacDonald made no such claim, but there were witches alive when he was a boy and ghosts went out a-haunting in locales close by. Hogg first made a name for himself by collecting ballads for a volume of Sir Walter Scott's *Border Minstrelsy* and then, inspired by those, he sat down to compose his own in the same tradition. After a shaky start he enjoyed popular success with *The Queen's Wake* (which includes *Kilmeny*) and his career was launched.

MacDonald also set out to be a poet, beginning with *Within and Without,* which ran to two editions. He also composed ballads, notably within the structure of his rambling novels. These are also in a traditional style, but usually contain a theological and didactic emphasis in line with MacDonald's own priorities. MacDonald's ballads, it must be said, are notoriously bad. Often they are no more than thumping, jingling lines of undistinguished doggerel. Yet, on the one hand they play a fascinating intertextual role within the structure of his own novels and, on the other hand, it should be pointed out that the tradition of the "bothy ballad" was strong and peculiar to Aberdeenshire. In bothy ballads, ordinary people made up rhymes about their friends, employers, and events in everyday life. MacDonald was not just following a romantic impulse in writing ballads, he was doing something which would have come naturally to him from boyhood.

Ballads hold a unique and important status in the literature of any country. They are generally anonymous, being passed on by oral tradition in various forms, and this secures their place as poetry of the people. They usually tell a story and often deal with important events such as birth, death, and love. In their own peculiar way, just as fairy tales do, ballads help people integrate their identity and order their inner experiences. It is true that ballads often include aspects of legend and fairy tale and vice versa. What Bruno

Bettelheim writes of the fairy tale in his book *The Uses of Enchantment* may also hold good for the ballad:

> It is here that fairy tales have unequalled value, because they offer new dimensions to the child's imagination which would be impossible for him to discover as truly his own. Even more important, the form and structure of fairy tales suggest images to the child by which he can structure his daydreams and with them give better direction to his life (7).

Even more suggestive is what Jung writes of fairy tales in *The Archetypes and the Collective Unconscious:*

> As in alchemy, our fairy tale describes the unconscious processes that compensate the conscious, Christian situation. It depicts the workings of a spirit who carries our Christian thinking beyond the boundaries set by ecclesiastical concepts, seeking an answer to questions which neither the Middle Ages nor the present day have been able to solve (251).

In other words, fairy tales benefit us by helping us order our unconscious, inner processes. Surely, in the same way, the ballad, legend, and folktale tradition that both Hogg and MacDonald were drawing on, helps to do the same thing. Ballads are anonymous products of an imaginative consciousness. They exist outside of the church and the taboos of religion as expressions of ancestral voices, voices which reach out of the past and into the here and now. MacDonald, for one, was very conscious of his ancestral voices and knew them to be speaking in his writing. He allowed them to do this and did not always try to control what they were saying. Often, partly because of this, he did not give a meaning to his fantasy writing, but allowed the reader to draw his own from it, as from a well. This, especially in the area of his children's writing, is one of his chief characteristics. Of these voices of the past, however, MacDonald wrote:

> In each present personal being we have the whole past of our generation enclosed, to be redeveloped with endless difference in each individuality. Hence perhaps it comes that, every now and then, into our consciousness float strange odours of

feeling, strange tones as of by-gone affections, strange glimmers as of forgotten truths, strange mental sensations of indescribable sort and texture. Friends, I should be a terror to myself, did I not believe that wherever my dim consciousness may come to itself, God is there (*Paul Faber, Surgeon* 203-204).

MacDonald felt strongly that his ancestral voices be contained by his faith lest, perhaps, he succumb to their power.

If MacDonald's writing appears, however, to be romantic, that is because it is. Both Hogg and MacDonald had the example of Burns before them, that forerunner of the Romantics, the ploughman poet who became the voice of Scotland. Hogg actually knew Wordsworth and corresponded with Byron. In addition, both found that, owing to the currency that Wordsworth's and Coleridge's theories received, the form of poetry they were most familiar with, the ballad, was thrust into the forefront of public taste. The ballad was heralded as the poem of the people, to be written in the language of the people and, along with the lyric, dislodged the forms of poetry, such as the epic, which had been popular in previous times. MacDonald found a theory therefore to give a spur to his writing of ballads, and it was a theory that served him well. Poetry in general became more "musical" with the poet as both player and instrument, recording his own *feelings* about the world around him. Poetry became, therefore, an invitation to *feel* with the poet and there was a return to the contemplation of nature accompanied by the sighing melancholic music of the Aeolian harp. These views found their way into MacDonald's essay "The Fantastic Imagination," which dealt with the fairy tale as a literary form: "The best way with music, I imagine, is not to bring the forces of our intellect to bear on it, but to be still and let it work on that part of us for whose sake it exists" (*A Dish of Orts* 321-322).

Similarly, in his preface to *Dealings with the Fairies* (1867), a pocket-size book of the fairy colors of gold and green, MacDonald wrote: "Where more is meant than meets the ear." In effect, MacDonald married his folk tradition to Romantic theory and brought both of them to his children's writing. What is startling is that in his children's fiction he succeeded superbly, whereas in his poetry he failed. But, it must be asked, how did he succeed, and how did his Scottishness help him?

First of all, there is nothing very apparently Scottish about *At the Back of the North Wind*. Indeed, there are only a few details. Diamond's odd bedroom above the stable in The Mews is clearly a *chaumer* of the kind in which Aberdeenshire farm workers would sleep (those same men who sang the bothy ballads), and a connection is made with the traditional Scottish ballad *Tam Lin* when North Wind tells Diamond: "Nay, Diamond, if I change into a serpent or a tiger, you must not let go your hold of me, for my hand will never change in yours if you keep a good hold" (14). [2]

In *Tam Lin,* Janet must hold on to Tam Lin while he changes into a variety of terrifying shapes and animals before turning back into a human knight. If she lets go, she will lose him; if she keeps hold then she can marry him. This motif is repeated in MacDonald's *The Carasoyn* where Colin must hold on to Fairy who turns successively into a snake, a white rabbit, a cat, a wood pigeon, and a dove.

But this is not enough to build a whole Scottish theory on. In MacDonald's other fiction, his children's books, *The Princess and the Goblin* and *The Princess and Curdie* seem to be set in a distant, Scottish landscape, and the goblins in the first of these books possess unindividuated toes, a traditional Scottish feature. Ranald Bannerman's nurse is nicknamed "Kelpie" (a wicked fairy creature) in the book of the same name; while MacDonald's short fairy tale, *The Carasoyn,* with its portrayal of the queen of the fairies and the changeling girl, seems to owe a great deal to border legend. Sir Gibbie, in MacDonald's Scottish novel, is a brownie, and MacDonald's continual connection of the wizard, the horse, and the devil (in *Malcolm,* for example) owes much to local color quite apart from anything else. The Horseman's Word, a local secret society of farm workers, actually claimed to possess a word of power enabling its members, with the devil's backing, to hold sway over both horses and women. This society, active until the 1930s in Aberdeenshire and beyond, was particularly strong in Huntly. MacDonald must have known about it, and its supernatural elements, even though so far removed from the bounds of the kirk, must have intrigued him.

Yet, all these are ingredients, it could be pointed out, and not *substance*. And where is the bearing on MacDonald's *children's* fiction? A clue is to be found, perhaps, in the ballad of "Thomas the Rhymer." At the beginning of "Thomas the Rhymer," Thomas, a noted seer, is sitting by the Huntly bank when the Queen of the Fairies (surely at least a cousin of Princess Irene's great-great grandmother) appears to him and takes him off to Elfland. She tells him:

> O see not ye yon narrow road,
> So thick beset with thorns and briers?
> That is the path of righteousness,
> Tho after it but few enquires.
>
> And see not ye that braid, braid road,
> That lies across yon lillie leven?
> That is the path to wickedness,
> Tho some call it the road to heaven.
>
> And see not ye that bonny road,
> Which winds about the fernie brae?
> That is the road to fair Elfland,
> Where you and I this night maun gae
> (*English and Scottish Ballads* 65).

Thus there are *three* roads, not two, and the third, which is not an evil path, is the road to fairy land, or to the imagination. It exists between good and evil, heaven and hell, and appears to belong to neither realm. Whatever fairies are (and whether they exist or not), they do show human imagination at work. There had been a time in Scottish history, before the Reformation, when the folk traditions and the old religion (where there was any religion) had been contentedly mixed up. T. C. Smout, the social historian, in his authoritative *A History of the Scottish People 1560-1830* writes:

> Medieval Scotland believed in saints, whose favour could be procured by sacrifice and pilgrimage: it believed in devils and fairies, whose quiescence at least could be procured by a libation of milk on the hillside, or by leaving a little grain in the ground for the "Old Gudeman." It believed in the power of priests, who served the saints, and likewise the power of witches, who were in communication with the devil and could control some of his supernatural powers either to do good by healing or to do evil by cursing and destruction (199).

The Reformation and the arrival of Calvinism in Scotland ended this truce between the church and the fairy folk. From then on there was no distinction between a good witch and a bad witch. The Mosaic text "Thou shalt not suffer a witch to live" was ruthlessly enforced and many women were put to death. The bright third way, the way of the imagination, was accordingly suppressed, to the continuing detriment of the arts in Scotland, and the fairies retreated to the woods and hills and vanished out of sight. But, perhaps it is a truth that while fairies can be hidden, they cannot be extinguished. They remained alive in ballads and stories, passed from mothers and nurses to each new generation of children and, though outlawed, they remained stubbornly in evidence. What this meant for writers like Hogg and MacDonald, growing up in rural areas where ballads and folktales were probably at their strongest, was that they imbibed, as children, a mixture of the Bible and fairy. Hogg, for example, recounted that his father was a strict religious man, while his mother was well versed in folklore and taught him ballads on her knee. He learned to read the Bible at an early age and memorized the ballads and the metrical psalms alongside each other. MacDonald, for his part, must have had similar childhood memories. Though he was better educated than Hogg, he would have heard folktales and learned ballads as a child, and it was this base which was galvanized into action when he finally encountered the library of German and romantic literature at Thurso Castle in 1842. *Within* met *Without* and the result was mingling of imagination, Romantic theory, and religion which was to serve him well in writing his children's fiction. In the fairy tale, as in poetry, MacDonald found that he did not have to be bound by the tenets of realistic fiction and was able to make his tales open-ended, Aeolian, as he pleased. At the same time, the subject of his children's books, the child, is also Jung's primal child. He is wise, eternal, and androgynous. This is a being who combines a knowledge of this world with an awareness of the other and is "given to metaphysics" (*North Wind* 83) just as Diamond is, and so is truly "father to the man," as Wordsworth claims.

In the Victorian era, children's fiction was largely prosy and instructive. Children were licked into shape in the nursery and anything to do with 'the imagination, especially fairy tales, was considered immoral and firmly out of bounds. Yet MacDonald was able to participate in removing these prejudices and there seem to be several reasons for this. On the one hand, his childhood acceptance of the fairy and the religious may have helped stifle any inhibition he may have felt against the fairy tale had he been brought up in the town. This is mere speculation, of course, but it might be true. It was also true that MacDonald was writing at a period when fairy tales were becoming more and more acceptable to the public at large. Yet, at the same time, it is MacDonald's legacy to have taken the fairy tale, in English, and given it a moral vision and to have written fairy tales and children's books which have never been out of print. This is a singular achievement and not a purely accidental one, as his essay on "The Fantastic Imagination" bears witness. For MacDonald considered what he was about, and this particular essay marks the first time that someone has dared to posit a theory as to how a fairy tale should be written. Much of this essay draws on MacDonald's understanding of Romantic theory, but, at the same time, MacDonald's morality is equally important. As in all his writing, MacDonald was aiming at a religious form. Interestingly, one of MacDonald's favorite poets was Sir Philip Sidney (whom he anthologized in *A Cabinet of Gems* in 1891). Sidney's aim "to teach and delight" was one MacDonald took to heart and perhaps it helped his work become fit matter for the nursery. For, if MacDonald was imaginative, he was also religious and if he was a strong defender of the supernatural, he was also a teacher. This balance of apparent contradictions (contradictions to the Victorians, at least) is what may have helped his children's writing gain approval in the starchy world of the nineteenth century nursery. As a Scot, with his own flavor of the fairy and religious, he was able to respond imaginatively to the German and English Romantics and begin to reclaim that area of the imagination, that third way, which had been denied to children for so long.

MacDonald, the London dweller of the 1860s or the Sage of Bordighera of the 1880s, seems far removed from the country boy running around his father's farm. Yet it is the early years which are often the most formative in any life, something MacDonald was more than aware of as he wrote so powerfully and with such effect for children. In a period when interest in MacDonald is growing and when Hogg, too, is having more attention paid to him, perhaps that third way that they both learned about as children is one which needs pointing to again.

Notes

1. David Robb's book *George MacDonald* in the Scottish Writers Series at last makes a beginning in examining MacDonald's heritage, purpose, and achievement as a Scottish writer.
2. MacDonald's treatment of the animal in the human is given an evolutionary and spiritual aspect in *The Princess and Curdie,* where Curdie is given the gift of feeling the animal growing within, under the skin of a human hand (*see The Princess and Curdie,* Puffin Books, England, 1982, pp. 70-1). A more mystical, Swedenborgian twist is given to this idea in *Lilith,* where Mr Raven tells Vane

> Every one, as you ought to know, has a beast-self and a bird-self, and a stupid fish-self, ay, and a creeping serpent-self too, which it takes a deal of crushing to kill! In truth he has also a tree-self and a crystal-self, and I don't know how many selves more—all to get into harmony. You can tell what sort a man is by his creature that comes oftenest to the front (30).

Works Cited

Bettelheim, Bruno. *The Uses of Enchantment: The Meaning and Importance of Fairy Tales.* London: Thames and Hudson, 1976.

Child, F. J. *English and Scottish Ballads.* London: Harrop, 1922.

Hogg, James. *James Hogg: Selected Poems.* Ed. D. S. Mack. Oxford: Clarendon, 1970.

Jung, C. J. *The Archetypes and the Collective Unconscious.* New York: Pantheon, 1959.

MacDonald, George. *At the Back of the North Wind.* London: Strahan, 1871.

_____. *A Dish of Orts.* London: Sampson, Low, Marston, 1895.

_____. *Lilith.* Tring: Lion Publishing, 1982.

_____. *Paul Faber, Surgeon.* London: Hurst and Blackett, 1879.

Robb, David. *George MacDonald.* Edinburgh: Scottish Academic Press, 1987.

Smout, T. C. *A History of the Scottish People 1560-1830.* London: Collins, 1969.

Language and Secret Knowledge in *At the Back of the North Wind*

By Roderick McGillis

I take as my starting point the rhyme Diamond's mother reads on the beach at Sandwich in chapter 13 of George MacDonald's *At the Back of the North Wind*. The verse is a seemingly endless account of a running river, dipping swallows, bleating sheep, and merry breezes. It is interminable! Diamond's mother—and it is difficult to blame her—stops reading out of sheer exasperation. Diamond asks, "Why don't you go on, Mother dear?" And she replies, "It's such nonsense! I believe it would go on forever." Diamond isn't consolatory: "That's just what it did," he says, referring to the river mentioned in the poem which he associates with the river he saw at the back of the North Wind. Mother and son fail to communicate. She is too concerned with the fact of her son's health, and also with a language that deals with a stable reality, as her reaction to the rhyme testifies. Her fear for her son's health is a metonymy for her fear of instability. Diamond, on the other hand, is with Christ in not caring for the morrow. He has befriended the spirit of change, North Wind, and he knows that change and instability are not synonymous. He knows that change is eternal and yet ephemeral, and the poem is merely a way of reminding him of this. It is North Wind's message to him, as several indications in the chapter make clear. At the outset Diamond and his mother look eastward while a "sweet little wind blew on their left side, and comforted the mother without letting her know what it was that comforted her." Later the wind flutters some paper, drawing their attention to a book of nursery rhymes half buried in the sand. And when Diamond's mother tries to find a more congenial rhyme than the one she first begins to read, "the wind blew the leaves rustling back to the same verse" (132-144).

Two questions occur: what is it about these particular verses that is important? And why does the North Wind choose to communicate to Diamond through poetry instead of, say, through the beauty of the sea and sky? Answers to these questions should allow us to share the secrets Diamond shares with those he will later meet in London. The first question is quickly answered if we refuse to judge the poem as a poem. Although graced with the epithet "nursery rhyme," it is a doggerel. But the fact that it is supposed to work as nursery rhyme—and there are later in the story revised versions of "Little Boy Blue," "The Cat and the Fiddle," and "Little Bo Peep"—ought to warn us that form is as important as content. First, content: the river metaphor communicates the life cycle (it recurs in the penultimate chapter) as it "flows for ever" through hollows and meadows. Sheep and swallows live and multiply by the singing river, changing as it flows, dependent upon it for nourishment. Sheep, swallows, breeze, grasses, daisies, and growing river are interdependent, continuous, and constantly moving, passing. Second, form: this establishes constant movement. There is no reason why this poem cannot go on forever; it has no beginning or ending and no interrupting punctuation. It consists of repeated rhyming that has no pattern other than verbal repetition and the recurring two-line, three-line, and four-line rhymes. The form of the poem intrudes with its insistent repetitions and rhymes; it impedes Diamond's mother. She fails to see "meaning" in a verse that appears endless. Like most readers, she seeks for a point, an end to what she reads. Language drawing attention to itself is nonsense to her. But our answers are clear: it is the metaphors that are important, and North Wind's medium is poetry since through poetry (language parading as metaphor) another world takes shape. Diamond is freed from the tyranny of poverty and nature through language.

Poetry truly never ends. The idea of the endless story is strong in MacDonald. For example, the final chapter of *Lilith* is "The Endless Ending," and in the final paragraph of *The Lost Princess* (1875), the narrator writes: "If you think it [the story] is not finished—I never knew a story that was" (142). In another book, *Castle Warlock* (1882), the poet Cosmo writes works that do not end: "to him the end of things never came; nothing that has an end was worth employing his art upon" (327). The reader supplies the sense of an ending if he participates in the action of the poetic language. To Diamond's mother, the poem is mere endless cycle; to Diamond, the circularity of the verse contains secret knowledge. Diamond chants bits of the verse; his mother fears for his health. Diamond's chant evolves into the repeated phrase, "home again, home again, home again," and this carries with it metaphoric suggestions of that place back of the north wind.

The poem then is a manifestation in the actual of that dreamlike place Diamond visits with the help of North Wind. The verse's improvised form dissolves into an incantation of repetitions suggesting what commentators of children's literature often refer to as "magic." Magic is evident in the repeated words and phrases, in the riddling quality that exasperates Diamond's mother. (There is, we remember, a riddle later in the book invented by Mr. Raymond. He lights the world with the music of language.) And magic, as Northrop Frye points out, "means secret wisdom, the keys to all knowledge" (31). Such knowledge takes Diamond to a centre of serenity in a world of chaos. The centre of serenity—what MacDonald refers to as "the community of the centre" in *Phantastes* (1858)—is clearly evident both in the noumenal world of fantasy and in the phenomenal world of London. In the important sixth chapter, North Wind takes Diamond out in a storm. As they remain suspended on the hayloft roof, they converse about North Wind's apparent duality: with one arm she intends to protect Diamond, with the other she intends to sink a ship. North Wind convinces Diamond that she is—in his words—the "kindest, goodest, best me in the world." Then North Wind rushes into the stormy night with Diamond clutched to her heart. The lengthy passage that follows is worth quoting since it complements the previous discussion between Diamond and North Wind by insisting on paradox. What MacDonald never tires of showing is that when opposites are perceived as complements—North Wind is a beautiful lady and a ferocious wolf—they do not only complete, but they also contain each other. This is reconciliation. No longer do we have "simply the clash opposites but the passage of each into the other" (Ricoeur 88). The passage is typical of MacDonald's style.

> And as if the clouds knew she had come, they burst into a fresh jubilation of thunderous light. For a few moments, Dia-

mond seemed to be borne up through the depths of an ocean of dazzling flame; the next, the winds were writhing around him like a storm of serpents. For they were in the midst of the clouds and mists, and they of course took the shapes of the wind, eddying and wreathing and whirling and shooting and dashing about like grey and black water, so that it was as if the wind itself had taken shape, and he saw the grey and black wind tossing and raving most madly all about him. Now it blinded him by smiting him upon the eyes; now it deafened him by bellowing in his ears; for even when the thunder came he knew now that it was the billows of the great ocean of the air dashing against each in their haste to fill the hollow scooped out by the lightning; now it took his breath quite away by sucking it from his body with the speed of its rush . . . It is quite impossible for me to describe what he saw. Did you ever watch a great wave shoot into a winding passage amongst rocks? If you ever did, you would see that the water rushed every way at once, some of it even turning back and opposing the rest; great confusion you might see nowhere except in a crowd of frightened people. Well, the wind was like that, except that it went much faster, and therefore was much wilder, and twisted and shot and curled and dodged and clashed and raved ten times more madly than anything else in creation except human passions . . . And Diamond felt as the wind seized on his hair, which his mother kept rather long, as if he too was part of the storm, and some of its life went out from him. But so sheltered was he by North Wind's arm and bosom that only at times, in the fiercer onslaught of some curl-billowed eddy, did he recognize for a moment how wild was the storm in which he was carried, nestling in its very core and formative centre.

Present and past participles abound, generating movement. Simile and metaphor strive to communicate constant movement. Syaesthesia adds its effect. Language fails. "It is quite impossible for me to describe what he saw," writes the narrator. The whole passage is a complex of contradictions. Paradox is the stuff of language and metaphor. "An ocean of dazzling flame" is an impossibility outside our imaginations. But inside our imaginations such a pairing of opposites is reasonable; in fact, it accomplishes the impossible description. This passage clarifies the meaning of duality by illustrating the importance of our mind's willingness to accept metaphor as a meaningful activity, as a mediator between Diamond's unmediated experience and the reader. Diamond's experience is of paradox, stasis in movement; he is surrounded by a storm, and he is "a part of the storm." He shares its energy and it shares some of his life; we receive but what we give. Diamond is both at the still centre and at the circumference of the storm. This is apocalypse! A revealing of chaos and its centre! Diamond experiences what Shelley calls "the deep truth" which is necessarily imageless (*Prometheus Unbound,* act 2, scene 4, 1. 116). Images are man's means of communicating this deep truth. And they come alive, Coleridge reminds us, only when "they have the effect of reducing multitude to unity, or succession to an instant" (177). This is what MacDonald's language attempts to do here. We can call it poetic language.

Poetic language for MacDonald appeals first to the ear and like speech it contains resonance, tone, ambiguity, and subtlety. Through hearing a poem the reader is induced to search for meaning: "A poem is a thing not for the understanding and heart only, but likewise for the ear; or rather, for the understanding and heart through the ear" (*A Dish of Orts* 216). In *England's Antiphon,* written three years before *At the Back of the North Wind,* MacDonald uses the analogy of music: "The heart of poetry is indeed truth, but its garments are music, and the garments come first in the process of revelation" (174). Reading the storm passage in *At the Back of the North Wind,* we realize the importance of language to MacDonald. Its effect on the reader is intended neither to suspend intellect nor to direct intellect, but rather to motivate it. Metaphor is that aspect of language that expresses the ineffable by envisaging an impossibility. Analogic thought becomes available to intellect through metaphor.

This explains MacDonald's interest in poetry as the central human concern. It seeks not to proselytize, but merely to quicken. As North Wind says, "A poet is a man who is glad of something, and tries to make others glad of it too." He spreads relationship and love through "poetic suggestiveness" (*Unspoken Sermons* I, 120). According to MacDonald this typifies Christ's way of teaching. As Louis MacNeice notices in *Varieties of Parable* (apparently without having read MacDonald's sermons), MacDonald equates poetry and parable, the poet and Christ. Christ is a "living lyre" whose parables present ideas "in subdefined, suggestive shapes, yielding no satisfactory meaning to the mere intellect" (*Unspoken Sermons* II, 41). "The form of parable," MacDonald says elsewhere, "is the first in which truth will admit of being embodied" (*Unspoken Sermons* I, 130). This surely is because parable defeats rational theology. It teaches through hyperbole, paradox, and metaphor.

This is why North Wind communicates with Diamond through poetry, and it also explains her method of teaching which (as always in MacDonald) consists in troubling her pupil, in disorienting him. For example, in chapter 7 the following exchange between Diamond and North Wind (Diamond speaks first) takes place:

> "How kind you are, North Wind!"
> "I am only just. All kindness is but justice. We owe it."
> "I don't quite understand that."
> "Never mind; you will some day. There is no hurry about understanding it now."

North Wind deliberately reverses Diamond's expectations. Early in the book she remarks that "Nobody is cold with the North Wind." Diamond reacts as we would: "I thought everybody was," he says. To this North Wind replies: "That is a great mistake. Most people make it, however. They are cold because they are not with the North Wind, but without it." Later in the chapter Diamond understands what North Wind means, and the narrator remarks: "How it was that he should have guessed what she meant at that very moment I cannot tell . . . " Diamond is at the very moment freezing; he learns through experience.

Diamond's night excursions with North Wind represent his experience of deep truth, and that is why he has difficulty remembering and recounting what happens to him. He constantly fears his relationship with North Wind is a dream, partly because her manifestations appear random. Colin Manlove compares the visits of North Wind to the randomness of the wind's visits to an Aeolian harp (80). But North Wind's visits are not as random as this suggests. Her arrival invariably announces Diamond's illness. The first third of the novel presents North Wind and her night world. This is the period in which Diamond catches his fever and falls seriously ill. His recovery in the seaside town of Sandwich is a prelude to renewed health and adventure as a cabdriver in London. The London section of the book is much the longest and ends with the recovery of wealth and happiness by the Colmans and with the attainment of security of Diamond's family. Diamond now becomes ill again. His illness allows him to re-establish unmediated contact with North Wind.

Between his early rambles with North Wind and his final illness Diamond communicates with her through his poetry. The verses found on the Sandwich beach introduce him to poetry and reveal his understanding. They also spark his own poetic talents. He now becomes "God's baby," a Christ figure who spreads his message of love, obedience, and duty through his actions and his words. His poetry is a sign of secret knowledge, his relationship with North Wind; it is a reminder that the Diamond who encounters the roughness of London lowlife has been to the back of the north wind.

In London, Diamond's dreams maintain his contact with North Wind and her poem of the running river. The narrator informs us that each morning Diamond wakes with "something in his mind" reminiscent of the "endless song his mother had read to him on the seashore," "a song in which the words and the music somehow appeared to be all one." Unfortunately the lines of the song fade until all that remains is "some lovely picture of water or grass or daisies . . . with all the commonness polished off it." This picture motivates Diamond to sing his own odd but lovely songs to his baby brother. The first two examples of Diamond's songs—both in chapter 16, "Diamond Makes a Beginning"—are reformulations of the endless song with "baby" as the focus around which swallows fly and lambs gambol.

These songs mark Diamond's beginning. (Later he will invent original compositions and parodies of traditional nursery rhymes.) He begins to be a poet; in other words, he "utters deeds." In Diamond, as in Jesus, "Poet and poem [are] one indivisible fact" (*Poetical Works* I, 257). The best example of this is the "Drunken Cabman" chapter in which Diamond, roused in the middle of the night by the voice of the drunken cabman, ventures across the yard to intervene in the row. From an interpretive standpoint this incident is crucial, since it is clearly open to the criticism of those who see a divorce between the "fantasy" and "reality" aspects of the book. H. J. C. Grierson confesses that "the good little boy and his exploits with his father's cab are trying, in the very worst style of Victorian edification" (10), and Colin Manlove lectures us by saying "we must feel that the supernatural episodes are so divided from the natural as to suggest that the whole book is the result of two quite separate imaginative acts" (81). Stephen Prickett simply does not like Diamond. He hastily claims that Diamond's "preternatural goodness . . . instead of arousing respect of gratitude in those he has helped, causes contempt. He *is* a prig" (246). Even MacDonald's son Greville speaks of a "two-world consciousness" in *At the Back of the North Wind* (361). It is worth examining this notion.

It is true that MacDonald is both poet and preacher and often the two persona clash. There are moments in *At the Back of the North Wind* in which MacDonald, or his narrator at least, mounts the pulpit, and these occur both in the supernatural and in the realistic episodes. For example, in chapter 2, Diamond cries when North Wind disappears, leaving him "with his bare feet on the stones of the paved yard." MacDonald takes the opportunity to preach.

> But for my part, I don't mind people crying, so much as I mind what they cry about, and how they cry—whether they cry quietly like ladies and gentlemen, or go shrieking like vulgar emperors, or ill-natured cooks; for all emperors are not gentlemen, and all cooks are not ladies—not all queens and princesses for that matter, either.

A more egregious example occurs in chapter 5. Diamond is playing in the Colman's garden, and MacDonald cannot forbear telling us that he "never touched any of the flowers or blossoms, for he was not like some boys who cannot enjoy a thing without pulling it to pieces, and so preventing everyone from enjoying it after them." Much later in the book when Diamond and his family suffer hard times, Diamond's father, Joseph, becomes irritable with his wife, and MacDonald intones:

> It is a strange thing how the pain of seeing the suffering of those we love will sometimes make us add to their suffering by being cross with them. This comes of not having faith enough in God, and shows how necessary this faith is, for when we lose it, we lose even the kindness which alone can soothe the suffering.

This is MacDonald of the unspoken sermons, the graduate of Highbury College. Such passages are for our edification. But this style occurs throughout the book and ought not affect our reaction to Diamond and his London exploits.

What these illustrate is MacDonald's belief that the natural and the supernatural are the same. While Diamond's actions and reactions are unbelievable as those of a real child, his personality is believable. He is simple, trusting, and well-spoken. That Diamond shows no influence of the vulgar language of the cabmen proves that MacDonald is not attempting naturalism in his depiction of Diamond's life in London. Diamond is an *exemplum*; he has been to the back of the north wind. Still he fears North Wind may be a dream; he would like to play with Nanny and Jim; and he suffers chill and fever from the cold wind. Through Diamond MacDonald wishes to fit together two worlds: that behind North Wind and that of London. Consequently, Diamond, for all his preternatural goodness remains a real child. He does not die because he is too good for the world; rather he dies because of his frailty, his susceptibility to illness. Although MacDonald has James Hogg's "Kilmeny" in mind (and perhaps Tieck's "The Elves," an account of a similar child disappearance, but lacking the Christian implications of "Kilmeny"), he does not suggest that Diamond is no longer at home with his family. For Kilmeny, this world "wasna her home, and she couldna remain" (l. 328). Diamond, however, is a little boy who dies; his death is a natural and sorrowful event.

To ignore this interconnection between fantasy and reality is to miss MacDonald's point. Diamond's fantasies make him a poet; they accomplish for him what is lacking in the "baffled poet," Cosmo Cupples, of *Alec Forbes of Howglen* (1865). Cosmo fails as a poet because of his

> incapacity for assimilating sorrow, his inability to find or vent a theory of the universe which should show it still beautiful despite of passing pain ... He had yet to learn that through "the heartache and the thousand natural shocks that flesh is heir to," man becomes capable of the blessedness to which all the legends of a golden age point (173).

Diamond succeeds as a poet because North Wind introduces him to the goodness in adversity, and she shows him that a golden age awaits. Once back in London, Diamond perceives such truth in poetry, and being a child he proves himself a natural poet, a manifestation of what MacDonald elsewhere calls the "divine idea of childhood." The many hints at Diamond's angelic, indeed Christ-like, character suggest his role as metaphor. The narrator cautions the reader that if he "find it hard to believe that Diamond should be so good, he must remember that he had been to the back of the north wind. If he never knew a boy so good, did he ever know a boy that had been to the back of the north wind?"

This passage introduces the new stage in Diamond's life; his London "beginning." Clearly, MacDonald wishes us to see fantasy or the supernatural at work in the real London in the person of Diamond. Consequently, when Diamond crosses the yard to the drunken cabman's room, he is "as much one of God's messengers as if he had been an angel with a flaming sword, going out fight the devil." His flaming sword, however, is language and symbol. He first directs the baby's attention to the dingy yellow light in the yard. Although the glass of the lamp is dirty and the gas bad, light in any form symbolizes sunship and hope; MacDonald through Diamond is revealing the supernatural in the natural. Diamond's silly songs follow and peace descends on the squalid room; it becomes a centre of serenity. Diamond and his songs connect the natural and super-natural parts of the book; rather than being "separate imaginative acts," the two spheres depicted in the book are the within and the without of imaginative activity. Within, Diamond travels with North Wind; without, he puts to the test his travel experiences. And North Wind herself continally works in the without as a determining agent, in one instance blowing so hard that Miss Colman is afraid to leave her house, thus ensuring a meeting with Mr. Evans.

But what is North Wind? And what does MacDonald mean by the "back of the north wind"? Calling North Wind and the land at her back "supernatural" is hardly a satisfactory explanation, and in his depiction of them, MacDonald scrupulously avoids sermoniz-ing; he avoids the doctrinal. From what we have seen North Wind is an embodiment of paradox. In a formal sense she allegorizes the defeat of allegory; in a thematic sense she refuses paraphrase. The land at her back represents, among other possibilities, the source of poetry. Put another way, North Wind is the visiting Muse—MacDonald's version for children of the Romantic anima figure that visits the poet in dreams or visionary moments—bringing intimations of eternity. She is Diamond's poetic genius. Like the grandmother in MacDonald's *The Princess and the Goblin,* she puts Diamond in touch with the noumenal. And also like the grandmother, North Wind has a male counterpart who functions in the phenomenal world. He is Mr. Raymond. We learn that Diamond gets some of his poems from Mr. Raymond's books—these tend to be literary parodies like "The True History of the Cat and the Fiddle" and the fairy tale "Little Daylight," or what the narrator calls "tricks" like the tree riddle. The other songs Diamond sings he makes up himself, finds "somewhere," or gets at the back of the north wind.

We keep returning to poetry and its way of communicating. In fact it is not too much to say that the meaning of *At the Back of the North Wind* is simply the importance of poetry as a way of knowing. The language of dream and poetry punctuate the so-called realistic section of the book in order to remind us of the Muse's power. Our poetic genius is the mind's power to dream a world of star children or moon ladies, or to imagine a world in which a princess sleeps all day and dances by the light of the moon. Such words remind us that imagination frees us from the tyranny of fact. Fact depends on immutable shape, but the poetic genius perceives constant change. This is why MacDonald uses the wind as his central figure: it is *inspiritus.* North Wind is ineffable, but in order that we can know her, as she tells Diamond, she must take shape, a body. Logically, she assumes the shape of a beautiful lady who reminds Diamond of his mother. But she takes other shapes as well, so that he can know her completely. He does. But what Diamond knows of North Wind cannot be what we know.

This brings us to the most interesting aspect of the book: its narrative framework. MacDonald's awareness of point of view is complex. If we except the blatant didactic passages in the book, there is no consistent point of view in which the reader can feel secure. The opening paragraph sets the tone:

> I have been asked to tell you about the back of the North Wind. An old Greek writer mentions a people who lived there, and were so comfortable that they could not bear it any longer, and drowned themselves. My story is not the same as his. I do not think Herodotus had got the right account of the place. I am going to tell you how it fared with a boy who went there.

Who has asked the speaker to tell us about the back of the north wind? And why has he been asked? The text offers no direct answer to either question. All we learn is that the narrator tells us the story of Diamond, a young boy he has met and for whom he develops a friendship based on intellectual affinity. The story serves at least two purposes: to keep alive the memory of the boy who has died, and to reassure readers as to his death. Much of what the narrator relates is what he has learned, secondhand as it were, from Diamond.

But Diamond's experiences, although unique, are not private, as Stephen Prickett has noted (245-246). The narrator mentions three writers who have written of this place at the back of the north wind: Herodotus the ancient Greek historian, Dante the medieval allegorist, and James Hogg, the Scottish Romantic. Something common exists in all three accounts, and none of the accounts by itself is complete. This ought to alert us to the fact that Diamond's story, presented in the language of parable, is symbolic; that is, it reveals at the same time that it disguises. It offers whatever a reader wishes to find in it, and more.

As MacDonald says, "words are live things" (*A Dish of Orts* 318). He understands how words strive to become objects, but fail; they return to the possibility of meaning. Each reader must engage in interpretation. This may sound like a feeble attempt at phenomenology's hermeneutic circle, but there is ample evidence in the text of such a dialectic. MacDonald deliberately splits his persona putting something of himself in both the narrator of the story and in Mr. Raymond who has written "the story of the Little Lady and the Goblin Prince," clearly a reference to *The Princess and the Goblin*. Perhaps the narrator is MacDonald's speculative self and Mr. Raymond his poetic genius. In any case, the narrator often reminds us of the difficulty of knowing. When he arrives at the part of the narrative that relates Diamond's experience at the back of the north wind, he tells us he has "come to the most difficult part of my story." Why the most difficult? "Because I do not know enough about it." What he knows is what Diamond has related, and Diamond "had forgotten a great deal, and what he did remember was very hard to tell." The narrator even disagrees with part of Diamond's account, his belief that no one speaks at the back of the north wind. For Diamond essence had replaced language.

The experience of essences will "appear somewhat different to different people" and this is the reason MacDonald insists on ambiguity. Each account of truth is rich in content and effect. Diamond's story can mean many things to many people, and it can affect its readers in a variety of ways depending on their prior assumptions about themselves and their world. The narrative structure of *At the Back of the North Wind* invites the reader to share the secrets of poetry, its ambiguities and paradoxes. The book belongs to each reader the way Dulcimer belongs to Diamond: "Love makes the only myness." What this means is that a subjective response to the book need not be an anti-intellectual response or a submission to personal desires. Instead the book ought to test assumptions, reverse expectations the way North Wind reverses Diamond's expectations. It allows us to share Diamond's secret, what the narrator calls "the secret of life" that Diamond possesses.

"Secret" suggests MacDonald's notion of revelation and mystery: "There must be revelation before mystery. I take it that mystery is what lies behind revelation, that as yet revelation has not yet reached" (Qtd. in Joseph Johnson 77). Poems and fairy tales reveal and disguise, but first they must capture our interest. Each reader must decide whether the book succeeds, but sound interpretive insight is possible in even the most impressionistic responses to it. Take, for example, the *Athenaeum* review of *At the Back of the North Wind:*

> *At The Back of the North Wind* is a poet's own book. Whether children will understand the whole of it or not, they will be sure to love it for the sake of the lovely spirits by which it is animated, and for the charming sights and sounds from Fairyland and Dreamland which come and go like the colours of the sky at sunset . . . The mystery that hangs over his [Diamond's] strange intercourse with the North Wind is never violated or explained away though the veil is sufficiently transparent for those who have the eye to see and the heart to understand (303).

The reviewer ignores the fact that the book is fiction; he calls MacDonald a poet who animates his fictional world by appeals to sight and sound, the apocalyptic senses. Furthermore, he notices MacDonald's confusion of dream and reality: Fairyland is "real" in the sense that it is a conscious imaginative creation, while Dreamland is "unreal," since it is a creation of the unconscious mind. More important still, however, is the acute perception of the book's central paradox: its open secret or knowable mystery. A mystery exists, but a certain few can understand it. Perceptive readers will be secret sharers in a mystery, a mystery shared with Diamond, Mr. Raymond, and the narrator. And happily, perceptive readers do not form an exclusive group; rather, the reviewer continues, the "whole work is woven into a lovely tissue, partly dream, partly vision, and partly a story which will be charming for readers of all classes and all ages." All that is required for participation in this secret is a willing suspension of self. We must submit to the book's charm, its *carmen,* its song. MacDonald would appreciate this, since for him, music offers a useful analogy for literature's effect on the reader. This charm, however, does not close our responses; it opens them. As interpreters we are not forced into a struggle to save our independence through misinterpretation; our independence finds validity in differing repetitions.

We cannot answer with certainty the question—who asked the narrator to tell us the story? The best we can do is approach truth. But one thing is clear: the narrator feels the subtlety of Diamond's story. He tells us in the last chapter that "consequential, priggish little monsters" ought to be stuffed like "big-headed fishes" after they die. In other words, they are all corpse, material self only. Diamond deserves a book because his imaginative (or spiritual, if you will) self is what is important. That is his real self. Listening to Diamond recounting his conversations with North Wind, the narrator allows that he did "not find myself at all in a strange sea, although certainly I could not always feel the bottom, being indeed convinced that the bottom was miles away." It is Newton, who, in Wordsworth's *Prelude* (book 3, line 61), swims in strange seas of scientific thought. Diamond's poetic metaphysics, however, are not strange, and although they prove impossible to explain, interpretation senses the possibility of explanation. This is what makes them worth preserving and rereading. The narrator's Muse, then, is Diamond, as Diamond's is North Wind, and the Muse asks, or prompts, the storyteller. We can now posit an answer to the second question: why has he been asked. To share the secret of poetry; to experience language as creativity; to know the certainty of uncertainties. This explains the difference between "thinking" and "knowing" with which the book ends: "They thought he was dead. I knew that he had gone to the back of the north wind."

Works Cited

Athenaeum. Review of *At the Back of the North Wind*. March 11, 1871, 77.
Coleridge, S. T. *Biographia Literaria*. London: Everyman, 1965.
Frye, Northrop. *The Critical Path*. Bloomington, IN: Indiana UP, 1971.
Grierson, H. J. C. "George MacDonald." *Aberdeen University Review* xii (1924): 1-13.
Hogg, James. *The Poems of James Hogg*. Ed. William Wallace. London: Isbistes, 1903.
Johnson, Joseph. *George MacDonald*. London: Sir Isaac Pitman and Sons, 1906.
MacDonald, George. *Alec Forbes of Howglen*. London: Hurst and Blackett, n. d.
_____. *At The Back of the North Wind*. New York: Garland, 1976.
_____. *Castle Warlock*. London: Kegan Paul, Trench, 1883.
_____. *A Dish of Orts*. London: Sampson, Low, Marston, 1895.
_____. *England's Antiphon*. London: Macmillan, 1868.
_____. *The Lost Princess*. (1875) London: Dent, 1967.
_____. *Unspoken Sermons*. First Series. London: Alexander Strahan, 1867.
_____. *Unspoken Sermons*. Second Series. London: Longmans, Green, 1886.
MacDonald, Greville. *George MacDonald and His Wife*. London: Allen and Unwin, 1924.
MacNeice, Louis. *Varieties of Parable*. Cambridge: Cambridge UP, 1965.
Manlove, Colin. *Modern Fantasy*. Cambridge: Cambridge UP, 1975.
Prickett, Stephen. *Romanticism and Religion*. Cambridge: Cambridge UP, 1976.
Ricoeur, Paul. "Hermeneutics: The Approaches to Symbol." *European Literary Theory and Practice*. Ed. Vernon W. Gras. New York: Dell, 1973, 87-117.

Old Wine in New Bottles
Aspects of Prophecy in George MacDonald's *At the Back of the North Wind*

By Lesley Smith

George MacDonald's *At the Back of the North Wind* (1871) is the story of a little boy, Diamond, who makes friends with death, in the person of North Wind, and, while still a child, matures and then dies—fulfilling Job's melancholy prophecy:

> Thou liftest me up to the wind; thou causest me to ride upon it, and dissolvest my substance. For I know that thou wilt bring me to death, and to the house appointed for all living (30:22-23).[1]

Throughout the book, Old Testament prophecies of punishment are lived out—but in a way so irradiated by the New Testament ideal of love that by the time Diamond dies, it is a case of, "O death, where is thy sting?" (1 Cor. 15:55). MacDonald shows us the love behind the sternness mainly through the agency of the hero, a child whose role is angelic ("I do somehow believe that wur an angel just gone," says the drunken cabman [*North Wind* 183]), priestly (North Wind reminds him that his name is the sixth stone in the high priest's breastplate in the Book of Exodus [13]), and prophetic. Diamond is both a prophet himself, as is underlined by his many links with the prophet Daniel, and the sacrificial victim demanded by much Old Testament prophecy.

Diamond's relationship with North Wind begins when his family is living in The Wilderness and develops further when he (apparently) visits the country at her back. But, though North Wind's influence is considerable during the Bloomsbury section of the book, personal contact between the two is suspended; the boy never sees her when Horse Diamond is present or playing a key role, and in Bloomsbury, Joseph, who has taken to cab driving, is reunited with the horse, and Diamond must come fully to terms with the animal after which he was named. Paradoxically, it is during this period that Diamond's prophetic role develops, as his association with Daniel suggests. The process by which he fixes on a name for his baby sister is revealing:

> The baby had not been christened yet, but Diamond, in reading his bible, had come upon the word *dulcimer,* and thought it so pretty that ever after he called his sister Dulcimer (323).

The word *dulcimer* occurs three times in the Bible—all three in the third chapter of the Book of Daniel. This is not the first reference to Daniel, for near the beginning of *At the Back of the North Wind* Diamond's mother feels that "she would have gone into a lion's den . . . to help her boy" (27).

There are several resemblances between the two books, though there is no precise allegory here or elsewhere; it is on the symbolic power of biblical myth that MacDonald draws. The most important links between Diamond and Daniel are not in the sphere of allusion but in those of character and role. What Diamond has gained from his sojourn at the back of the north wind is understanding—not the cleverness to which Mr. Raymond is at first inclined to attach too much importance ("Genius finds out truths, not tricks," says MacDonald [213])—and not the street wisdom of Nanny and Cripple Jim, but the understanding which can be derived only from reflection on intensely lived experience. In *The Hope of the Gospel,* MacDonald says: "Our whole life, to be at all, must be a growth in understanding." And he adds something which is clearly borne out in the life of Diamond: "Upon obedience our energy must be spent; understanding will follow" (19). Diamond is both obedient and consequently understanding, and this produces the Diamond "full of quiet wisdom" (345) vitally linked to Daniel, for the prophet is above all a man of understanding—"I am now come forth to give thee skill and understanding," says the Angel Gabriel (Dan. 9:22)— a man who is more sensitive to others than they are to themselves and who awakens them to the word which God is speaking to them as well as to him.

It is long before Diamond reaches this point, but from the very first chapter North Wind, through her nocturnal visits, begins to initiate him into the mysteries of life and eternity just as, in the Bible, "the secret [was] revealed unto Daniel in a night vision" (2:19). And Diamond, like Daniel, has "seen the vision, and sought for the meaning" (8:15). Daniel's role at first seems to be that of a good psychiatrist, helping Nebuchadnezzar bring his most deeply buried ideas into consciousness, and it is doubtful whether this can be said of Diamond. His association is basically with the interpreter of dreams who becomes a visionary, though in his case it is the other way round; he sees visions long before he becomes, not quite an interpreter of Nanny's dream of the moon, but a commentator who tries to convince her of its fundamental truth (297-98). Going one better than Nebuchadnezzar, Nanny does at least remember her dream—but Daniel has the advantage of dealing with someone who believes that his dreams have meaning. By the Mound section of *At the Back of the North Wind,* Nanny can say, "I never dreamed but that one [dream], and it seems nonsense enough, I'm sure . . . . Dreams ain't true." But her dream, rejected as it is, is not wasted, for Diamond meditates on it: "It wasn't nonsense," he answers Nanny. "It was a beautiful dream—and a funny one too, both in one" (355). From this time, his own interest in the moon increases significantly.

The apocalyptic passages of the Book of Daniel have no place in *At the Back of the North Wind,* but during the Bloomsbury section they are represented by allusions to the Book of Revelation (itself influenced by Daniel) which manifest themselves through the horses. Diamond's first assay at driving a cab is made with Mr. Stonecrop and his "nameless horse" (163), a mysterious animal whose color is not specified but who bears some affinity to the "pale horse" of Revelation: "His name that sat on him was Death, and Hell followed with him" (6:8).

> "What's the horse's name?" whispered Diamond, as he took the reins from the man.
> "It's not a nice name," said Mr. Stonecrop. "You needn't call him by it. I didn't give it him. He'll go well enough without it. Give the boy a whip, Jack. I never carries one when I drives old—"
> He didn't finish the sentence (162).

There is a suggestive parallel here with a subsequent conversation between Diamond and North Wind:

> "Sometimes [people] call me Bad Fortune, sometimes Evil Chance, sometimes Ruin; and they have another name for me which they think the most dreadful of all."
> "What is that?" asked Diamond, smiling up in her face.
> "I won't tell you that name" (363-64).

Soon after Diamond drives out of the yard, he narrowly avoids colliding with his father's cab:

> "Why, Diamond, it's a bad beginning to run into your own father," cried [Joseph].
> "But, father, wouldn't it have been a bad ending to run into your own son?" said Diamond in return; and the two men laughed heartily (163).

Father and son have narrowly escaped fulfilling one of the death prophecies of Jeremiah: "I will dash them one against another, even the fathers and the sons together, saith the Lord" (Jer. 13:14).

In Revelation, the rider of the red horse, and thus by association the horse itself, represents destruction; in *At the Back of the North Wind*, "Things . . . did not go well with Joseph from the very arrival of [the horse] Ruby. It almost seemed as if the red beast had brought ill luck with him" (309-10). The worst misfortune, Ruby's month of lameness, is brought about by his deliberate spraining of his own ankle. His mission, as he sees it, is clearly spelled out: "It was necessary I should grow fat, and necessary that good Joseph, your master, should grow lean," he tells Horse Diamond (320), sounding remarkably like Isaiah: "And . . . it shall come to pass, that the glory of Jacob [Joseph's father] shall be made thin, and the fatness of his flesh shall wax lean" (Is. 17:4). Subsequently it transpires that Ruby has misjudged his duty; his owner exclaims that he is "as fat as a pig" (327), which is undignified for an angel—but then, as Job says, "the price of wisdom is *above* rubies" (28:18; italics mine).

Horse Diamond has religious significance too. MacDonald does not specify his color, but he must be dark for a white lozenge to stand out on his forehead, and he certainly appears so in the Arthur Hughes illustrations. Revelation 6 goes on:

> And I beheld, and lo a black horse; and he that sat on him had a pair of balances in his hand. And I heard a voice in the midst of the four beasts say, A measure of wheat for a penny, and three measures of barley for a penny; and see thou hurt not the oil and the wine (6:5-6).

The black horse and its rider represent famine, and if Horse Diamond does not cause it, he certainly suffers from it in London. When Mr. Raymond inspects Ruby and Horse Diamond, they form an astonishing contrast:

> Beside the great red round barrel Ruby, all body and no legs, Diamond looked like a clothes-horse with a skin thrown over it. There was hardly a spot of him where you could not descry some sign of a bone underneath. Gaunt and grim and weary he stood, kissing his master, and heeding no one else (328).

But much more important than the apocalyptic overtones of the Bloomsbury episode is Diamond's growth in wisdom and maturity. The trials endured by his family in London help him "[take] his place as a man who judged what was wise, and [do] work worth doing" (251), and the value of suffering is underlined by MacDonald's reference to 2 Corinthians: "Diamond could not help thinking of words which he had heard in church . . . : 'Surely it is good to be afflicted,' or something like that" (254; *see* 2 Cor. 1:6).

The most important resemblance between Diamond and Daniel is that both are especially loved—a quality they share with Benjamin, "The beloved of the LORD." When North Wind carries Diamond in her hair, she is treating him as Moses prophesied Yahweh would treat Benjamin: "The Lord shall cover him all the day long, and he shall dwell between his shoulders" (Deut. 33:12). And Daniel is unique among Old Testament prophets not only in being visited by the Archangel Gabriel but also in being described as a man "greatly beloved" (Dan. 9:23, 10:11, 19). The Archangel's reasoning is crucial: "I am come to shew thee," he says, "*for* thou art greatly beloved: *therefore* understand the matter, and consider the vision" (Dan. 9:23; italics mine). Love is the key to all his prophetic gifts—and so it is to Diamond's.

Paradoxically, the fact that Diamond is loving and loved makes him an acceptable sacrifice in the Mound section of the book; and

The Mound, though one of the little hills singled out in the Bible as places of rejoicing—"The little hills rejoice on every side," sings King David (Ps. 65:12)—is clearly to be Diamond's grave. It is here that the sternest prophecies are fulfilled, and many of them relate to those who, like Diamond, build their nests (at least figuratively) in tall trees—though their motives are very different from his: "Woe to him that coveteth an evil covetousness to his house, that he may set his nest on high, that he may be delivered from the power of evil!" says Habbakuk (2:9). And the nest-builders are usually told that they will be forced to descend: "Though thou shouldest make thy nest as high as the eagle, I will bring thee down from thence, saith the LORD," proclaims Jeremiah (49:16), and Obadiah is even more emphatic: "Though thou exalt thyself as the eagle, and though thou set thy nest among the stars, thence will I bring thee down" (v. 4).

To Diamond his nests—one in the beech tree and one in the tower—are, as they have been ever since the night he flew in the "woven nest" of North Wind's hair (39), simply vantage points, and although he dies his fate is closer to the one hoped for by Job than to the downfall of those attacked by the prophets. If Diamond does not, like the man from the land of Uz, expect to "multiply [his] days as the sand" (Job 29:18), since he not only feels that he "should like to get up into the sky" (344) but that "the earth is all behind [his] back" (345), he fulfils Job's youthful anticipation that "I shall die in my nest" (Job 29:18).

The fall of the rotten elm tree in The Wilderness signifies the end of the status quo; the fall of a branch of the beech tree, struck by lightning at The Mound, foretells Diamond's death—as he recognizes when he immediately sings:

> The clock struck one,
> And the mouse came down.
> Dickery, dickery, dock! (351).

The identification of a tree or a branch with a man is so frequent in the Bible that the word *Branch* is used as a Messianic title (Is. 11:1). And in both testaments the severing of a branch from the tree suggests a curse: "The Lord, the LORD of hosts, shall lop the bough with terror" declares Isaiah sternly (10:33), and Jesus says that any branch that does not bear fruit will be cut away from the vine and burnt (*see* John 15:6). But in *At the Back of the North Wind* the curse is defused, although the seriousness of the situation is emphasized by the tutor's reflections: "I turned my steps a little aside to look at the stricken beech. I saw the bough torn from the stem. . . " (352). Death, which seems the ultimate curse, is Diamond's beloved, and he looks forward to nothing more than her visits through the window of his tower room. When he finally goes to the land at her back, some of Jeremiah's most frightening words are fulfilled without their sting: "Death is come up into our windows, and is entered into our palaces, to cut off the children from without" (Jer. 9:21).

St. Paul says of Jesus that "Christ hath redeemed us from the curse of the law, being made a curse for us" (Gal. 3:13), and through Diamond, too, a curse is transformed into a blessing.[2] He does not bear the guilt of others, like Jesus, but he absorbs the fearfulness of death; the ultimate message of the book is that, no matter what happens, there is nothing to be afraid of (cf. Reis, *George MacDonald* 84). Though there is great poignancy in the realization that North Wind can never share the eternity for which she has lovingly prepared Diamond, since she can never enter the country at her back—"There shall be no more death" in the New Jerusalem (Rev. 21:4)—Diamond has learned, as the tutor puts it, that "there is a still better love than that of the wonderful being you call North Wind" (376).

George MacDonald makes no attempt to elucidate the mystery of eternity, and it is intensified by the fact that Diamond's direct relationship is not with God, but with a creature who does not understand this mystery herself. The whole movement of the book is towards trust, which Diamond attains in such measure that he can peacefully let go of everything—even North Wind, even life. Though he goes to the "something that nobody knows" that the old princess sings of in *The Princess and Curdie* (67), we are not afraid for him; for the message of *At the Back of the North Wind* is to promise, as the final and culminating sentence of the Book of Daniel expresses it, that "thou shalt rest, and stand in thy lot at the end of the days" (12:13).[3]

Notes

1. Kathy Triggs, in *The Stars and the Stillness: A Portrait of George MacDonald*, cites a review of one of MacDonald's lectures which appeared in the Pittsburgh *Methodist Recorder* in February 1873 and which included the information that Mrs. MacDonald identified their son Maurice as "the lad who suggested ... by his quaint sayings, that weird writing, 'On the Back of the North Wind'" (122). This was sadly prophetic in view of Maurice's premature death in 1879 at the age of fifteen.

2. There are several references to Diamond as a Christ figure in Roderick McGillis's "Language and Secret Knowledge in *At the Back of the North Wind*." Robert Lee Wolff, in *The Golden Key,* also considers Diamond Christ-like (291)—even to the extent of identifying his parents as Joseph and Mary instead of Joseph and Martha—but he diminishes the comparison by remarking that MacDonald "leaves somewhat ambiguous the question of young Diamond's sanity" (285).

3. The Book of Daniel is the first in the Old Testament to teach, specifically and in detail, the doctrine of the resurrection—which is no doubt one reason why MacDonald draws on it.

Works Cited

MacDonald, George. *At the Back of the North Wind.* London: Scripture Union, 1978. Facsimile of first edition. London: Strahan, 1871.

———. *The Hope of the Gospel.* London: Ward, Lock, Bowde, 1892.

———. *The Princess and Curdie.* London: Chatto & Windus, 1883.

Reis, Richard. *George MacDonald.* New York: Twayne, 1972.

Wolff, Robert Lee. *The Golden Key: A Study of the Fiction of George MacDonald.* New York: Yale UP, 1961.

Kore Motifs in *The Princess and the Goblin*

By Nancy-Lou Patterson

In *That Hideous Strength,* when Jane Studdock has escaped from the torture chambers of Fairy Hardcastle to St. Anne's Manor, she asks for something to read as she recovers: "I'd like the *Curdie* books, please," she says (198). Though C. S. Lewis devoted a complete anthology to his "master," George MacDonald, he never paid him a prettier compliment than this, in which he included MacDonald's fantasies in a fantasy of his own.

When I first read those words—"the *Curdie* books"—I was surprised, because I had always thought of *The Princess and the Goblin* (1872) and *The Princess and Curdie* (1883) as being about the princess. The first of these books begins with Princess Irene and her discovery of her great-great grandmother, who is Queen Irene. This discovery and this fact are the kernel of the book. There is a sense in which every daughter *is* her mother (and her grandmother). This profound truth lies at the heart of the great archetype, both literary and psychological, which in Western culture is embodied in the myth of the *Kore,* the Maiden. The Kore myth is a quintessentially female story.

George MacDonald anticipates the principles of modern depth psychology, writing of them in terms of his own period: "our consciousness is to the extent of our being but as the flame of the volcano to the world-gulf whence it issues: in the gulf of our unknown being God works behind our consciousness" (cited in Manlove 66). C. S. Lewis noted MacDonald's awareness "that the conscious self, the thing revealed by introspection, is a superficies.

Hence the cellars and attics of the King's castle" in *The Princess and the Goblin* (*George MacDonald* 20).

The "*Curdie*" or Princess books, written seven years apart, present a dichotomy of feminine and masculine. In the feminine world of *The Princess and the Goblin,* the mysterious realm is within the immediate environs of the heroine; it is within her own house (her "father's house") that her adventures begin, and she never strays far from that beginning until the end of the novel, when she leaves to take her place in the King's palace at the capital city. In the masculine world of *The Princess and Curdie,* the hero goes out to meet his adventures. He is sent on a quest, whereas the Princess was guided by her thread when she went out or down or in or up. Curdie's extended, horizontal travel is essential to the structure of this second book. The structure of the two works is thus centripetal (feminine) for *The Princess and the Goblin,* and linear (masculine) for *The Princess and Curdie.*

The present study will concentrate upon *The Princess and the Goblin,* of whose heroine Roderick McGillis remarks, "she need fear no harm from the goblins" (150). This fact presents a central clue to understanding the meaning of the story. McGillis sees a set of opposites reconciled in the "garden of the king's house," where "wilderness (nature) and civilization (art)" are reconciled (149). He searches for opposites in his essay; I shall search for correspondences and equivalents.

The garden, to which the Princess returns on a number of significant occasions, may serve as a good beginning. It consists of hardy mountain flowers combined with pleasant garden flowers. The floral motif offers a first and central parallel with the figure of Persephone, the Kore of the myth. In the Homeric Hymn, Persephone is wandering for pleasure in a meadow of flowers—roses, crocuses, violets, irises, and hyacinths—when a god places a supernal narcissus of "a hundred blossoms" before her.

In Persephone's garden, all nature is represented in her flowers, and these are contrasted with the infinitely attractive, literally ravishing supernatural narcissus:

> a wonderful and radiant narcissus, an awesome sight to all, both immortal gods and mortal men. From its stem a hundred blossoms sprouted forth and their odor was most sweet. All wide

heaven above, the whole earth below, and the swell of the salt sea laughed (*Classical Mythology* 199).

Compared to this blossom, all the rest are natural flowers, but they too have a symbolic significance, for nearly all of them, with the exception of the rose and the violet, are bulbs, mysterious plants which thrust themselves out of the bare earth in the early spring, as from the underworld.

The late eighth- or early seventh-century Homeric Hymn to Demeter begins this way: "I begin to sing about the holy goddess, Demeter of the beautiful hair, about her and her daughter, Persephone of the lovely ankles, whom Hades snatched away; loud-thundering Zeus, who sees all, gave her to him." Thus sings the poet, summarizing his matter for his hearers. Persephone is innocently picking flowers when the giant narcissus appears before her. Reaching out to pluck it, she finds herself rapt away by the Lord of the Underworld, whose golden chariot comes bursting out of the earth. Hecate, a moon goddess, and Helius, a sun god, hear her cries, as does her mother Demeter, who begins a frantic search of nine days. She beseeches Hecate and Helius for help, and learns of her daughter's capture.

Disguising herself as an old woman, Demeter walks among humankind until she meets at Eleusis the "daughters of Celeus," who invite her to become the nurse of their infant brother. When Demeter visits the household, she sits in sadness until Iambe amuses her with coarse jests. When the goddess cares for the child, Demophoon, each night she plunges him into the fire, preparing him for eternal life. When the child's mother discovers, she protests, and Demeter reveals herself as a goodess, returns the still-mortal child to his mother, and commands that a temple and altar be erected to her in that place.

Demeter then continues in her sorrow, causing "a most terrible and devastating year on the fruitful land" (*Classical Mythology* 205). Not a sprout can grow; ploughs are dragged and barley is sown in vain. At last Zeus relents and orders Erebus to "appeal to Hades . . . and bring chaste Persephone up from the murky depths to the light." Hades consents, but forces his wife to eat three pomegranate seeds. Joyously reunited, the mother and daughter can remain together two-thirds of the year, but because of the seeds eaten in the underworld, Persephone must spend a third of every year with her husband. Immediately fruit, leaf, and flower spring out, and Demeter instructs the kings of Eleusis in the rites to be practiced henceforth: only "those who are initiated into the holy rites" are "destined to a similar joy when . . . dead in the gloomy realm below" (*Classical Mythology* 199-200). The dead in this ancient thought-world are beneath the earth. Their world is the underworld, and consequently a descent to the underworld is a descent to the afterworld.

In the Eleusinian rite as reconstructed by scholars, after Persephone is raised to her mother's arms, she shows forth her son, Brimos, born from her marriage in the underworld. This son is often identified with Dionysus: "The growth of the grain seed to fruition is the Eleusinian symbol of rebirth" (*The Road to Eleusis* 107). Brimo, as the mother of Brimos is called, is both Hecate and Persephone; that is, she is the Queen of Death. In the culminating ritual event, "the goddess of death had borne a son in the fire," just as Demeter had intended to make Demophoon immortal by placing him in the fire.

In Mircea Eliade's interpretation, "the rape,—that is, the symbolic death—" made it possible for Persephone to annul "the unbridgeable distance between Hades and Olympus." She thus became "the Mediatrix between two divine worlds" (Eliade 293), who could "intervene in the destiny of mortals" (Jung and Kerenyi 105). In *The Princess and the Goblin,* it is Irene who travels between the tower world and the goblin world, carrying the power of her mother and her great-great-grandmother as she goes. No wonder McGillis can say that she is never really in danger.

The Demeter-Kore myth, as it is expressed in its Homeric form, presents a number of motifs which appear in *The Princess and the Goblin.* First, as we have seen, Persephone is associated with flowers. There is in *The Princess and the Goblin* a striking scene in chapter 17, "Spring-Time," which depicts Irene searching for primroses "opening an eye of light in the blind earth." She tends each blossom "as tenderly as if it had been a new baby." Perhaps these are the children of Princess Irene.

C. Kerenyi calls Persephone herself "a bud," and states that she is the goddess of the "borderline situation" (Jung and Kerenyi 125). One who travels or crosses a borderline can serve as mediatrix between the realms divided by that border, and the border-place is depicted as a garden. In the same way, spring is a borderline period between winter and summer, so that Persephone embodies a borderline season. Irene's garden which combined wild mountainside flowers with the domesticated plants of a deliberately planted garden, is a borderline garden indeed.

A second motif is the placing of Demophoon in the fire by Demeter; the grandmother in *The Princess and the Goblin* possesses a brazier of burning roses into which she places the ball of thread she has spun for Irene, before giving it to the Princess. She "put her hand in the fire, brought out the ball, glimmering as before, and held it toward her."

A third motif in the myth is Kore's rape or capture: she is swept away to marry the "Zeus of the Underworld" (Jung and Kerenyi 125). The elements of rape and marriage appear in *The Princess and the Goblin* when the Goblin Queen plots unsuccessfully to steal Irene as a bride for her son, Harelip. The Goblin Queen is the queen of the underworld, and Persephone in her archaic form was also a chthonic goddess, a doublet of Hecate, whose lunar associations included the so-called "dark of the moon." The moon in this sense is the "dying and returning moon" (Jung and Kerenyi 131), which appears in three forms—waxing, full, and waning—and also fails to appear during its period of occultation. Irene not only undergoes a descent into the underworld, where she goes to rescue Curdie, but also a period of absence, when Curdie is unable to find her in the castle, for she has been led to safety in his mother's cottage.

The most archaic aspects of Persephone took monstrous form, "the nocturnal aspect of what by day is the most desirable of all things." She assumed various animal forms. This motif finds a correspondence in the "Cobs' Creatures," the goblins' animals of *The Princess and the Goblin,* who want to play with the Princess (though they frighten her), and who enter the upper world through an opening in Irene's garden.

In the underworld descent of Greek thought, a labyrinthian or spiral dance led the way downward. The labyrinth is the "primordial image" of what "men have to pass" through "when they die" if they are to reach the Queen of Hades and then return to life (Jung and Kerenyi 133). Theseus was freed from the Labyrinth by Ariadne, who saved him by means of her thread, like the thread by which Princess Irene leads Curdie safely from the caves of the goblins. The movement of this dance is first downward into death and then upward into birth, and the emergence is a significant part of the sequence, as Curdie and Irene emerge in her garden.

Persephone, because she is associated with the underworld, is also associated with water, which comes out of the earth in the form of springs and wells: "The Primordial Maiden can only be conceived as the primal being born of the primal element," as Kerenyi puts it (150). The great flood ruled by the grandmother's moon, which washes away the goblins and cleanses mines and castle, echoes this motif.

Irene's grandmother is also named Irene: she represents what Kerenyi calls "the Demetrian aspect," which is "the abyss of the nucleus." "Every grain of wheat and every maiden contains . . . all its descendants and all her descendants—an infinite series of mothers and daughters in one" (Jung and Kerenyi 153). As MacDonald says in the first chapter of *The Princess and the Goblin,* "Every little girl is a princess."

C. G. Jung has described his finding of Kore motifs in his practice of psychology: "the figure of Demeter and the Kore in its three-fold aspect as maiden, mother, and Hecate [is] not unknown to the psychology of the unconscious," he writes. "The 'Kore' has her psychological counterpart in those archetypes which I have called the *self* or *supraordinate personality* on the one hand, and the *anima* on the other" (Jung and Kerenyi 156). In women whose psyches were studied by Jung, the Kore "often appears . . . as an unknown young girl" (158). A young girl is of course the central figure of *The Princess and the Goblin,* Princess Irene. Jung adds significantly that sometimes there is "a true *nekyia,* a descent into Hades," to which the "innocent child," the young maiden, "falls victim" (158).

Jung reports Demeter and Hecate figures appearing in women's dreams, and also remarks upon "the Baubo type" (159). Baubo is the Latin name for the Iambe of the myth, who by her earthy antics rouses the mournful Demeter to laughter. A Roman Baubo statue showed a female torso with a woman's face set in it. This aspect of the female personality talks with its belly, one might say. The character of Lootie, Irene's nurse, comes closest to this figure, with overtones of Juliet's bawdy Nurse not entirely silent for the adult reader: Lootie is worried about Irene's desire to kiss Curdie, thus calling attention to the only implicitly sexual event, however innocent an embrace it may have been, in the book.

Jung states that the "Earth Mother is always chthonic" and is related to the moon. He writes:

> Demeter and Kore, mother and daughter, extend the feminine consciousness both upwards and downwards. They add an "older and younger," "stronger and weaker," dimension to it and widen out the narrowly limited conscious mind bound in space and time, giving it intimations of a greater and more comprehensive personality, which has a share in the eternal course of things (162).

This expansion of consciousness certainly occurs for a young girl reading *The Princess and the Goblin.* Jung states, "Every mother contains her daughter in herself and every daughter her mother, and . . . every woman extends backwards into her mother and forward into her daughter" (162).

It is important to remember that Kore is a goddess. She is the mediatrix between the world of Demeter and the world of Hecate, and she moves between these august deities and their worlds like the movement of Spring in its eternal return, like the yearly waning and waxing of the sun, and the monthly waning and waxing of the moon. The divinity of Kore comes from her mother, but it becomes hers, and she is last seen in the Eleusinian mysteries as the august and terrible Queen of Death, Holy Brimo.

The Princess and the Goblin begins with the Princess tired, frustrated, and "very miserable as she would say herself." When the novel concludes, she is happily triumphant over disaster, and her father is taking her to court to take her mother's place. She has moved from being a child under care of her nurse to one capable of taking charge of the entire castle staff. She has matured, moved from childishness to a serene prefiguration of young womanhood.

Irene's path from child to young woman begins when she leaves her toys and finds a stairway which leads her up, after many delays, to a tower. There she discovers a Lady at a spinning wheel, spinning with "a sweet, bee-like humming." Bees are an attribute of Demeter. MacDonald says "Guess what she was spinning." Later, Irene tries to visit her grandmother again, but this time, "she had not gone high enough."

Curdie the miner-boy meets the Princess and her nurse, when, staying out on the mountainside too long, they are surprised by goblins. He later discovers the goblins tunneling near the mine shaft where he works. Later, Irene is "playing on a lawn in the garden" when she hears a bugle announcing her father's arrival on a visit. She and the King walk in this garden together, and Irene tells her father about the goblins.

After the King's departure, Autumn too comes and goes. There are "no more flowers in the garden." One night Irene pricks her finger on an old brooch and is put to bed in pain. Awakened by the moon, she mounts the staircase again and finds her grandmother at her spinning. In "The Sleeping Beauty," a princess at the age of fifteen pricks her finger on a spindle used by an old lady hidden in a remote part of her castle; MacDonald has cautioned his reader that "*More old ladies than one have sat spinning in a garret,*" but there is a parallel. The drawing of blood suggests the onset of puberty, that absolute moment of transition from one state of life to another which manifests itself as a spot of blood.

MacDonald now reveals that the Lady is spinning "spider-webs—of a particular kind." There is a traditional association of the spun thread with the spider, expressed in Greek mythology through the story of Arachne. Irene's wounded hand is healed, and lying with her head in her great-great-grandmother's bosom, she dreams of "summer seas and moonlight and mossy springs and great murmuring trees and beds of wild flowers."

The bliss is not to last, for a few days later, the goblins' monstrous animals break out of their underworld precisely in the garden, where they enjoy "a romp on a smooth lawn." Irene is terrified by a long-legged cat; she runs outside and up the mountainside, where the sight of her grandmother's moonlike lamp leads her safely back to that lady's door.

This time she is given a ring with "a fire-opal," which matches the stones in the Lady's crown, and a "shimmering ball . . . about the size of a pigeon's egg," which represents all of her grandmother's spinning since Irene "came to the house." The reader has been told that Irene came to the "half-castle, half farm-house" soon after she was born, "because her mother was not very strong." The grandmother completes her task by casting the ball in the fire of burning roses and drawing it out again. She then places the ball in her own cabinet, saying that one end is fastened to the ring Irene has been given, and telling her to "follow the thread." The path upon which it leads her may be, she says, "a very roundabout way indeed." This way, the way of the labyrinth, is Irene's by right, for when she awakens in her own room, her nurse remarks, "I think it must have been your mother gave it you," as if she had seen it every day.

Spring, returning to the mountainside, finds the King returning to visit his daughter. When she asks him about the ring, he says, "It was your queen-mama's once." The mother, in other words, has died, perhaps the very night the great-great-grandmother gave the ring to the Princess. The King says of Irene's mother, "she's gone where all those rings are made."

After her father's second departure, the Princess goes out on the mountainside to visit the primroses blooming "in the warmer hollows." This passage, redolent with new life, ends with its opposite, a "kind of sheep" the goblins keep, coveted by their creatures, who "knew they should have their bones by-and-by." We are reminded by this that Irene is very near the door of the underworld.

Curdie's confrontation with and capture by goblins in the caves follows. He has gone in confidently with his "clue," a ball of string his mother has given him. But he loses hold of it in encountering a "knot of the cobs' creatures." As a parallel, a noise "of creatures snarling and hissing and racketing about" awakens Irene, and following her grandmother's instructions, she puts her ring beneath her pillow and feels for her thread. It leads her out of doors and up a mountain path to a hole in the rocks, which leads her into the "total darkness" of the underground world and directly to Curdie, who is closed into a cave chamber behind a pile of rocks.

The Princess patiently clears these away one by one "with aching back, and bleeding fingers and hands," like Psyche at her impossible tasks, or any housewife struggling with her endless daily chores. She tells Curdie, "My great-great-grandmother sent me." Irene combines her wisdom—"Now, Curdie! I think if you were to give a great push, the slab would tumble over" with his strength. Though he cannot see her thread, "You've saved my life, Irene!" he says, and now, in the role of Ariadne, she leads the doubting boy safely out of the caverns. She is not afraid of the underworld because "my grandmother is taking care of us."

When they emerge into the light, "they stood in her own garden." When she leads Curdie into the castle, they mount to the tower, but Curdie still does not believe. Even when taken to the grandmother's room, he sees only squalor and a sunbeam and hears only the warbling of pigeons.

The conclusion of the book describes the invasion of the castle by the goblins. Curdie pursues them down into the castle cellar, where suddenly his own hand comes upon a taut thread. It leads him to the Princess, safe in his own mother's arms. The miners close up the goblins' holes with masonry, and a great subterranean flood destroys the goblins, pouring out "from the doors and windows of the king's house," which is later drained, revealing the Goblin Queen dead in the cellar.

In the story outlined above, the Princess is surrounded by significant female figures. Of these the most powerful, the one who most attracts the female reader, is Queen Irene, the great-great-grandmother. Of her many attributes which are derived from those of the Great Mother, most significant for the Kore theme is her constant spinning of spiderweb, tempered in rose-fire. This motif may have been derived by MacDonald from Novalis, whose "Klingsohr's Fairy Tale" included the sentence, "You must soak the thread in spiderjuice . . . and work flowers into it that have grown in fire" (36).

The thread being spun as a parallel to a life is an ancient motif, expressed in the Three Fates of Greek mythology. These divinities, the *Moirai*, made use of a distaff, a drop spindle, and shears. Their names were *Lachesis* ("draw off" or "apportioner"), *Clotho* ("twist and spin" or "spinner"), and *Atropos* ("cutting" or "cutter"). The meaning of these figures and their relation to the story is based upon the fact that the action of spinning with a drop spindle is not continuous. One must repeatedly stop, wind off a spun segment, reloop the portion around the top of the spindle, and recommence to spin. On the other hand, as MacDonald himself points out, a spinning wheel twists and pulls the thread in a continuous motion. In the primary myth the thread represents an individual human life, spun, measured, and severed in death.

The fact that the grandmother uses a wheel means that, in contrast, she can control the length as she chooses and that her thread is continuous. Her measure begins not when Irene is born but when she enters the house, and ends not with the death of the Princess, but when her mother has died. Irene receives it as a completed ball on the night of her mother's death, and she is then ready to descend into the underworld to rescue her eventual husband. The measurement then is of Irene's life as a child. We may see here that the descent to the underworld is itself a kind of death, a death of girlhood.

The Hecate figure in *The Princess and the Goblin* is the Goblin Queen, mother of the goblin who seeks Irene for his bride. In MacDonald's words she is a grotesque figure, with every feature distorted and wrongly proportioned. The Goblin Queen "had the misfortune to be born of a sun-mother," that is, a human, which means that she has toes, a feature considered monstrous by the other goblins. It also suggests that a woman has already been rapt away to the underworld to marry a goblin. The Goblin Queen wears a stone *sabot* to hide her hybrid trait, a many-toed foot.

When Curdie and the Princess are escaping, they pass a rock platform upon which "the king and queen of the goblins" lie asleep. Curious to see if the rumours are true, Curdie withdraws the granite shoe of the sleeping Queen, revealing "six horrible toes." But as he attempts to remove the other shoe, "the queen gave a growl and sat up in bed." Irene dashes her light to the ground in order to extinguish it, and she and Curdie escape, running hand in hand, with the Goblin Queen bellowing behind them. When she is last seen dead in the flood, the Queen lies "with skin shoe gone, and the stone one fast to her ankles," drowned, perhaps, by its weight, through her own pride. There is something oddly pitiable in this poor vanity about the part of herself most in touch with humanity.

In his list of opposites in *The Princess and the Goblin,* McGillis contrasts the thread of spiderweb, Irene's clue, with the string of Curdie's clue. This clue is given to him by his mother, Joan Peterson, and she is his guide not only underground, but in moral matters. We first hear of her when we learn that he is working late in the mines because he plans to "buy a very warm red petticoat for his mother, who had begun to complain of the cold in the mountain air sooner than usual this autumn." She is a very human mother, then, who both feels the cold and complains of it.

Curdie's mother appears in person in "A Short Chapter About Curdie," where MacDonald remarks, "Mrs. Peterson was such a nice good mother!" She makes her cottage "a little heaven" for her husband and son, working with hands of the Princess when she rescues Curdie. Her special use for these hands is to disentangle Curdie's string, which he uses to keep his way underground. She guides him by disentangling his thread, and this work is performed at night. When asked how she does it, she replies, "I follow the thread," exactly as the grandmother has advised Irene to do.

Mrs. Peterson has something to say to Curdie when he returns home after his rescue by Irene, complaining about the invisible grandmother. She wins him over to belief by telling him how she herself was frightened by tormenting goblins and rescued by the appearance of the grandmother's lamp and the intervention of one of her pigeons.

When Curdie finds the Princess safe at his mother's house after the goblin invasion, "the faces of the mother and the princess shone as if their troubles only made them merrier." There is thus a close relationship between these two, as well as between both of them and the grandmother. And "Then Curdie's mother laid her in Curdie's bed," from which Irene can see "her grandmother's lamp shining far away beneath." Here the mother herself prepares the Princess symbolically to be Curdie's eventual bride.

Joan Peterson accompanies the young couple down to the castle, where the King awaits them. She last appears in *The Princess and the Goblin* when the Princess rides away with the royal party. Curdie, his father and mother, and Lootie, Irene's nurse, who is now homeless and no longer employed, go home together. The character of Lootie is interesting because she is unobtrusive but ubiquitous. Outside of Irene and Curdie, she appears in more chapters than any other character. She represents Irene's childhood dependency and is thrown off rather like an outworn garment when the Princess leaves that childhood behind.

Lootie's first action in the story is prophetic of her future, for we read in the second chapter that "her nurse goes out of the room." This departure triggers the first discovery by Irene of her grandmother, for a moment later the Princess is darting up a "curious old stair" and the story has truly begun. Lootie has a chapter title to herself, "What the Nurse Thought of It," *It* being Irene's adventure upstairs. Lootie is a doubter. "'Oh, I dare say!' remarked the nurse," when the Princess has told her "what a beautiful mother of grandmothers I've got upstairs."

Lootie continues her pattern of absence when, as she says, she "could not be every moment in the room," and she leaves. Again Irene "was off and up the stairs," though this time she does not find her grandmother. Lootie also provides the occasion upon which Irene first meets the goblins and, luckily, Curdie. When the miner-boy drives the goblins away, the nurse is "offended at the freedom with which he spoke." Though he escorts them to within sight of the lights of the castle, she refuses to let the Princess kiss him.

Lootie also provides the occasion for Irene's second visit to her grandmother: "One morning the nurse left her with the housekeeper for awhile." This time, Irene plays with "a curious old-fashioned brooch," and runs "the pin of it into her thumb." Lootie is fetched, and the doctor too. Irene is put to bed. This experience leads her to her grandmother, who heals the wound, and asks the Princess to visit her again in one week's time. Irene's pensiveness as she waits for the time to pass causes Lootie to remark upon "What an odd child she is!" Once again, her absence creates the occasion for Irene's visit to the tower, and this time the Princess consciously awaits Lootie's departure. When Lootie "was longer in returning than she intended," so that the long-legged goblin cat is let in, the Princess is led to the tower and receives her mother's ring and her grandmother's ball of thread.

This time, when Lootie remonstrates with the Princess upon her absence, Irene reminds her of the previous episode upon the mountainside, and Lootie goes for fresh tea and bread and butter "without a word." Irene is beginning to gain authority over her nurse and to use their relationship for her own ends. Lootie does not appear again for seven chapters, and when "Irene Behaves Like a Princess," we see a new, mature Irene who is ready to take charge not only of her own affairs, but also those of the whole household. "Up to this moment, they had all regarded her as little more than a baby."

Finally, Lootie is present when Irene gives Curdie his promised kiss, and even joins "in the praises of his courage and energy." But as Irene departs with her father in sight of a "silvery globe," sign of the grandmother's overwatching presence, "of which all but Lootie understood the origin," the nurse remains in her state of mental darkness to the last.

The Princess and the Goblin begins, continues, and ends with Irene as the dominant element, presenting with remarkable power a female structure and meaning. And what is that meaning? It is the meaning of the Eleusinian Mysteries and the Demeter-Kore myth: the daughter—the Kore—becomes the mother. The role of the Kore's mother is to seek and find, but never finally to get back her daughter, who has moved beyond her and is reborn as a new person, an adult woman. Life, literally the life of the human race, depends upon this continually forward-moving pattern of daughter becoming herself a woman in her own right. This womanhood is presaged in the blood-spot, but the true womanhood is won by the young girl herself, taking authority from supernatural and subnatural and making that authority her own. Her male relationships bring about the death of her girlhood, and in her new status as queen of the world of death, she will, if may be, bring forth a new child to begin the process all over again. This is the meaning of the Kore myth and the story of *The Princess and the Goblin*.

Works Cited

Eliade, Mircea. *A History of Religious Ideas*. Vol. 1. Chicago: U of Chicago P, 1978.

Jung, C. G., and C. Kerenyi. *Essays on a Science of Mythology*. New York: Harper/Bollingen, 1963.

Lewis, C. S. *George MacDonald: An Anthology*. New York: Macmillan, 1948.

_____. *That Hideous Strength*. London: The Bodley Head, 1945.

MacDonald, George. *The Princess and the Goblin*. New York: Airmont, 1967.

McGillis, Roderick. "High Seriousness: George MacDonald's 'Princess' Books." *Touchstones*. Ed. Perry Nodelman. West Lafayette, IN: ChLA Publications, 1985: 146-162.

Manlove, Colin. *Modern Fantasy*. Cambridge: Cambridge UP, 1975.

Morford, Mark P. O., and Robert Lenardon. *Classical Mythology*. New York: David McKay, 1971.

Novalis, "Klingsohr's Fairy Tale." *Hymns to the Night and Other Selected Essays*. Trans. Charles E. Passage. New York: The Liberal Arts Press, 1960.

Wasson, R. Gordon, Carl A. P. Ruck, and Albert Hoffman. *The Road to Eleusis*. New York: Harcourt, 1978.

The Diamond in the Ashes
A Jungian Reading of the "Princess" Books

By Joseph Sigman

Some years ago I wrote a rather elaborate article on George MacDonald's *Phantastes* in which I argued that this work retold, in Victorian dress, the ancient myth of the hero's descent into the underworld and his confrontation with the creative and destructive power of his own unconscious. I tried to show how MacDonald's protagonist, Anodos, struggled with projections of his own regressive desires and finally moved toward a stronger ego-consciousness and an adult sense of responsibility. I mention that article because I think it is useful to see the "Princess" books in relation to *Phantastes*. Coming as *Phantastes* docs at the beginning of MacDonald's career, it is his initial and basic articulation of his personal version of the hero myth, and this myth continued to be of great importance to him.

In this analysis, I will assume the unity of the Princess books, dealing with them as two parts of one pattern, two episodes in one myth. I will limit my discussion to three elements in the books: first, the basic symbolic contrast between them; second, the archetypal myths that structure them, and third, Curdie's development in the course of them.

At the beginning of *The Princess and the Goblin,* we are told that the Princess Irene, "soon after her birth," was sent "to be brought up by country people" because her mother was "not very strong." This odd piece of family history is very like the illogical family history in *Phantastes*. The fact that it doesn't make sense points to its symbolic importance. Why should Irene be sent away because her mother isn't "very strong"? Aren't there any servants to do the cooking and the washing? After all, her mother is a queen. And if Irene did have to be sent away, why of all places to a mountain inhabited by Goblins? The King knows they are there, for there is a rule that Irene isn't to go out after dark. And anyway, what does it mean that the mother isn't "very strong"? Not sick, just not "very strong." She never does appear and later has evidently died. It becomes clear that this material is important when we notice that in the second book, the father's strength has failed; he is confined to bed, unable to perform his royal duties. The themes of the two books are defined, therefore, by the weakness of the mother in the first case and the weaknesses of the father in the second.

It is a basic principle of Jungian thought that the ego is poised between the unconscious inside of us and the social world outside of us. Health and integration as understood by Jungians are a matter of balancing the demands of these two realms. If the ego is closed off from its instinctual basis in the unconscious, the result is a loss of direction and a sense of meaninglessness. If, on the other hand, the unconscious dominates the ego, the result is neurosis or madness.

According to Jung, a man personifies the unconscious in dreams by female figures —especially the mother and the beloved, while the social world is symbolized by male figures —one's father and companions. We have here a basis for beginning to understand the "Princess" books. In *The Princess and the Goblin,* the mother's weakness indicates an enfeebling of the female side of the personality and defines a world in which the individual is losing touch with the inner realm.

Such a state of psychic alienation was long a concern of MacDonald and appears to have been central to his understanding of the late nineteenth century. At the beginning of *Phantastes,* the death of Anodos's mother and the lack of information about his female ancestors are symbols of his dissociation from his own inner life. His consciousness, therefore, is empty and without direction. Similarly, in *Adela Cathcart,* Adela, whose mother is also dead, is suffering from a disease that is imaginative and spiritual rather than physical. "I wake wretched every morning," Adela tells Smith. "Nothing seems worth anything. I don't care for anything"(27). In *The Princess and the Goblin,* the dissociation of the conscious from the unconscious appears in Irene's boredom at the beginning of the book and, more importantly, in the inability of Curdie to see the

Grandmother or to believe Irene's reports of her. If the weakness of the mother in the first book defines in a very general way the theme of the ego's loss of contact with the instinctive source of life in the unconscious, the weakness of the father in the second book indicates the general theme of social breakdown resulting from this loss of contact. The King, we are told, is "a real king." He rules not by the cynical manipulation of power but through traditional values and loyalties that bind men together into a community. However, it is precisely these traditional values and loyalties, supported by a cultural canon of symbols and rituals mediating between the ego and the unconscious, that have been undermined by the intensification of consciousness in the modern world. The result is the superficiality of life and the atomistic individualism that characterizes MacDonald's Gwyntystorm, which is, of course, a thinly disguised picture of Victorian England.

This bring me to the second topic I want to discuss: the archetypal myths that structure the "Princess" books. *The Princess and the Goblin* is organized around the myths of Persephone and Theseus. Irene is, like Persephone, in danger of being carried off to become the bride of a prince of the underworld. Curdie, on the other hand, is a Theseus who enters the labyrinth, while Irene becomes an Ariadne who provides the thread that enables him successfully to find his way out again. The complexity of the book derives in large part from the double perspective afforded by these two archetypes. We can begin to sort out the varied implications by a consideration of the significance of the goblins.

Robert Lee Wolff has said that the goblins are *Elementargeister* (i.e. elemental spirits) like those in German Romantic literature (Wolff 165-166). But they aren't. The elemental spirits are, technically speaking, a race separate from men. MacDonald's goblins, however, are degenerate human beings; they have chosen to live underground. This has caused them to become both deformed and cunning: "as they grew misshapen in body they had grown in knowledge and cleverness." The goblins see their degeneration as progress; they are proud of their hard heads (as Glump says, "the goblin's glory is his head"), and they hate poetry. In Jungian terms, they are projections of the shadow of Victorian society, an externalization of its inner deformity —its materialism, cruelty, scepticism, and megalomania.

But what precisely would the goblin's abduction of Irene mean? Like Persephone, Irene is associated with flowers and spring, and her abduction would presumably result in some sort of a winter. In order to understand the nature of this winter, we must turn to the myth of Theseus and the image of the labyrinth.

The Princess and the Goblin is filled with labyrinths. People constantly take wrong turns, get lost, are unable to find their way back to where they started. Historically, the labyrinth is an ancient symbol associated with the mother goddess and the underworld. In Jungian terms, it is a depiction of the unconscious, particularly at the time when it is first encountered at the beginning of a process of individuation. Since the unconscious is potentially both creative and destructive, the labyrinth can either indicate an initiation leading to rebirth on a higher level of existence or else a loss of direction leading to regression and incapacity.

MacDonald more than once imaged the unconscious as a double labyrinth. In *The Princess and the Goblin,* there is an upper labyrinth of doors and halls leading to the Grandmother's room and an underground labyrinth of caves dominated by the demonic goblin queen. In *Phantastes* we find the same pattern. The father's secretary is a kind of labyrinth with a "multitude of little drawers and slides and pigeon-holes" in which Anodos for the first time encounters his fairy godmother. Later, Anodos falls into an underground labyrinth (with goblins, I might add) where he encounters a demonic old woman. It seems clear that MacDonald intended to associate the labyrinths in *Phantastes* and *The Princess and the Goblin* for when the Grandmother shows Irene her pigeons, we see "a great many pigeon holes with nests," a phrase echoing the description of the earlier desk-labyrinth with its "pigeon-holes." In both books, MacDonald places his hero between the same symbolic poles: the unconscious as nourishing mother who fosters growth toward maturity and spiritual vision and the unconscious as devouring mother (remember that the goblin queen intends to eat Curdie, or at least to feed him to her beasts) who draws the personality backward toward incapacity. The association of the goblins not only with the Pluto of the Persephone myth but also with Milton's fallen angels[1] further identifies their caves as the hellish underworld into which the hero must descend to experience the dark side of his own personality and confront his own self-destructive impulses. Curdie does this when, in the darkness of the cave, he is forced to accept

Irene's guidance even though he cannot see her thread or believe in its existence. Here, the self-destructive impulse the hero faces is the same one that threatens Victorian society: an overintensification of ego-consciousness leading to a dissociation from the inner world and a tendency to trust only what can be seen. If in *Phantastes,* Anodos's fear of life was the regressive impulse that stood between him and maturity, Curdie's rationalistic Victorian distrust of the inner world is the impediment to his spiritual growth.

At this point in my discussion, it is important to emphasize that the "Princess" books are about Curdie. Although the first book initially focuses on Irene, it is Curdie's struggle with unbelief that comes to be the dramatic center. The second book is, of course, totally devoted to Curdie, and in it Irene is reduced to a very minor character. Taking an overall perspective on the books makes it easier to see that Irene functions as what Jungians call an *anima* figure. She is Curdie's guide to the world within. She mediates between his ego and the unconscious. She externalizes his developing awareness of the inner realm. She embodies the intuitions by which he must be guided. In the first book, when Curdie's mother tells him that he should not have rejected Irene's story when he had no better explanation, he says "that is what something inside of me has been saying all the time." When in the second book he wounds the pigeon, "its last look reminded him of the princess —he did not know why." The reason clearly is that he is destroying that in himself which Irene represents. If, therefore, Irene were carried away by the goblins, her loss would be the loss of a meaningful goal for Curdie's life. Theseus would be trapped in the labyrinth. The winter implied in the Persephone myth would descend, freezing Curdie's personality and rendering him incapable of growth and spiritual vision.

When we turn to *The Princess and Curdie,* we find two very different archetypes: the return of Odysseus to Ithaca and the second coming of Christ. Curdie, entering the palace secretly in order to discover which servants are faithful and which unfaithful, is clearly a kind of Odysseus. He, too, fights a battle in a "hall," and his punishment of the wicked servants is analogous to the destruction of the suitors, the hanging of the maidservants and the killing of Melanthios in the *Odyssey.*[2] Co-ordinated with this archetype is the more important one of the return of Christ. The housemaid is called a "prophetess," and she functions as a kind of John the

Baptist, even being thrown into prison like John. The theme of the faithful and unfaithful servants recalls not only the *Odyssey* but a number of the gospel parables as well (*see especially* Luke 12:42-48). The wicked servants driven into the night correspond to various figures in the parables who are locked out of the wedding feast or cast out into exterior darkness. The final battle recalls the Book of Revelation in its horses of different colors, its birds, and its trumpet. Even Curdie's pickax comes to seem the sickle Christ carries for the great harvest of nations.

These archetypes suggest that Curdie has fully matured and achieved the status of a semidivine hero. We have moved beyond the stage of the hero myth in which the hero has to descend into the underworld to struggle with his own dark side. We are now at the point of the hero's return to society. The archetypes emphasize, however, that he returns as an avenger.

Already in *The Princess and the Goblin,* the goblins, in so far as they were images of the sceptical and materialistic tendencies in Victorian society, indicated that this society was headed for destruction. Any reader of the Bible would recognize the goblin's tender feet as an allusion to the "great image" with feet "part of iron and part of clay" in Nebuchadnezzar's dream. The feet of the image, Daniel tells Nebuchadnezzar, symbolize a divided kingdom that will be destroyed by the Lord (Daniel 2:31-45). Similarly, the drowning of the goblins at the conclusion of the book suggests the biblical deluge, which destroyed a sinful world. In *The Princess and Curdie,* Gwyntystorm is identified with Homer's Ithaca and the Jerusalem of the New Testament, corrupt societies upon which judgment falls. In Jungian terms, they are societies that have turned their backs on the deeper realities of the psyche. The hero, therefore, comes as a representative of that which lies outside the world of ego-consciousness. This is particularly evident in Curdie's role as master of the beasts. Their grotesque deformity indicates that they are, in Jungian terms, the collective shadow of Gwyntystorm, externalizations of its inner deformity. This, I think, is why MacDonald felt the need to illogically relate them both to the goblin beasts of the first book and to humans punished for wickedness. They are, it should be remembered, associated a number of times with nightmares, being described, for example, as "forms wilder and more grotesque than ever ramped in nightmare dream." Like the apocalyptic symbols later in the book, they are examples of emotional and archetypal material that will not remain repressed and eventually precipitates a psychological crisis. In order better to understand Curdie's role as a semi-divine avenger and representative of deep psychic forces, we must turn to the third topic I want to discuss: Curdie's development.

As I indicated earlier, the "Princess" books are about Curdie, or more precisely, about his development. If we step back and look at the overall pattern of imagery in the two books, we see a movement from a female-oriented childhood world of family relationships, nighttime rural settings, water and caves to a male-dominated adult world of companionship in battle, daytime urban settings, fire, and social institutions. Almost precisely the same shift of images occurs in *Phantastes* and is basic to MacDonald's concept of individual development. In *A Dish of Orts,* MacDonald has an essay entitled "A Sketch of Individual Development" in which he outlines the stages of a typical life very elaborately. He was much interested in such progressions, and his fantasies illustrate this clearly. In *The Princess and the Goblin,* Curdie's ego gradually opens to the inner world. At the end of the book he finally sees the Grandmother in a dream —the normal way for unconscious material first to enter consciousness. In the Wordsworthian opening of *The Princess and Curdie,* Curdie has grown older and the "Shades of the prison-house have begun to close on the growing Boy." He consciously feels the absence of Irene: the goal of his life has been mislaid. However, as MacDonald would say in his "Sketch of Individual Development," "conscience" speaks to him and brings about "the birth of the Will" (47). Curdie consciously affirms what the Grandmother represents, and this commitment is finalized when he steps through the door of her room, even though he can't see any floor. The emphasis on conscious moral choice in the second book reflects Curdie's maturing ego-consciousness. No longer is the Grandmother discovered inadvertently in moments of boredom and fear, in dreams, or in fevered delirium.

The high points of Curdie's development are symbolized as a series of baptisms: Irene's immersion in the Grandmother's silver tub in the first book, Curdie's immersion of his hands and later the King's total immersion in the Grandmother's rose fire in the second. The relevant biblical passage is this statement by John the Baptist in Matthew, with parallel passages in Mark and Luke: "I indeed baptize you with water unto repentence: but he that cometh after me is mightier than I, whose shoes I am not worthy to bear: he shall baptize you with the Holy Ghost and with fire" (Matthew 3:11). The baptisms of water and fire define the movement from a state of blissful union with nature and the unconscious to the painful entry into the world of experience and finally to the achievement of a state of higher innocence through the integration of the conscious and the unconscious.

The King's fire baptism symbolizes the final stage. The crucial point (from my point of view) to be made about that event is that, on one level of the narrative, Curdie dreams it. This is clear if we look at MacDonald's description of the events. That night, Curdie leaves the housemaid with the King and goes to sleep in front of the King's door. In the middle of the night, he awakes and sees a glow under the door. Opening it, he witnesses the baptism. He then returns to the corridor and goes back to sleep. In the morning, the housemaid is still in the King's room, and there is no sign that anything unusual has occurred. The scene, therefore, should be seen as analogous to Curdie's dream of the Grandmother, which is the culmination of the first book, and it should be interpeted as an event in his psychic life, marking his arrival at the goal toward which his development aimed. In "A Sketch of Individual Development," MacDonald calls movements to a new stage of life "births." Fire, like water, is traditionally part of the imagery of rebirth—the baptism font, the alchemical retort, the furnace are all wombs in which the personality is purified in order to be reborn on a higher level of existence. But what precisely is the nature of Curdie's final rebirth?

Here again I think Jungian thought can help us. According to Jung, the goal of an individual's development is the integration of the personality and the realization of the self. The *self* is Jung's word for the core of the personality, the regulating center that is the source of the impulse to growth and development. According to Jung, a woman personifies the self in dream as a female figure, e.g., Cinderella's fairy godmother. A man, on the other hand, personifies the self as a male figure, e.g., the wise old man of the fairy tales about whom Jung has written a well-known essay. When Curdie dreams of the King, therefore, it is a vision indicating his own attainment of a state of higher innocence through the experience of the self.

When the self is realized and lived in an integrated personality, this constitutes the achievement of psychological wholeness through the synthesis of the conscious and the unconscious. Therefore, in dreams and myth, the realization of the self is commonly symbolized by the union of opposites. Appropriately, the King's fire baptism unites fire and water as the Grandmother weeps over the King:

> the water of her weeping dropped like sunset rain in the light of the roses. At last she lifted a great armful of her hair, and shook it over the fire, and the drops fell from it in showers, and they did not hiss in the flames, but there arose instead as it were the sound of running brooks (326).

This union of opposites is complemented by a classic archetypal image of the self when we see "the face of the king, which shone from under the burnt roses like a diamond in the ashes of a furnace." The structure of the self, like that of a diamond, reflects the inner order of nature. The conscious realization of the self, therefore, harmonizes the ego with the transpersonal pattern of the world. The diamond also, of course, recalls Little Diamond, MacDonald's representative of the state of pure innocence in the earlier *At the Back of the North Wind*. The image of the diamond is complemented by another cosmological image when we are told that Curdie "awoke like a giant refreshed with wine." The giant referred to here is not an evil giant like that killed by Anodos in *Phantastes*. Such an evil giant was in Victorian devotional literature an image of sin and weakness.[3] Rather, this is a good giant, the archetype of the primordial cosmic man, image of the self that extends beyond the ego in time and space and includes the entire world. The reference to wine continues the communion motif in the book and again suggests the union of the ego with the body of the divinity. The diamond, the cosmic giant, and the communion wine all suggest the transcendant and permanent aspect of the personality revealed when the superficial ego orientation is burned away.

For MacDonald, the individual could only realize this eternal aspect of the personality through the sacrifice of the ego. The chapter describing the King's fire-baptism is entitled "The Sacrifice." The table on which the King lies is a "table-altar." MacDonald also has a sonnet entitled "The Burnt Offering" in which sleep, in so far as it strips away the superficial ego, is described as a sacrifice in imagery identical to that of the fire-baptism sequence. This makes it clear that the fire-baptism should be seen as a kind of Old Testament sacrifice. Curdie's stepping into the room that seemed to have no floor and his thrusting his hands into the fire were earlier and partial sacrifices. Now, the ashes on which the diamond lies symbolize the total destruction of an ego-oriented personality organization.

The apocalyptic final battle between good and evil follows the fire baptism. The thing to be noted here, however, is that the victory has very little effect on society. After the King and his strange army ride out of the city, the inhabitants gather flowers with which to welcome their enemies. Eventually, of course, the greed of the people of Gwyntystorm destroys the city. The battle, therefore, is not truly apocalyptic. It does not transform the world. It is better to see it simply in terms of Curdie's development, apocalyptic in the sense of the transformation of his personality.

The final battle is part of the constellation of images indicating the achievement of wholeness. A final image of the union of opposites as a synthesis of the male and female aspects of the personality occurs as the various characters join in battle. This parallels to some degree a scene near the end of *Phantastes*. Both scenes are examples of the Jungian "quaternity," the four-sided mandala, which is the archetypal image of psychic wholeness. In MacDonald's version of this configuration, the ego is united with the mother, the father, and the anima. In *Phantastes,* the Knight and the Marble Lady stand beside the grave in which Anodos has re-entered the womb of mother earth. In *The Princess and Curdie,* Curdie joins with the Grandmother, the King Father, and Irene in battle. There are, however, great differences between the two scenes. Anodos is never able fully to separate the archetypes of the mother and the beloved. His relationships with the female characters, therefore, always have a regressive and incestuous character. As a result, the mother image cannot be integrated into the world of consciousness and social institutions. At the end of *Phantastes,* the mother is located beyond the grave and Anodos's relationship to life is tenuous. In *The Princess and Curdie,* however, the one sexually charged image of incest (when the Grandmother takes Irene to bed with her) is part of the imagery of innocence. In *The Princess and Curdie,* the Grandmother is clearly distinguished from

Irene and can, therefore, play an active role in the masculine world of ego-consciousness. Unlike Anodos, who could establish a genuine relationship only with the mother, Curdie marries Irene and founds a kingdom, integrating the wisdom gained in the depths into the social world, precisely as the hero myth requires.

In all, then, I do not see *The Princess and Curdie,* as other critics have done, as a falling off from the first book or as evidence that MacDonald was in a state of despair, convinced, as Wolff has maintained, "that evil triumphs in the end" (176). I rather see the second "Princess" book as evidence that MacDonald was at the height of his powers and that his insight into life had developed significantly beyond the immature and rather adolescent stage that we find in *Phantastes.* The apocalyptic element in *The Princess and Curdie* may be uncomfortable to a society that has since MacDonald's time increasingly lost touch with the deeper levels of existence, but the sureness and force of MacDonald's psychological insight and mythological imagination in this book cannot, I think, be denied.

Notes

1. The history of the goblin's fall into the underworld is recounted at the beginning of *The Princess and the Goblin* with suggestive vagueness. It has a general similarity in structure to Milton's account of the fall of the rebel angels. For example, we hear that the goblins "so heartily cherished the ancestral grudge against those who occupied their former possessions, and especially against the descendants of the king who had caused their expulsion, that they sought every opportunity of tormenting them...." In addition, some details are identical. The goblins are "greatly altered" by their fall, and so are the angels.

Satan's first words to Beelzebub are

> If thou beest hee; But O how fall'n! how chang'd
> From him, who in the happy Realms of Light
> Cloth'd with transcendent brightness didst outshine
> Myriads though bright. . . (*Paradise Lost*, I, 84-87).

2. This parallel with the *Odyssey* clarifies at least one further element in *The Princess and Curdie.* After the battle in the hall, Curdie and the beasts "clean house": "there was such a cleaning and clearing out of neglected places, such a burying and burning of refuse, such a rinsing of

jugs, such a swilling of sinks, and such of flushing of drains as would have delighted the eyes of all true housekeepers and lovers of cleanliness generally." That this is not merely a Victorian passion for tidiness is clear if we compare Odysseus's cleansing of his hall:

> Then they first carried away the bodies of those who were dead
> And they set them down under the portico of the well-fenced court,
> Propping them on one another. Odysseus gave the orders,
> Urging them on himself. They bore them out by constraint.
> And then the tables and the beautiful armchairs
> They cleaned off, with water and the porous sponges.
> Then Telemachos, the oxherd, and the swineherd
> Scraped down the floor of the stoutly built house with shovels.
> The servants kept carrying the scrapings and put them outdoors
>
> *The Odyssey,* trans. Albert Cook, XII, 448-456.

3. *See,* for example, Richard Newton, *The Giants and How to Fight Them* (London: Nelson, 1886).

Works Cited

MacDonald, George. *Adela Cathcart.* London: Edwin Dalton, 1908 (1864).
———. *A Dish of Orts.* London: Sampson, Low, Marston, 1895.
———. *Phantastes and Lilith.* Grand Rapids, MI: Eerdmans, 1964.
———. *The Princess and the Goblin; The Princess and Curdie.* Oxford: World's Classics, 1990.
Sigman, Joseph. "Death's Ecstasies: Transformation and Rebirth in George MacDonald's *Phantastes.*" *English Studies in Canada* II (Summer 1976): 203-226.
Wolff, Robert Lee. *The Golden Key: A Study of the Fiction of George MacDonald.* New Haven: Yale UP, 1961, pp. 165-166.

The Princess and the Wizard
The Fantasy Worlds of Ursula K. LeGuin and George MacDonald

By Cordelia Sherman

George MacDonald was a Scot, a clergyman, and an evangelical Christian. Ursula K. LeGuin is an American, a writer and teacher, and a self-confessed "congenital non-Christian" (*Language* 55). Yet the Curdie books and the Earthsea trilogy share a commonality of symbol and tone which transcends their differences. Like priests or shamans of their own religions, MacDonald and LeGuin in these fantasies teach their readers the universal truths of individual morality: you, too, they tell us, can be as wise as Ged, as good as Curdie or Irene, if only you are willing to learn to know and master your self.

The common tone of the Curdie books and the Earthsea books comes primarily from their common purpose, which is indeed the purpose of most serious children's literature: to teach children by dramatic example what it means to be a good adult. Each series recounts the emotional and moral coming-of-age of a boy and a girl, which is achieved by overcoming a number of hardships. MacDonald, who comes right out and tells you what he wants you to learn from the adventures of Curdie and Irene, is not as subtle an instructor as LeGuin, who puts the didactic bits in the mouths of mentor figures like Ogion and Nemmerle in *A Wizard of Earthsea* and Ged himself in *The Tombs of Atuan* and *The Farthest Shore*. But neither writer wishes to leave the reader in any doubt as to the moral and personal implications of what he has just read, and both sets of books are as full of aphorisms as an egg is of meat.

The nature of the moral tests Ged, Tenar, and Arren must pass on their way to adulthood is more equivocal than that of the tests Curdie and Irene encounter, for MacDonald's universe is more absolute than LeGuin's, his idea of goodness easier to apprehend. To MacDonald, an adult is physically clean, mindful of his or her place in the social hierarchy, honest, cheerful, essentially innocent. These virtues are both taught and exemplified by sympathetic and supportive adult characters: Irene's numinous great-great-great-Grandmother and her king-papa, and Curdie's parents, especially his mother.

Curdie's mother is what MacDonald imagines all women potentially to be: a sort of Grandmother-in-training. Like the old Princess, she is a loving protector whose words and example gently lead her husband and son onto the paths of righteousness. Both explicitly and implicitly, MacDonald identifies Curdie's mother as the Grandmother's chosen mediator between the practical world of the mines and the mystical world of the attic. If a girl cannot hope to achieve the Grandmother's perfect, mutable beauty, she can, MacDonald shows us, hope to achieve Mrs. Peterson's more homely grace.

In *The Princess and Curdie,* Irene does in fact emulate Curdie's mother, protecting, caring for, and feeding her king-papa as a wife or a mother would. This maternal role and her essentially adult speech patterns, so different from the artless prattle MacDonald puts into her mouth in the earlier novel, encourage the reader to think of Irene not as a nine-year-old child, but as an adolescent or even as a grown woman. The narrator tells us that her sufferings have aged her prematurely, but like the Grandmother—indeed like all of MacDonald's virtuous women—Irene is actually ageless, her wisdom a function of gender and character, not of chronological or biological age.

Curdie, on the other hand, must overcome the inclinations of his gender and character in order to achieve wisdom. Boys, MacDonald suggests, are just not naturally spiritual. Despite his good heart, his courage, and his kindness, which allow him to accompany Irene to her Grandmother's attic, the Curdie of *The Princess and the Goblin* is spiritually commonplace, insensitive to beauty, and impatient of mystery—which is why he sees only an empty garret when he gets there. The subject of *The Princess and Curdie* is

Curdie's merging and tempering the manly virtues of absolute faith, pleasure in beauty, and the impulse to bring order and renew life.

LeGuin does not find one sex fundamentally more moral than the other, cares nothing about physical cleanliness, cheerfulness, or the social hierarchy, and implies that innocence, if coupled with ignorance, is at best limiting. In *The Farthest Shore,* Prince Arren begins where Curdie ends up—trusting, honest, faithful, responsive to beauty and mystery, ready to do what authority defines as his duty without question or doubt. If *The Princess and Curdie* is about Curdie's conscious surrender of his ego and imagination to the old Princess, *The Farthest Shore* is about Arren's conscious separation of his ego and imagination from externally set expectations and models. Arren's path to this end is more lonely than Curdie's, for Curdie always has the emotional support and guidance of the Grandmother and the physical support of the monster Lina. As benefits LeGuin's philosophy of self-determination, Ged teaches Arren responsibility by refusing to pass judgment on his actions. When Arren reasonably expects praise for asking the right question or blame for falling asleep on guard duty, Ged simply refuses to comment. It takes some time and soul-searching before Arren can understand the purpose behind Ged's seeming indifference: "Arren saw then that what he had done and what he had not done were not going to receive judgment from Sparrowhawk: He had done it; Sparrowhawk accepted it as done" (*Farthest Shore* 65). For LeGuin, calling an action good or evil is something an adult must learn to do for himself by judging that action's consequences and its place in the grand pattern of life.

Ged's own coming-of-age, recounted in *A Wizard of Earthsea,* is a more self-directed process than Arren's, for Ged does not wish to be taught. Like Curdie, he is willing to learn facts—he is the quickest student of spells and names on Roke—and, like Curdie, he is impatient of learning concepts that have no observable purpose. If a mage has the power to avert rain, turn into a hawk or raise the dead, Ged argues, why doesn't he just do it? The Master Hand answers him: "A wizard's power of Changing and of Summoning can shake the balance of the world. It is dangerous, that power. It must follow knowledge, and serve need. To light a candle is to cast a shadow" (*Wizard* 44). Ged learns his lesson by upsetting the balance and releasing the Shadow, by pursuing it, and ultimately by accepting it as part of himself.

Weighing Ged's long, lonely, physically and emotionally demanding odyssey against Curdie's relatively brief, amply guided, and supported quest seems an unbalanced comparison, but although their duration and hardship are unequal, their narratives are fundamentally similar. Curdie, too, achieves salvation by breaking a prohibition. He shoots one of the Grandmother's pigeons, takes the bird to her, repents, and cements his repentance by accepting her mission and holding his hands in her fire of roses. According to MacDonald's standards, Curdie comes as close to utter ruin as Ged: losing his belief in the Grandmother's reality is tantamount to losing his soul. And the lesson he learns from his sin is, at bottom, the same: "I was doing the wrong of never wanting or trying to be better" (*Princess and Curdie* 30) is no less an expression of accountability for one's actions than "To light a candle is to cast a shadow."

A similarly complex relationship exists between LeGuin's and MacDonald's definitions of evil. Superficially, the two differ profoundly. To LeGuin, evil is shadowy and shifting, difficult to grasp and difficult to define. It is also, to some extent, divorced from human agency. When Ged releases the Shadow into Earthsea, it is not the precipitating action—calling up the ghost of a long-dead queen—that is evil. The art of Summoning is as morally neutral as any other wizardry. But Ged summons Elfarran because he is driven to do so by the most flawed parts of his character: pride, hatred, and social insecurity. Ged is a strong wizard, so Elfarran comes. But he is not yet an emotionally mature man, so the Shadow comes with her. LeGuin makes it clear that the Shadow is not in itself evil, nor is Ged evil for having released it. The evil comes of the Shadow's not being restrained or tamed by Ged, its creator and alter ego. Like Curdie, Ged repents and recognizes his faults. But rather than shedding them all at once in a ritual of purification, as Curdie does, Ged must spend the next three years of his life learning control, balance, patience, and humility. His Shadow is destructive, greedy, deceitful—attributes both of MacDonald's goblins and the King's treacherous advisers. But the Shadow is also formless, physically mutable, difficult for Ged to see clearly or to touch (although it can certainly touch him). Evil to MacDonald is at once more internal and more separable from its human host than Ged's Shadows.

In both Curdie books, evil is physically repellent and easily recognized by those who have eyes to see it. The goblins' stone heads and tender feet reflect their lack of imagination and their touchy vanity. The King's treacherous counsellors in *The Princess and Curdie* are even more symbolically ugly. The Chamberlain is "a lean, long, yellow man, with a small head, bald over the top. . . His eyes were very small, sharp, and glittering, and looked black as jet. He had hardly enough of a mouth to make a smile with" (147). He is already more than half the bird of prey his hand reveals him to be.

The gift the Grandmother gives Curdie—the ability to judge the state of a man's soul by the form of his hand—is MacDonald's strongest metaphor of the willful and separable nature of evil. Unlike Ged, who learns that an adult must acknowledge his baser instincts in order to harness and tame them, Curdie learns that an adult must cast his baser instincts from him. The Grandmother explains sin to Curdie as a kind of devolution: "Since it is always what they *do,* whether in their minds or their bodies that makes men go down to be less than men, that is, beasts, the change always comes first in their hands—and first of all in the inside hands. . . " (*Princess and Curdie* 70). MacDonald wants to excise the beast both from the individual human soul—by means of the symbolic flames of the Grandmother's fire of roses—and from society at large—by means of the flooding of the goblins' mines and the scouring of the King's castle. No matter its degree, sinfulness must be rooted out, lest it undermine the foundations of good.

In their treatments of the nature of evil and sin, then, these two writers have used very different approaches to the process of spinning straw into gold. Indeed, MacDonald's categorical rejection of human weakness and LeGuin's qualified acceptance of it delineate most of the philosophical differences between the two writers. Yet the symbols which inform their narratives are constant. We do not need MacDonald or LeGuin to tell us that evil belongs in dark, subterranean places; we are predisposed to judge anything living in such a place as being frightening, destructive, greedy: evil. LeGuin tries to remove the moral burden from physical darkness by taking the Jungian view that the Nameless Ones who dwell in the *Tombs of Atuan* are simply a part of Earthsea, as the Shadow is part of Ged, no more evil in themselves than a tidal wave. Human beings, however, can master their shadows; the world cannot master its tidal waves or its Nameless Ones. Given power by humanity, they encourage evil. On the one hand, Ged calls the Nameless Ones "the ancient and holy Powers of the earth"; on the other, he tells Tenar "They are dark and undying, and they hate the light: the brief, bright light of our mortality. They are immortal, but they are not gods. They never were. They are not worth the worship of any human soul" (*Tombs of Atuan* 106).

So darkness is naturally the habitation of evil, whether evil be defined as loss of self or loss of God. Equally naturally, light is the habitation of good, whether good is defined as union with and surrender to God or as personal integration and freedom. A journey is an archetype of a child's psychological and moral development, which brings him in the end to stand in the light or be swallowed by the darkness. LeGuin and MacDonald know that the path to darkness is as torturous and difficult to chart as the path to light; LeGuin and MacDonald know that a child must tread both in the process of choosing between them. And both writers set at least a part of their narratives in physical labyrinths and mazes that serve as backgrounds to and figures of the children's choices.

Because of its mythological associations with Minotaurs, secrets, and death, the labyrinth seems to be more naturally a symbol for the path to darkness than for the path to light. However, the symbolic associations that have accreted around the figure of the labyrinth over the centuries are complex. There is evidence that natural labyrinths were the locus for coming-of-age rituals in paleolithic tribes. The Cretan labyrinth itself was connected with the worship of the sun. In the Middle Ages, churches in France and Italy frequently had mosaic mazes set into their floors. They were all specifically identified as figures of man's journey through life, but in some cases, the center medallion contained a representation of the Minotaur—death—and in some cases, it contained the words *Sancta Eglise* or *Ciel* or *Jerusalem*.[1]

In a larger sense, the world in which each child lives and through which he or she must journey in order to find his or her adult self is a labyrinth of light and dark blended in rich and inextricable confusion. In *The Princess and Curdie,* for example, MacDonald sets the King's castle, as it is when the King lies poisoned and dying within it, against the same castle after Curdie has cleansed it of the treacherous counsellors. But one of the prerogatives of the fantasist is to present good and evil, light and dark, as separable and separate entities, similar in outward form, perhaps, but profoundly different in effect. Thus, Irene and Curdie,

Ged, Tenar, and Arren all journey toward adulthood through mirroring pairs of labyrinths, some dark and belowground, some light and aboveground. In *The Princess and the Goblin,* MacDonald sets the goblins' mine against Irene's rambling house. And, on a grander scale, LeGuin sets the lightless Tombs of Atuan against the watery geography of Earthsea itself.

In each case, since the maze of light is not always strictly part of the world it anchors, it is more tenuous, more abstract than the dark labyrinth, and its center is harder to achieve.[2] The heart of the great maze of water and islands that is Earthsea is the Immanent Grove on the Island of Roke, which lives at the geographical center of the archipelago. "It is said that no spells are worked there, and yet the place itself is an enchantment. Sometimes the trees of that Grove are seen, and sometimes they are not seen, and they are not always in the same place and part of Roke Island" (*Wizard* 72). Despite its illusiveness, the Grove is the center upon which Earthsea is balanced, the fulcrum of the magic that keeps the water from flooding the islands.

The heart of Irene's house is her great-great-great-Grandmother's attic, which even Irene cannot always find, and which, when found, is not always there. Curdie's mother reminds him,

> ... when the princess took you up that tower once before, and there talked to her great-great-Grandmother, you came home quite angry with her, and said there was nothing in the place but an old tub, a heap of straw ... a withered apple, and a sunbeam. According to your eyes, that was all there was in the great, old, musty garret (*Princess and Curdie* 38).

Curdie cannot immediately see the beauty of the Grandmother's bedroom for the same reason that Jasper cannot come to the Immanent Grove: both grove and attic are spiritual as much as they are literal, and those who would reach them must be sensitive to their power. Such sensitivity can be inborn, as it seems to be for Vetch and Irene, or it can be cultivated through study and discipline, as Ged does, or achieved through faith and suffering, as Curdie does. It can be called goodness or it can be called magic, but in either case, this sensitivity is necessary to achieve transcendance.

The aboveground mazes are both easy of entrance—indeed in both cases most of the characters, good and evil, live their daily lives in their outer corridors. But the underground labyrinths of MacDonald and LeGuin must be entered deliberately. Those who dwell in them, hoping to feed from their power, are swallowed by the darkness and become one with their sterility and despair.[3] Thus, the community dedicated to the worship of the Nameless Ones is, because of the object of its worship, stagnant, barren, and meaningless. When she is chosen as Arha, the Eaten One, Tenar loses her family, her individuality, her hope of achievement, her freedom, her very name. All around are images of sterility and dryness: the tombs are in a desert, her companions are virgins and eunuchs, her only function in life is to perform the rituals of forgotten meaning before an Empty Throne. Lightless, cold, and barren, the labyrinth of the Tombs of Atuan is a power symbol of evil. Unfortunately, since it is protected and served by priestesses, a comparison between it and Roke, with its creative and supportive community of men, is inescapable. The subliminal message of *The Tombs of Atuan* seems to be that women living without men must become twisted and purposeless, while men living without women can be productive and strong. In his model of a girl's coming-of-age, MacDonald initially seems far more positive.

Women are the moral backbone of MacDonald's world. When men's daring leads them into sin or despair, women are always there to lead them back to righteousness, if they are willing to be led. The Grandmother performs this function for mankind, and on a smaller scale, Mrs. Peterson performs it for her husband. Irene performs it for Curdie on a literal as well as metaphorical level when she follows the Grandmother's thread into the goblins' mine where Curdie has been imprisoned.[4] She is a child, a very young child in this book, sheltered, cosseted, brought up by servants. She enters a mine which she has good reason to fear and physically digs Curdie out of his prison, rock by rock. Yet the dramatic effect of her accomplishment is mitigated by the fact that both the reader and Irene know that she is safe wherever she goes. The reader knows that the danger of the mines cannot affect her, because she is innocent and trusting. Irene knows she is safe because the Grandmother's ring would not lead her into mortal danger. Because she is part of the Grandmother, Irene is practically guaranteed strength and faith, and her possession of these qualities is hardly a virtue in her, any more than having blue eyes or rosy fingers is a virtue. We are told she matures, but MacDonald does not show us the process of her maturation.

Tenar, who is just as essentially innocent as Irene, just as ignorant of the reality of evil, must learn to fight against forces of the labyrinth, and is therefore allowed as much psychological complexity as her male counterpart. Ged must convince her that the Nameless Ones are evil and support her in her attempts to throw off their influence. But Tenar is not entirely passive in her rescue. The Tombs of Atuan hide not only the Nameless Ones, but also the missing half of the Ring of Erreth-Akbe, the talisman that binds the diverse world of Earthsea into a harmonious whole, and Ged cannot find or remove it without Tenar's help and guidance. In the process of leading him to the hidden door of the tombs, Tenar learns the use and control of the darker side of her personality, and begins to take an active part in the formation of her own character.

In MacDonald's world, it is possible to defeat the darkness, to flood the mines, to clean the castle, and to use the treasure wisely. In LeGuin's world, it is possible only to comprehend the nature of the dark, to accept its immortality, and to go about one's business. Yet at the end of LeGuin's trilogy, order is restored to Earthsea, and the language of the last paragraph, which refers to all the preceding events as if they were ancient history, suggests that order remains stable. At the end of *The Princess and Curdie,* Irene and Curdie's children undermine the castle their ancestors saved, and "the very name of Gwyntystorm . . . ceased from the lips of men" (*Princess and Curdie* 221). In view of the bleakness of this final image of destruction, MacDonald's doctrine of salvation is finally no simpler or more comforting than LeGuin's doctrine of self-reliance and accountability.

There are other corresponding images in the Curdie books and the Earthsea books: symbolic death and rebirth at a higher level of wisdom; the ambiguous role of animals as guides to both wisdom and loss of humanity; the idea that in order to be a whole human being, an adult must not reject his child-self, but incorporate it into his personality. In each case, the symbolic trappings of these themes have complex similarities, even though the philosophies that inform them are as different as philosophies can be. Consistently, MacDonald writes of developing the Christian virtues of humility and perfect faith in and obedience to the will of God; LeGuin writes of developing a sense of balance and taking full responsibility for all one's words and actions. But the superficially divergent paths they trace lead ultimately to the same center—wisdom and maturity. Both Curdie and Ged learn that appearances can be deceiving and that all actions have consequences.

Both Irene and Tenar learn to trust their instincts as well as their training. And all four children learn that it is better, if harder, to choose to act from their own internal sense of right and wrong than simply to follow the dictates of others.

Notes

1. Joseph Campbell discusses the ritual significance of labyrinths in paleolithic culture in *The Masks of God*, 65-70 *passim*. Descriptions of church-floor mazes appear in W. H. Matthews, *Mazes and Labyrinths*, 54-70. Matthews quotes an inscription found next to a maze set in the floor of the tenth-century church of San Savino at Piacenza: *"Hunc mundm tipice laberinthus denotat iste / Intranti largus, redeunti set nimis artus / Sic mundo captus, viciorum molle gravatus / Vox valet ad vite doctrinam quisque redire."*

2. In *Le Mythe de l'éternel retour*, the French philosopher Mircea Eliade describes the idea of the "Centre of the World," which he conceives as a sacred place connecting Heaven, Earth, and Hell. His examples of such centres include sacred mountains such as Sinai and Parnassus, cities such as Jerusalem and Mecca, objects such as the Grail and the Golden Apples, places such as the heart of a Labyrinth. Of such centres, he writes:

> Le "Centre" est donc la zone du sacré par excellence, celle de la réalité absolue... Le chemin est ardu, semé de périls, parce qu'il est, en fait, un rite de passage du profane au sacré; de l'éphémère et de l'illusoire à la réalité et à l'éternité, de la mort à la vie; de l'homme à la divinité. L'accès au "centre" équivaut à une consécration, à une initiation, à une existence, hier profane et illusoire, succède maintenant une nouvelle existence, réelle, durable et efficace (30).

3. In *The Masks of God*, Joseph Campbell traces a number of connections between labyrinths and passages to the underworld (60-70 and *passim*). A man entering a labyrinth always dies to his old life—either childhood or mortal existence—and is reborn into another—adulthood or an afterlife. In "Ancient Myths and Modern Man," Joseph Henderson

emphasizes the identification of the labyrinth with the anima, with the "entangling and confusing representation of the world of the matriarchal consciousness" which "can be traversed only by those who are ready for a special initiation into the mysterious world of the collective unconscious" (117).

4. Unlike Ariadne, Irene is more active in rescuing her hero, who merely supplies the clue but does not enter the labyrinth herself. Although Curdie rescues Irene from the goblins on the mountain and ends up marrying her, MacDonald never presents her simply as a damsel in distress or a prize, as Ariadne herself was.

Works Cited

Campbell, Joseph. *The Masks of God.* New York: Penguin, 1969.
Eliade, Mircea. *Le mythe de l' éternel retour.* Paris: Gallimard, 1969.
Henderson, Joseph L. "Ancient Myths and Modern Man." in *Man and His Symbols.* Ed. Carl G. Jung. New York: Dell, 1973, 95-156.
LeGuin, Ursula K. "Dreams Must Explain Themselves." *The Language of the Night.* Ed. Susan Wood. New York: Putnam, 1979, 47-56.
_____. *The Farthest Shore.* New York: Bantam, 1975.
_____. *The Tombs of Atuan.* New York: Bantam, 1975.
_____. *A Wizard of Earthsea.* New York: Bantam, 1975.
MacDonald, George. *The Princess and Curdie.* Harmondsworth: Penguin, 1966.
_____. *The Princess and the Goblin.* Harmondsworth: Penguin, 1966.
Manlove, C. N. *The Impulse of Fantasy.* Kent, OH: Kent State UP, 1983.
Matthews, W. H. *Mazes and Labyrinths: Their History and Development.* New York: Dover, 1922, reprinted 1970.
Rees, David. *The Marble in the Water.* Boston: Horn Book, 1983.
Swinfen, Ann. *In Defense of Fantasy.* London: Routledge & Kegan Paul, 1984.
Wolff, Robert Lee. *The Golden Key.* New Haven: Yale UP, 1961.

Duality Beyond Time
George MacDonald's "The Wise Woman, or The Lost Princess: A Double Story"*

By Melba N. Battin

> It was in . . . mythopoeic art that Macdonald excelled. . . . The great works are *Phantastes*, the *Curdie* books, *The Golden Key, The Wise Woman,* and *Lilith* (Lewis 17).

Not many critics agree with C. S. Lewis that "The Wise Woman" belongs among George MacDonald's "great works." For instance, Richard Reis and C. N. Manlove dismiss "The Wise Woman" as too didactic. This position, however, ignores the literary form which MacDonald chooses and which emphasizes in the subtitle of the first edition published in book form in 1875: "The Wise Woman: a parable." The accepted purpose of the parable in biblical times, as well as in MacDonald's day, was that of setting forth "the truth spiritual and heavenly" (*OED* 2071). In the Synoptic Gospels, Christ explains to the disciples why and for whom he speaks in parables:

> . . . Because it is given unto you to know the mysteries of the kingdom of heaven, but to them it is not given. For whosoever hath, to him shall be given, and he shall have more abundance:

---

* This work was begun at Princeton University in a National Endowment for the Humanities seminar directed by U. C. Knoepflmacher. Helpful suggestions were provided by Roderick McGillis.

but whosoever hath not, from him shall be taken away even that he hath. Therefore speak I to them in parables: because they seeing see not; and hearing they hear not, neither do they understand (Matthew 13: 11-13).

Another scholar who criticizes this story is R. L. Wolff; he finds that

> the Wise Woman has cruelty as her only weapon. . . Grandmother has lost her power; she can do nothing now but strike out cruelly . . . [and] the story makes the social statement that the poor are sometimes even worse than the rich . . . (170).

In similar language, Mark Zaitchik also finds the "goddess figure unpleasant [with] more than a touch of cruelty" (vi), and he complains that MacDonald will not tell us "Why the princess is redeemed and the peasant girl left in darkness . . . " (viii). These psychological and socioeconomic concerns, however, seem outside the central issue of the story, which is that of the "truth spiritual," for MacDonald only incidentally shows us that one can be spiritually deprived in a cottage as well as in a castle. Indeed, his aim is to indicate that to those with insight, more understanding shall be given. Thus, the struggle to grow spiritually could just as easily have been shown by reversing the roles, making the peasant instead of the princess the character who achieves spiritual insight. In fact, MacDonald could have developed the spiritual journey of both girls instead of merely hinting at Agnes's future growth in the final paragraph of the tale; but then, of course, we would have a novel.

In *Varieties of Parable,* Louis MacNeice expands the definition of parable to encompass those works which rise to mystical, dreamlike, poetical heights. In his introduction he lists the terms which he rejects; for example, symbolism, allegory and myth, and says:

> I did think of using "fantasy", which should be wide enough—almost too wide, though it would exclude the New Testament parables—but which suffers from the pejorative associations of Coleridge's "Fancy" . . . "(1).

Under this expanded definition of parable,[1] MacNeice discusses MacDonald's works, including "The Wise Woman," which are usually classified as fantasy. It is only fair to say that of all of MacDonald's works of "fantasy," "The Wise Woman" is the most obviously a parable in the narrower sense of the New Testament. As MacNeice interestingly points out, however, "MacDonald does not talk about God, let alone Christ, in his parable writing" (97).

Nonetheless, one-half of "The Wise Woman" deals with defining and identifying "the truth spiritual"; the other half, with the process of changing and deepening the spiritual self. That MacDonald chooses mundane, everyday chores to illustrate how difficult it is to change, even after one's conscience is awakened, is no accident, for the spiritual journey is fraught not only with temptation, self-delusion, and suffering, but also with tediousness. Although the central truth of a parable may be easy for some to understand, it may be difficult to put into practice, and MacDonald knows that religious terminology does not necessarily illuminate. Thus characters such as the Wise Woman (and Diamond in *At the Back of the North Wind*), like the disciples of Christ, who already possess spiritual awareness, serve to point the way to others.

As Roderick McGillis's metaphor aptly points out, "The Wise Woman's function is to break up the ice of fixed ideas and expectations, for she knows that without conflict, without the piquancy of fear, there will be no progression" (21).

It is doubtful that MacDonald would have argued with critical analysis of "The Wise Woman," for he understood that interpretation of a work of art is an individual matter. In his essay "The Fantastic Imagination," he states: "Everyone ... who feels the story, will read its meaning after his own nature and development: one will read one meaning in it, another will read another" (*A Dish of Orts* 164).

But elsewhere MacDonald clarifies the major intent of his literary works; for instance, in his dedication to *The Portent* he says: "Truth to Humanity, and harmony within itself, are almost the sole unvarying essentials of a work of art" (v).

And in the preface to Adolph Valdemar Thisted's *Letters from Hell,* MacDonald elaborates on what he means by "truth":

> I do not mean either truth of theory or truth in art, but something far deeper and higher—the realities of our relations to God and man and duty—all, in short that belongs to the conscience. Prominent among these is the awful verity, that we

make our fate in unmaking ourselves, that men in defacing the image of God in themselves, construct for themselves a world of horror and dismay; that if a man will not have God, he never can be rid of his weary and hateful self (vi-vii.)

This concern with the inner and outer, the spiritual and the physical, dominated both MacDonald's life from his childhood and his works from the earliest published long poem, *Within and Without* (1855). In "The Wise Woman" the concept of duality remains constant in the titles, despite the five changes of title. In fact, duality is explicit not only in the literary form as discussed above, but also in the setting and characters.

The duality implicit in the title and literary form is immediately reinforced in the two dominant settings—one pastoral, one urban. A golden rain is falling at the palace at the moment that Princess Rosamond is born, the sun turning "all its drops into molten topazes" (*Wise Woman* 2). Despite the fact that her father was king, her mother, queen and so she was "Somebody," the first thing Princess Rosamond "did was to cry" (3). By contrast, "while the same cloud was dropping down golden rain all about the queen's new baby [it] was dashing huge fierce handfuls of hail upon the hills" (3-4). "And, among the hailstones, and the heather and the cold mountain air, another little girl [Agnes] was born, whom the shepherd her father, and the shepherdess her mother and a good many of her kindred too, thought Somebody. . . . And yet . . . she cried the very first thing" (4).

Despite the difference in setting and socioeconomic environment MacDonald, nevertheless, makes clear that each child has in common her physical female form, her natural instincts (each "cries"), and her psychological attitudes of self-importance (each thinks of herself as "Somebody"). Later in the story, MacDonald contrasts the castle and pastoral settings with that of the Wise Woman's magical cottage, where operate values other than those of thinking oneself "Somebody" in physical, psychological, and socioeconomic terms. And it is at the Wise Woman's cottage that the two girls begin their spiritual education—the central theme of the parable.

Rosamond and Agnes provide the dominant duality among the characters. Of the two, Princess Rosamond is the more important, for her character and journey are more fully developed. Rosamond is one of the most obnoxious of prepubescent princesses in MacDonald's work. Her moods, whims, and demands change with electric rapidity, "wanting everything she could and everything she couldn't have" (5). Memorable are her demands to play with a lighted candle and her tantrums, in one of which she smashes against the chimney a gold repeater encrusted with jewels, the least of which are diamonds, and several of which fall into the ashes. So when Rosamond asks that the moon be given her in hand, the reader anticipates the rage which follows the discovery that the silver disk which her parents substitute is only a copy. In utter exasperation, the King and Queen summon the Wise Woman from her country cottage among the pine trees and complain to her that they have given Rosamond "every mortal thing she wanted" (8). The Wise Woman is quick to point out that they should have given this Rose of the physical world "a few things of the other sort" (8). As the Wise Woman is making this distinction, Rosamond appears clutching a rabbit from which she is pulling out fur by the handfuls. As the Queen shouts "Rosa, Rosa*mond!*" (9) in an attempt to stop this barbarism, she receives as reward a rabbit flung into her face. The Wise Woman, who is able to see the spiritual even in this stunted wordly "Rose," helps Princess Rosamond escape the environment which encouraged this ugly behavior by grappling her firmly under her magnificent magical cloak, gliding down the marble steps, carrying her out into the night, across the fields, through the woods filled with hyenas and wolves from which the Wise Woman rescues Rosamond by fearlessly catching the largest, meanest "wolf by the throat half-way in his last spring" (18). Finally, she places Rosamond outside her own cottage in the company of the real moon, "two white faces in the cone of the night" (19).

In his essay, "True Christian Ministering," MacDonald refers to conscience as "The candle of God within . . . " (*A Dish of Orts* 309). So it is not by chance that Rosamond craves a candle and the moon and that she is careless of diamonds—all of which represent in nature those things which shine and which in the context of the story point up the paucity of her own inner light, with which her parents, themselves spiritually bankrupt, were unable to provide her. And in facing the solitary moon outside the Wise Woman's cottage, Rosamond for the first time, simultaneously faces her self-centeredness and the emptiness of her own conscience and soul. Her spiritual education is at zero (that very shape which the full moon and the silver disc take); and if her journey is to proceed beyond this unenlightened stage, it must do so out of her own choice, for the Wise Woman's admonition is that "No one ever gets into my house who does not knock at the door, and ask to come in" (19).

Although the Wise Woman watches lovingly from within the cottage, Rosamond still "understands terror better far than tenderness" (12). When she decides to take the chance of entering the cottage of the "Ogress" and finds "A cottage without a door!" (21) her frustration turns to roars and screams, which are to no avail. Now she thinks of her parents for the first time and "a feeble flutter of genuine love for her parents [awakes] in her heart" (23). These twinges of love carry over to the Wise Woman, and Rosamond remembers that she must ask to enter the Wise Woman's cottage. Since there is no door, she does the best she can and knocks on the wall, from which materializes a door through which Rosamond enters the cottage. And then,

> ... what with the sufferings and terrors she had left outside, the new kind of tears she had shed, the love she had begun to feel for her parents, and the trust in the wise woman, it seemed to her as if her soul had grown larger of a sudden (23).

But the narrator immediately cautions us against optimism, for "people are so ready to think themselves changed when it is only their mood that is changed!" (23). And almost directly, Rosamond, warming herself at the Wise Woman's hearth, becomes absorbed in self-admiration: "how very good she had grown, and how extremely good she must always have been that she was able to grow so very good as she now felt she had grown" (23). However, natural forces outside the cottage interfere with this self-admiration: the wind blows out the fire, lightning strikes, thunder resounds. As so often happens in MacDonald, this storm on the outside reflects the chaos or nightmare going on inside Rosamond. The Wise Woman, offering calm, order, and love, remains the stately vessel that she is and weathers the chaotic inner turmoil which Rosamond projects. When the Wise Woman, for instance, returns to the cottage to find that Rosamond has allowed the fire to go out, has not kept the heather bed watered, has not dusted, but *has* eaten the food which has magically appeared in the hole by the chimney, she merely holds before Rosamond a mirror in which Rosamond sees "a child with dirty fat cheeks, greedy mouth, cowardly eyes ... stooping shoulders, tangled hair, tattered clothes and smears and stains everywhere. That was what she had made herself" (33).

Refusing to accept responsibility for her own actions, Rosamond throws the mirror into the fire, where it shatters into splinters. But the Wise Woman's love is constant and Rosamond is given many other chances, one of which leads her to find the tall eight-day clock, behind which she squeezes into an "enormous stately room lighted only from above ... its walls strengthened by pilasters, and in every space between—a large picture, from cornice to floor" (37). Vascillating between wonder at the room and rage at the Wise Woman, whom she calls "a cheat" (38), Rosamond returns again and again to one picture in particular of

> A blue summer sky, with fleecy clothes floating beneath it ... hung over a hill green to the very top and alive with streams ... flocks of sheep ... shepherd ... two dogs ... a girl with bare feet in a brook ... the wind ... blowing her hair back from her rosy face ... a sheep dog ... trying to reach her hand and lick it ... (38).

Rosamond's wish to be that girl is fulfilled as she steps out into the picture frame shouting, "I am free, I am free!" (39). Thus the Wise Woman's magical pictures give Rosamond (and later Agnes) the opportunity of rejecting her cottage, and the hard work of spiritual development it represents, in favor of a situation which on the surface appears idyllic. In fact, this choice is a setback for Rosamond, who must eventually return to the Wise Woman's cottage to complete her spiritual journey.

Of course, as Rosamond moves into the pastoral setting which she envies, Agnes takes her place at the Wise Woman's cottage, where she finds herself placed naked as a baby into "a great hollow sphere made of a substance similar to that of the mirror which Rosamond had broken.... It had neither door nor window, nor any opening to break its perfect roundness" (48). Again, as with Rosamond and the moon, the sphere represents the beginning of Agnes's solitary spiritual journey. And since Agnes "cared only for Somebody ... now she was going to have only Somebody" (48). By the third solitary day, Agnes becomes aware "that a naked child is seated beside her . . . her chin sunk on her chest . . . her eyes staring at her toes . . . her color of pale earth, with a pinched nose, and a mere slit in her face for a mouth. 'How ugly she is!' thought Agnes" (50). In her abject loneliness, Agnes is even willing to play with this ugly child, but as she reaches toward her, the girl moves away and when Agnes talks to her, the girl only repeats Agnes's words. Then "Agnes lost her temper, and put out her hands to seize the little girl; but lo! the little girl was gone, and she found herself tugging at her own hair" (51).

The orb into which Agnes is placed functions in the same way that the moon and the mirror had previously functioned for Rosamond: revealing spiritual emptiness in each. For the Wise Woman insists that it is necessary to face this truth before the soul can expand. The Wise Woman, however, rescues Agnes from the horror of this realization, admonishing her to remember that she must not yet consider herself cured. And although Agnes has no difficulty with the household chores given her to do, she, too, long before she is spiritually ready to be a "true princess," finds her way into the picture gallery and is dazzled before the palace scene, with its proclamation in gold letters that "every stray child found in the realm shall be brought without a moment's delay to the palace" (53-4). Not listening to the Wise Woman or concerning herself with "killing the ugly things in her heart" (56), she resolves to be "more careful of her face, that is . . . to become a hypocrite as well as a self-worshiper" (56-7); so she sets out to make her material way at the palace, confirming that she, too, is "lost."

Agnes's step backward in the spiritual journey is no worse than the setbacks endured by Rosamond. Her major function in the plot—that of providing range and resonance—is accomplished, for the generalization which MacDonald makes early in the story that "every boy and girl in [this odd kingdom] was rather too ready to think he or she was Somebody" (3) is substantiated in the examples Rosamond and Agnes provide. Agnes also widens the number of ways in which spiritual growth can be circumvented, adding hypocrisy and material greed to the list already set forth by Rosamond or reiterated by Agnes. Similarly, the parents function as concrete examples of adults who, out of their own underdevelopment, provide little spiritual guidance to their children. For example, the King and Queen lie to Rosamond, "pretend[ing] to do what they [can] not" (5) when they substitute material things for spiritual needs, and they downgrade Rosamond's "hideously ugly rages" (6) to "little tempers" (6). Equally important, the shepherd and shepherdess flatter Agnes when they "praise . . . things in her which in another child . . . would . . . have disgusted them altogether" (40). The Wise Woman believes that such flattery and untruth does not allow a child to look within her conscience for blame; depriving the individual of squarely facing inner lacks, of mastering them, and of becoming "a princess over herself" (82). Thus with great economy MacDonald conveys the impression that greatness of spirit is the exception rather than the rule in this "peculiar country" (4).

Agnes never does develop her inner self in this story. When Agnes steps out of the frame into the city scene, parallels with Rosamond (except for the finale) largely cease. However, despite setbacks, Rosamond does widen her understanding and love of others. The spiritual deepening which occurs during her sojourn with the shepherds prepares her for the penultimate part of her journey and for the return to the palace as a "true" rather than a "lost" princess.

MacDonald, however, reiterates the difficulty of genuine inner change, for some of Rosamond's former behavior reappears. But Rosamond is rescued again and again by the Wise Woman who, as one of the tests, requires that Rosamond run through a pack of wolves on the strength of her trust in the Wise Woman. From this success with the wolves, Rosamond learns that trust has a power of its own and that she does not have "to open the cottage door of her heart" (82) to let in evil. But the Wise Woman cautions that "Nobody can be a real princess . . . until she is a princess over herself" (82), and Rosamond must endure three more painful but imaginatively rendered trials before she incorporates within her heart the moral of the parable, which is that she "must not do what is wrong, however much she is inclined to do it, and she must do what is right, however much she is disinclined to do it" (83). To bypass these three additional trials, each of which is represented by a room in the gallery of pictures, is to miss some of the most vivid scenes in the tale, including a tug-of-war over a tantalizing water lily which results in a dead friend staring wide-eyed at Rosamond from the bottom of the pond and an enchanting snow-white horse with "living sails of blue" (92), not to mention the fairy princess who gives life to flowers by tossing them away. These final trials are the last pieces placed in the puzzle of Rosamond's spiritual development, and they complete her understanding of what it means to be a "true" princess.

When in that flash of recognition Rosamond understands that the life-giving princess is the Wise Woman whom she previously had thought a witch, an ogress, and a cheat, she simultaneously sees that the stages of spiritual growth that have been shown to her are not only aspects of Rosamond's inner self, but also former stages which the Wise Woman has herself experienced. It is at this moment that the "or" in the title ("The Wise Woman or The Lost Princess") fully becomes clear: the Wise Woman was once spiritually "lost" in the same way as Rosamond and Agnes. Yet Rosamond, by developing her inner self, is assured of becoming a "wise woman" in this world and of continuing her spiritual growth in the next. For as MacDonald observes of Agnes, unless she cultivates her inner self,

> her growing would be to a mass of distorted shapes all huddled together; so that, although the body might grow up straight and well-shaped and comely to behold, the new body that was growing inside of it, and would come out of it when she died, would be ugly, crooked this way and that, like an aged hawthorn that lived hundreds of years exposed upon all sides to salt sea-winds (41).

Thus, through the gropings of his characters, MacDonald clarifies some of the steps necessary for spiritual growth. Furthermore in the finale, as the Wise Woman reveals herself in her dazzlingly white gown, it is only the dusting woman, the shepherd, and Rosamond who recognize her true identity, for only those with inner purity are able to understand and withstand this light. On this day of spiritual reckoning, it is not the poor who fare worse than the rich, for the King and Queen are at the bottom of the ladder and the woman who dusts is at the top, followed closely behind by Rosamond and the shepherd who catches a glimmer of the Wise Woman's spiritual light. And although Agnes was not able to see the Wise Woman in her purity, nevertheless, "she felt the presence upon her like the heat of a furnace seven times heated" (107). Thus it is the shepherdess (who sees only Agnes) and the King and Queen (who are blinded) who neither see nor feel the light of the Wise Woman. Presumably the shepherd will help Agnes and her mother when he returns from the Wise Woman's cottage; and the King and Queen, whose physical blindness is symbolic of their previous inner blindness, are left in the care of Rosamond, whose responsibility it is to develop the spiritual awareness of her parents.

Also, in the final paragraph MacDonald invites the reader to find his or her niche among the characters who now form a spiritual hierarchical arrangement. Thus in this final insight, as in Rosamond's previous instant of recognition, all the characters spin out of their places of duality and realign themselves on a continuum—a continuum which pays little attention to the intellectual, the psychological, the physical, the socio-economic dimensions, but focuses all upon the "truth spiritual"—a continuum which folds over much like a Mobius band and continues beyond death.

Notes

1. MacNeice ennumerates eight parts to his expanded definition of parable. I refer the reader to the original for a worthwhile experience. At the risk of reducing four pages of delineation to meaninglessness, I paraphrase MacNeice as follows. The parabolist creates a special inner world which is often strongly spiritual or mystical and often merges worlds and personalities, as do dreams. The major concerns in these works are with identity and with theme, rather than character. As in dreams, the parabolist tempts the reader to look below the surface, yet regardless of point of view, one is left with irreducible elements. Although the parabolist cannot be restricted to one particular style, in general, he uses the poetic rather than the documentary. Furthermore, he has a clear worldview of his own.

Works Cited

The Holy Bible, Old and New Testaments. King James Version. Cleveland and New York: World Publishing Co., n.d.
Lewis, C. S. *George MacDonald: An Anthology.* London: Geoffrey Bles, 1946.
MacDonald, George. *A Dish of Orts.* New York: Edwin Dalton, 1909.
_____. *Phantastes and Lilith.* Grand Rapids, MI: Eerdmans, 1964.
_____. *The Portent.* New York: Harper & Row, 1979.

———. *The Wise Woman and Other Stories.* Grand Rapids, MI: Eerdmans, 1980.
MacNeice, Louis. *Varieties of Parable.* Cambridge: Cambridge UP, 1965.
Manlove, C. N. *Modern Fantasy: Five Studies.* Cambridge: Cambridge UP, 1975.
McGillis, Roderick. "Fantasy as Adventure: Nineteenth Century Children's Fiction." *Children's Literature Association Quarterly* 8.3 (1983): 18-22.
Oxford English Dictionary. Compact Edition. Oxford: Oxford UP, 1971.
Reis, Richard H. *George MacDonald.* New York: Twayne, 1972.
Thisted, Adolph Valdemar. *Letters from Hell.* New York: Funk & Wagnalls, 1887.
Wolff, Robert Lee. *The Golden Key: A Study of the Fiction of George MacDonald.* New Haven: Yale UP, 1961.
Zaitchik, Mark. "Preface," *The Wise Woman, A Parable.* New York: Garland, 1977.

Select Bibliography

Recent Editions of MacDonald's Fairy Tales

At the Back of the North Wind. Illus. E. H. Shepard. London: J. M. Dent, 1967 (1956).

The Day Boy and the Night Girl. Illus. Nonny Hogrogian. New York: Knopf, 1988.

The Fairy Fleet. Illus. Stuyvesant Van Veen. New York: Holiday House, 1936.

The Gifts of the Child Christ: Fairy Tales and Stories for the Childlike. 2 vols. Ed. Glenn Edward Sadler. Grand Rapids, MI: Eerdmans, 1973.

The Gold Key and the Green Life: Some Fantasies and Celtic Tales by George MacDonald and Fiona Macleod. Collected and edited by Elizabeth Sutherland. London: Constable, 1986.

The Golden Key. Illus. Maurice Sendak. Afterword by W. H. Auden. New York: Farrar, Straus, and Giroux, 1967.

The Golden Key and other Fantasy Stories. Illus. Craig Yoe. Grand Rapids, MI: Eerdmans, 1980.

The Gray Wolf and other Fantasy Stories. Illus. Craig Yoe. Grand Rapids, MI: Eerdmans, 1980.

The Light Princess. Illus. Dorothy P. Lathrop. New York: Macmillan, 1952 (1926).

The Light Princess. Illus. Katie Thamer Treherne. Adapted by Robin McKinley. New York: Harcourt Brace Jovanovich, 1988.

The Light Princess. Illus. Maurice Sendak. New York: Farrar, Straus and Giroux, 1969.

The Light Princess and other Fantasy Stories. Illus. Craig Yoe. Grand Rapids, MI: Eerdmans, 1980.

The Light Princess and other Tales. Illus. Arthur Hughes. Introduction Roger Lancelyn Green. London: Victor

Gollancz, 1967.
The Lost Princess: A Double Story. Illus. D. Watkins-Pitchford. Introduction by Elizabeth Yates. London: J. M. Dent, 1967 (1965).
Phantastes. Introduction David Holbrook. London: Everyman, 1983.
The Princess and Curdie. Illus. Charles Folkard. London: J. M. Dent, 1967 (1949).
The Princess and the Goblin. Illus. Charles Folkard. London: J. M. Dent, 1949.
The Princess and the Goblin and the Princess and Curdie. Ed. Roderick McGillis. London: Oxford UP, 1990.
The Son of the Day and the Daughter of the Night. Illus. Lyn Temple. La Jolla, CA: Green Tiger P, 1980.
The Wise Woman and other Fantasy Stories. Illus. Craig Yoe. Grand Rapids, MI: Eerdmans, 1980.

Bibliography

Bulloch, J. M. "A Centennial Bibliography of George MacDonald." *Aberdeen University Library Bulletin* 5 (1925): 679-747.
Hutton, Muriel. "The George MacDonald Collection. Brander Library, Huntly." *The Book Collector* 17 (1968):13-25.
_____. "Sour Grapeshot." *Aberdeen University Review* 41 (1965):85-88.
Shaberman, R. B. *George MacDonald's Books for Children: A Bibliography of First Editions.* London: Cityprint Business Centres, 1979.

Books on George MacDonald

Hein, Rolland. *The Harmony Within: The Spiritual Vision of George MacDonald.* Grand Rapids, MI: Eerdmans, 1982.
Higgins, James E. *Five Authors of Mystical Fancy for Children: A Critical Study.* New York: Columbia UP, 1965.
Johnson, Joseph. *George MacDonald: A Biographical and Critical Appreciation.* London: Sir Isaac Pitman and Sons, 1906.
Lochhead, Marion. *The Renaissance of Wonder in Children's*

Literature. Edinburgh: Cannongate, 1977.
MacDonald, Greville. *George MacDonald and His Wife*. London: Allen and Unwin, 1924.
Phillips, Michael R. *George MacDonald: Scotland's Beloved Storyteller*. Minneapolis, MN: Bethany, 1987.
Raeper, William. *George MacDonald*. Tring, Lion, 1987.
Raeper, William, Ed. *The Gold Thread: Essays on George MacDonald*. Edinburgh: Edinburgh UP, 1990.
Reis, Richard. *George MacDonald*. New York: Twayne's, 1972.
Robb, David S. *George MacDonald*. Edinburgh: Scottish Academic Press, 1987.
Saintsbury, Elizabeth. *George MacDonald: A Short Life*. Edinburgh: Cannongate, 1987.
Triggs, Kathy. *George MacDonald: The Seeking Heart*. London: Pickering and Inglis, 1984.
_____. *The Stars and the Stillness: A Portrait of George MacDonald*. Cambridge: Lutterworth, 1986.
Wolff, Robert Lee. *The Golden Key: A Study of the Fiction of George MacDonald*. New Haven: Yale UP, 1961.

Articles, Reviews and Chapters in Books

Adams, Gillian. "Student Responses to *Alice in Wonderland* and *At the Back of the North Wind*." *Children's Literature Association Quarterly* 10 (1985): 6-9.
Athenaeum. Review of *At the Back of the North Wind*. (March 11, 1871): 303.
_____. Review of *Phantastes*. (November 6, 1858): 580.
_____. Review of *The Princess and the Goblin*.(December 23, 1871): 835.
Bergmann, Frank. "The Roots of Tolkien's Tree: The Influence of George MacDonald and German Romanticism Upon Tolkien's Essay 'On Fairy Stories'." *Mosaic* 10 (1977): 5-14.
Blishen, Edward. "Maker of Fairy Tales." *Books and Bookmen* 19 (1974): 92-95.
Brewer, Derek. "Introduction." *Phantastes*. New York: Schocken, 1982, v-xi.
British Quarterly Review. Review of *Phantastes*. 29 (1859): 296-297.
_____. "Works by George MacDonald." 47 (1868): 1-34.

Carpenter, Humphrey. "George MacDonald and the Tender Grandmother." In Humphrey Carpenter. *Secret Gardens*. Boston: Houghton Mifflin, 1985, 70-85.

Chesterton, G. K. "The Sage: George MacDonald." *Daily News* (Sept. 23, 1905), 6.

Colvin, Sidney. Review of *The Princess and the Goblin*. *The Academy* (Jan. 15, 1872): 24.

Crago, H. "Charles Dickens and George MacDonald: A Note." *Dickens Studies* 5 (1969): 90-96.

Docherty, John. "A Note on the Structure and Conclusion of *Phantastes*." *North Wind: Journal of the George MacDonald Society* 7 (1988): 25-30.

Donoghue, Denis. "The Other Country." *The New York Review of Books* (Dec. 21, 1967): 34-37.

Douglas, Alison. "The Scottish Contribution to Children's Literature." *Library Review* 20 (1965): 241-246.

Douglass, Jane. "Dealings With the Fairies." *The Horn Book Magazine* 37 (1961): 327-335.

Edwards, Bruce L., Jr. "Toward a Rhetoric of Fantasy Criticism: C. S. Lewis's Readings of MacDonald and Morris." *Literature and Belief* 3 (1983): 63-73.

Fisher, Lenna W. "Mystical Fantasy for Children: Silence and Community." *The Lion and the Unicorn* 14 (1990): 37-57.

The Globe. Review of *Phantastes*. (December 30, 1858).

Hein, Rolland. "*Lilith*: Theology Through Mythopoeia." *Christian Scholar's Review* 3 (1974): 215-231.

Hetzler, Leo A. "George MacDonald and G. K. Chesterton." *Durham University Review* 58 (n.s. 37, 1976): 176-182.

_____. "G. K. Chesterton and the Myth-Making Power." *Seven* 3 (1982): 72-82.

Holbrook, David. "George MacDonald and Dreams of the Other World." *Seven* 4 (1983): 27-37.

_____. "Postscript: a Reply." *Seven* 5 (1984): 34.

Hutton, Muriel. "The George MacDonald Collection." *Yale University Library Gazette* 51 (1976): 74-85.

_____. "Writers for Children: George MacDonald." *The School Librarian* 12 (1964): 244-254.

Hutton, R. H. "*David Elginbrod*." *The Spectator* (Jan. 3, 1863, supplement): 20-21.

Kirkpatrick, Mary. "An Introduction to the *Curdie* Books of George MacDonald." *Bulletin of the New York C. S. Lewis Society* 5, v (1974): 1-6.

―――. "Lewis and MacDonald." *Bulletin of the New York C. S. Lewis Society* 5, vii (1974): 2-4.

Kocher, Paul H. "J. R. R. Tolkien and George MacDonald." *The Cresset* 8 (1981): 3-4.

Landow, George P. "And the World Became Strange: Realms of Literary Fantasy." In Roger C. Schlobin, Ed. *The Aesthetics of Fantasy Literature and Art.* Notre Dame, IN : U of Notre Dame P, 1982, 105-142.

The Leader. Review of *Phantastes.* (November 13, 1858): 1222.

Lewis, Naomi. "Children's Books: George MacDonald." *New Statesman* (Nov. 10, 1961): 693-694.

"Lilith." *The Critic* 25 (1896): 58.

"Lilith." *Pall Mall Gazette* (Oct. 18, 1895): 9.

Lochhead, Marion. "George MacDonald and the World of Faerie." *Seven* 3 (1982): 63-71.

MacDonald, A. "The Dialect of *Sir Gibbie.*" *Alma Mater* (Feb. 17, 1915): 182-183.

MacNeice, Louis. "The Victorians." In Louis MacNeice. *Varieties of Parable.* Cambridge: Cambridge UP, 1965, 76-101.

McGillis, Roderick. "The Abyss of His Mother-Tongue: Scotch Dialect in Novels by George MacDonald." *Seven* 2 (1981): 44-56.

―――. "The Beauty of Holiness." *Mythlore* 36 (1983): 39-41.

―――. "Childhood and Growth. George MacDonald and William Wordsworth." In James Holt McGavran, Jr., Ed. *Romanticism and Children's Literature in Nineteenth-Century England.* Athens, GA: Georgia UP, 1991, 150-67.

―――. "Fantasy as Adventure: Nineteenth Century Children's Fiction." *Children's Literature Association Quarterly* 8 (1983): 18-22.

―――. "George MacDonald's *Princess* Books: High Seriousness." In Perry Nodelman, Ed. *Touchstones: Reflections on the Best in Children's Literature.* West Lafayette, IN: ChLA Publications, 1985, 146-162.

―――. "If You Call Me Grandmother, That Will Do." *Mythlore* 21 (1979): 27-28.

―――. "*Lilith: A Romance.*" In *Survey of Modern Fantasy*

Literature. Vol. 2. Ed. Frank N. Magill. La Canada, CA: Salem Press, 1983, 880-886.

———. "The Logic of Dreams." *Fantasiae* 2 (1974): 1, 10-11.

McIntyre, J. *"Phantastes* into *Alice." Victorian Studies Association of Western Canada Newsletter* 3 (1977): 6-9.

Manlove, C. N. "Circularity in Fantasy: George MacDonald." In C. N. Manlove. *The Impulse of Fantasy Literature.* Kent, OH: Kent State UP, 1983, 70-92.

———. "George MacDonald (1824-1905)." In C. N. Manlove. *Modern Fantasy.* Cambridge: Cambridge UP, 1975, 55-98.

———. "George MacDonald's Fairy Tales: Their Roots in MacDonald's Thought." *Studies in Scottish Literature* 8 (1970): 97-108.

Marshall, Cynthia. "Allegory, Orthodoxy, Ambivalence: MacDonald's 'The Day Boy and the Night Girl.'" *Children's Literature* 16 (1988): 57-75.

Massingham, H. J. Review of *Lilith* and *Fairy Tales. Nation and Athenaeum* (August 2, 1924): 569.

Mendelson, Michael. "George MacDonald's *Lilith* and the Conventions of Ascent." *Studies in Scottish Literature* 20 (1985): 197-218.

Moss, Anita. "Sacred and Secular Visions of Imagination and Reality in Nineteenth Century British Fantasy for Children." In Joseph O'Beirne Milner and Lucy Floyd Morcock Milner, Eds. *Webs and Wardrobes.* Lanham, MD: University Press of America, 1987, 67-78.

Nicoll, William Robertson (Claudius Clear). "Dr. George MacDonald." *Bookman* 18 (1900): 116-118.

———. "Dr. Parker's New Novel—Others." *British Weekly* (Oct. 10, 1895): 395.

Page, H. A. "Children and Children's Books." *Contemporary Review* 11 (1869): 23-24.

Patterson, Nancy-Lou. "Archetypes of the Mother in the Fantasies of George MacDonald." *Mythcon 1 Proceedings.* Los Angeles: The Mythopoeic Society, 1971: 14-20.

Perrot, Jean. "Un Grand Victorien: George MacDonald." *La Revue des Livres pour Enfants* 137-138 (1991): 34-37.

Prickett, Stephen. "Adults in Allegory Land: Kingsley and MacDonald." In Stephen Prickett. *Victorian Fantasy.* Bloomington, IN: Indiana UP, 1979.

———. "Demythologising and Myth-making: Arnold versus Mac-

Donald." In Stephen Prickett. *Romanticism and Religion: The Tradition of Coleridge and Wordsworth in the Victorian Church.* Cambridge: Cambridge UP, 1976.

Rabkin, Eric S. "The Fantastic and Perspective." In Eric S. Rabkin. *The Fantastic in Literature.* Princeton, NJ: Princeton UP, 1976, 98-108.

Rigsbee, Sally. "Fantasy Places and Imaginative Belief: *The Lion, the Witch, and the Wardrobe* and *The Princess and the Goblin.*" *Children's Literature Association Quarterly* 8 (1983): 10-11.

Robb, David S. "The Fiction of George MacDonald." *Seven* 6 (1985): 35-44. This essay has also appeared in David Hewitt and Michael Spiller, Eds. *Literature of the North.* Aberdeen: Aberdeen UP, 1983.

_____. "George MacDonald and Animal Magnetism." *Seven* 8 (1987): 9-24.

Robertson, E. S. "A Literary Causerie: *Phantastes.*" *Academy* 70 (1906): 308-309.

Sadler, Glenn Edward. "*At the Back of the North Wind*: George MacDonald: A Centennial Appreciation." *Tolkien Journal* 4 (1970): 20-21.

_____. "The Fantastic Imagination in George MacDonald." In Charles A. Huttar, Ed. *Imagination and the Spirit.* Grand Rapids, MI: Eerdmans, 1971, 215-227.

_____. "George MacDonald." In D. L. Kirkpatrick, Ed. *Twentieth-Century Children's Writers.* London: St. James, 1978.

_____. "George MacDonald." In Jane Bingham, Ed. *Writers for Children.* New York: Charles Scribner's Sons, 1988, 373-380.

_____. " 'The Little Girl That Had No Tongue': An Unpublished Short Story by George MacDonald." *Children's Literature* 2 (1973): 18-34.

Saintsbury, George. "*Lilith.*" *Academy* (Oct. 12, 1895): 291.

Salmon, Edward. "Literature for the Little Ones." *Nineteenth Century* 22 (1887): 563-580.

Sendak, Maurice. "George MacDonald." *Caldecott & Co.: Notes on Books and Pictures.* New York: Farrar, Straus and Giroux, 1988, 45-49.

Shaberman, R. B. "Lewis Carroll and George MacDonald." *Jabberwocky* 5 (1976): 67-87.

Sigman, Joseph. "Death's Ecstasies: Transformation and Rebirth in

George MacDonald's *Phantastes*." *English Studies in Canada* 2 (1976): 203-226.
Spectator. Review of *Phantastes* (December 4, 1858): 1286.
Stott, Jon C. "George MacDonald." In Jon C. Stott. *Children's Literature From A to Z*. New York: McGraw-Hill,1984, 190-192.
Sutherland, D. "The Founder of the New Scottish School." *The Critic* 27 (1897): 339.
Sutton, Max Keith. "The Psychology of the Self in MacDonald's *Phantastes*." *Seven* 5 (1984): 9-25.
Swiatecka, M. Jadwiga. "Dean Inge, George Tyrrell and George MacDonald." In M. Jadwiga Swiatecka. *The Idea of the Symbol*. Cambridge: Cambridge UP, 1980, 151-168.
Tanner, Tony. "Mountains and Depths— An Approach to Nineteenth Century Dualism." *A Review of English Literature* 3 (1962): 51-61.
Triggs, Kathy. "Worlds Apart: The Importance of Double Vision for MacDonald Criticism." *Seven* 5 (1984): 26-33.
Walker, Jeanne Murray. "The Demoness and the Grail: Deciphering MacDonald's *Lilith*." In Robert A. Collins and Howard D. Pearce, Eds. *The Scope of the Fantastic - Culture, Biography, Themes. Children's Literature*. Westport, CT: Greenwood, 1985, 179-90.
Watkins, Gwen. "A Theologian's Dealings with The Fairies." *North Wind: Journal of the George MacDonald Society* 7 (1988): 5-14.
Westminster Review. "Review of *The Portent* and *Adela Cathcart*." 2 (1864): 258-259.
_____. "Review of *The Princess and the Goblin*" 41 (1872): 581.
Willard, Nancy. "The Nonsense of Angels: George MacDonald at the Back of the North Wind." In Jill P. May, Ed. *Children and Their Literature: A Readings Book*. West Lafayette, IN: ChLA Publications, 1983, 34-40.
Willis, Lesley. "'Born Again': The Metamorphosis of Irene in George MacDonald's *The Princess and the Goblin*." *Scottish Literary Journal* 12 (1985): 24-39.
Wilson, Keith. "The Quest for 'The Truth': A Reading of George MacDonald's *Phantastes*." *Etudes Anglaises* 34 (1981): 140-152.
Wolfe, Gregory. "C. S. Lewis's Debt to George MacDonald." *Bulletin of the New York C. S. Lewis Society* 15 (1983): 1-7.
Wolff, Robert Lee. "An 1862 Alice: 'Cross Purposes'; or *Which Dreamed It?*" *Harvard Library Bulletin* 23 (1975): 199-202.

———. "The Preacher in Fairyland." *Times Literary Supplement* (Nov. 15, 1974).
Woods, Katharine Pearson. "A Little Glory." *The Bookman* (New York, October 1895): 133-135.
Yates, Elizabeth. "George MacDonald." *The Horn Book Magazine* 14 (1938): 23-30.
Zipes, Jack. "Inverting and Subverting the World with Hope: The Fairy Tales of George MacDonald, Oscar Wilde and L. Frank Baum." In Jack Zipes. *Fairy Tales and the Art of Subversion.* New York: Wildman, 1983, 97-111.

Note: A useful selection of excerpts from various critics of MacDonald is available in the following publication:

"George MacDonald: 1824-1905." Vol. 9. *Twentieth-Century Literary Criticism.* Ed. Dennis Poupard. Detroit: Gale Research, 1983, 286-312.

List of Contributors

Celia Anderson is an Associate Professor of English at Eastern Connecticut State University. She is co-author of the recent book *Nonsense Literature for Children: Aesop to Seuss* (1989).

Melba Battin is an Assistant Professor of English at Bowie State University.

A. Waller Hastings is an Assistant Professor of Language, Literature and Communication at Northern State College. His interests are in the relationship between literature and ideology.

Cynthia Marshall is an Assistant Professor of English at Rhodes College. As well as publishing articles on George MacDonald, she has published on Renaissance literature and is the author of the forthcoming book *Last Things and Last Plays: Shakespearean Eschatology* (1991).

Roderick McGillis is a Professor of English at the University of Calgary. He is the former editor of the *Children's Literature Association Quarterly* and has recently edited the Oxford World's Classics edition of MacDonald's 'Princess' books (1990).

Michael Mendelson is an Associate Professor of English at Iowa State University. He has written on nineteenth-century fantasy, on children's fiction, on narrative theory, and on Greek and Roman rhetoric.

Nancy-Lou Patterson is a Professor of Fine Art at the University of Waterloo. She is book review editor for *Mythlore* and is the author of the fantasy *Apple Staff and Silver Crown* (1985).

Stephen Prickett is Regius Professor of English Language and Literature at the University of Glasgow. He is the author of many books, including *Romanticism and Religion* (1976) and *Victorian Fantasy* (1979). His most recent book is *Reading the Text: Biblical Criticism and Literary Theory* (1990).

William Raeper is a writer who lives in Oxford, England. He is the author of the biography *George MacDonald* (1987) and the editor of the volume of essays on MacDonald, *The Gold Thread* (1990).

Frank Riga is a Professor of English at Canisius College. He is the co-author of the *Index to the London Magazine* (1978) and the author of many papers on C. S. Lewis and St. Augustine. He also has an abiding interest in Keats.

Cordelia Sherman teaches writing and fantasy at Boston University. She has published in *The Magazine of Fantasy and Science Fiction* and has an adult fantasy novel titled *The Famous Flower of Serving Men* (Ace).

Joseph Sigman is a Professor of English at McMaster University. He has published articles on George MacDonald and Kurt Vonnegut, and he is the editor of the massive compilation of Ernest Hemingway's library.

Lesley Smith lives in Cornwall, England. As Lesley Willis, she has published articles on MacDonald, Kenneth Grahame, and L. M. Montgomery, and she is working on a book on George MacDonald.

Nancy Willard is a poet, author of *A Visit to William Blake's Inn, The Island of the Grass King,* and the Anatole Trilogy Series. In 1982 she won the Newbery Award.

Index

Abrams, M. H., 46, 61
Allegory, 22, 33, 44, 54, 78, 99, 104, 112, 114, 115, 116, 118, 119, 120, 123-28, 154, 162
Andersen, Hans Christian, 34, 35, 45, 76: "The Candles," 76; "The Little Match Girl," 76, 77; "The Story of Old Johanna Told," 76
Anderson, Celia, 4
Arachne, 176
Ariadne, 173, 177, 185, 205
Arthos, John, 93
Athenaeum, 54, 157
Auden, W. H., 42, 54, 105
Audience, 1, 6, 13, 52

Bakhtin, Mikhail, 13
Barfield, Owen, 24
Basile, Giambattista, 45
Battin, Melba, 6
Berggren, Douglas, 2, 27-28
Bettleheim, Bruno, 47, 138
Bible, the, 130, 166: Daniel, 5, 162, 163, 165, 167, 168, 188; Deuteronomy, 165; Habbakuk, 166; Isaiah, 164, 166; Jeremiah, 164, 166; Job, 102, 161, 166, 167; Obadiah, 166; Psalms, 166; 1 Corinthians, 161; 2 Corinthians, 165; Galatians, 167; John, 167; Luke, 73, 188, 189; Mark, 189; Matthew, 3, 9, 73, 100, 101, 104, 189, 190, 208; Revelation, 163, 164, 167
Blake, William, 20, 63, 78: "Crystal Cabinet," 58
Bloom, Allan, 129
Boehme, Jakob, 96
Bosch, Hieronymus, 73
Brimos, 172, 175
British Quarterly Review, 54
Brooke-Rose, Christina, 46

Buber, Martin, 36
Burns, Robert, 139
Butor, Michel, 45
Byron, Lord, 139

Campbell, Joseph, 204
Carlyle, Thomas: *Sartor Resartus*, 46
Carroll, Lewis, 36, 47: *Alice's Adventures in Wonderland*, 10, 42, 85; *Alice's Adventures Underground*, 38
Chamisso, Adalbert: *Peter Schlemihl*, 47
Chesterton, G. K., 21, 43, 44: *Victorian Age in Literature*, 21
Child reader, 6, 7, 12, 13, 14
"Cinderella," 41
Clark, George Kitson, 78
Coleridge, S. T., 24, 60, 139, 149, 208: *Rime of the Ancient Mariner*, 61; *Statesman's Manual*, 23

Dahl, Roald, 12
Dante, 4, 22, 23, 24, 28, 134, 156: *Paradiso*, 38; *Purgatorio*, 22
Demeter, 171-72, 174-75, 181
Demophoon, 171, 173
Diana, 68
Dickens, Charles, 78, 85
Dike, 68
Dionysus, 172
Docherty, John, 64

Ego, 5, 12, 44, 184, 187, 188, 193, 197
Eichhorn, Johann Gottfried, 21
Eliade, Mircea, 172, 204
Eliot, George, 21
Erasmus, Desiderius, 106
Eumenia, 68

Evil, 5, 6, 197-200, 202, 203

Feuerbach, Ludwig, 21
Folklore (folktales), 7, 8, 9, 22, 38, 40, 45, 80, 138, 142
Frau Berchte, 68
Freud, Sigmund, 25, 33, 37, 44, 55, 88, 107, 136
"Frog Prince," 41
Frye, Northrop, 45, 147

German Romantics, 4, 32, 87, 95, 104, 143, 185
Globe, the, 54
Goethe, Johann Wolfgang: "Marchen," 41, 47
Greeves, Arthur, *111, 112, 130*
Grierson, H. J. C., 151
Grimm, Jacob, 45, 68
Grimm Brothers, 7, 12, 32, 35, 76

"Hansel and Gretel," 38
Hastings, A. Waller, 3, 6
Hecate, 171, 172, 173, 174, 175, 179
Heine, Heinrich, 60
Helius, 171
Henderson, Joseph, 204
Herodotus, 4, 134, 155, 156
Hirsch, E. D., 105
Hoffman, E. T. A., 32, 35: "The Golden Pot," 47; "Princess Brambilla," 34, 46
Hogg, James, 133-39, 142-43, 153, 156: *Kilmeny*, 4; *The Queen's Wake*, 134, 137
Hughes, Arthur, 164

Iambe, 171
Ingelow, Jean: *Mopsa the Fairy*, 77

"Jack and the Beanstalk," 7
Johnson, Joseph, 157
Jung, C. G. (also Jungian), 5, 25, 55, 136, 138, 142, 172, 173, 174, 175, 184, 185, 186, 187, 188, 190, 192, 199

Kant, Immanuel, 47

Keats, John, 60: *La Belle Dame Sans Merci*, 61
Kerenyi, C., 172, 173, 174
Kermode, Frank, 101, 103
Kingsley, Charles, 84: *The Water Babies*, 77
Knoepflmacher, U. C., 46, 207
Kohut, Ernst, 55
Kotzin, Michael, 85

La Motte-Fouqué, Baron H. F. K. de: *Undine*, 32, 47
LeGuin, Ursula K., 5, 195-203: *The Farthest Shore*, 195, 197; *Language of the Night*, 195; *The Tombs of Atuan*, 195, 199, 200, 202; *A Wizard of Earthsea*, 195, 197, 201
Lewis, C. S., 2, 4, 37, 67, 111-31, 169, 207; *Abolition of Man*, 131; *Dymer*, 130, 131; *George MacDonald: An Anthology*, 112, 170; *The Last Battle*, 4, 122-23; *Moving Image*, 112; *Out of the Silent Planet*, 4, 115-19, 128; *Surprised by Joy*, 131; *That Hideous Strength*, 169; *They Stand Together*, 111; *The Voyage of the Dawn Treader*, 4, 119-20, 124; *Weight of Glory*, 123
Lüthi, Max, 34, 37, 40, 43, 45, 46

MacDonald, George: *Adela Cathcart*, 7, 11, 12, 46, 184; *Alec Forbes of Howglen*, 153; Arundel, 19, 20, 79; *At the Back of the North Wind*, 2, 4, 5, 6, 22, 33, 42, 77, 85, 120-21, 122, 130, 133-36, 140, 142, 145-59, 161-68, 190, 209; *A Cabinet of Gems*, 143; Calvinism, 18, 19, 20, 104, 108, 142; "The Carasoyn," 47, 140; *Castle Warlock*, 146; "Cross Purposes, " 3, 8, 13, 75, 79-85; *The Day Boy and the Night Girl* ("Photogen and Nycteris") 4, 10, 80, 124-28; *Dealings With the Faeries*, 1, 42, 139; *Diary of an Old Soul*, 111; *A Dish of Orts*, 46, 64, 91, 149, 209, 211; *England's Antiphon*, 87, 149; "The Fantastic Imagination," 33,

Index

37, 46, 104, 105, 108, 139, 143, 209; "The Giant's Heart," 6, 7-13, 47; *The Golden Key,* 3, 4, 10, 31, 38-42, 44, 47, 67, 69, 70, 71, 72, 75, 80, 81, 83, 84, 86, 87-97, 99-108, 115, 121, 122, 128, 207; *Good Words for the Young,* 42; Hastings, 18; Highbury College, 19, 153; *The Hope of the Gospel,* 162; Huntly, 18, 140; "The Imagination: Its Function and Culture," 34, 46, 60, 130; *The Light Princess,* 3, 13, 31, 34-38, 39, 46, 47, 85; *Lilith,* 2, 4, 17, 26, 32, 46, 55, 58, 121-22, 123, 144, 146, 207; "Little Daylight," 6, 85, 155; London, 18; *The Lost Princess* ("The Wise Woman"), 3, 4, 6, 67, 68, 69, 70, 71, 73, 119, 124, 146, 207, 208-17; *Malcolm,* 140; "Of the Son of Man," 54; *Paul Faber, Surgeon,* 139; *Phantastes,* 3, 17, 32, 51-64, 92, 111, 112, 131, 147, 183, 184, 186, 187, 189, 190, 191, 192, 193, 207; *Poetical Works,* 54, 151; *The Portent,* 209; *The Princess and Curdie,* 3, 5, 13, 44, 68, 72, 73, 140, 144, 167, 169, 170, 187-93, 197, 198-99, 200, 201, 203; *The Princess and the Goblin,* 2, 3, 5, 6, 8, 13, 21, 25, 31, 42, 56, 58, 68, 70, 71, 79, 140, 155, 156, 169, 170, 172, 173-82, 183-87, 188, 189, 193, 196; *Ranald Bannerman's Boyhood,* 140; "The Shadows," 4, 85, 114; *Sir Gibbie,* 140; "A Sketch of Individual Development," 189, 190; *Twelve Spiritual Songs* (Novalis), 19; University of Aberdeen, 19; *Unspoken Sermons:* First Series, 149, 150; *Unspoken Sermons:* Second Series, 87, 150; *Unspoken Sermons:* Third Series, 64; *Wilfrid Cumbermede,* 131; *Within and Without,* 135, 137, 142, 210
MacDonald, Greville: *George MacDonald and His Wife,* 20, 21, 23, 26, 46, 108, 152

MacDonald, Maurice, 168
MacNeice, Louis, 104, 149, 208, 209, 217
Manlove, Colin, 55, 78, 150, 151, 169, 207
Marshall, Cynthia, 3, 5, 10, 86
Matthews, W. H., 204
Maurice, F. D., 78, 84
McGillis, Roderick, 5, 168, 170, 172, 179, 207, 209
Mendelson, Michael, 2, 3
Metaphor, 2, 27, 28, 33, 39, 52, 53, 146, 147, 149, 150, 154, 199, 202
Milton, John: *Comus,* 4, 46, 87-97, 186; *Lycidas,* 88; *Paradise Lost,* 87, 193
Mysticism, 19, 20, 24, 25, 44, 105
Myth (mythopoetic), 3, 22, 25, 28, 32, 38, 41, 42, 183, 193

Neuse, Richard, 89, 90, 91
Newton, Richard, 194
Norman, Edward, 84
Novalis (Friedrich von Hardenberg), 19, 21, 32, 54, 60, 95: *Heinrich von Ofterdingen,* 41, 61; "Klingsohr's Tale," 41, 47, 177

Odyssey (Homer), 187, 188, 193-94
Opie, Iona and Peter, 41
Opposites, 2, 6, 10, 35, 43, 44, 147, 148, 170, 179, 191, 192
Orality, 6, 8, 34, 45, 46

Page, H. A. (A. H. Japp), 1
Parable, 76, 99, 103, 104-106, 149, 150, 156, 207-209, 215, 217
Parker, Patricia, 109
Patterson, Nancy-Lou, 5
Perrault, Charles, 35
Persephone, 170-74, 185, 186, 187
Plato, 23, 24, 40, 95, 106, 111-31: *Phaedo,* 129; *The Republic,* 4, 47, 112; *Symposium,* 112
Prickett, Stephen, 2, 3, 78, 106, 152, 156
Psyche, 177

Raeper, William, 1, 4, 7, 79

Reis, Richard, 7, 18, 36, 37, 54, 167, 207
Rhea, 68
Ricoeur, Paul, 147
Riga, Frank, 4, 47
Robb, David, 1, 4, 144
Robertson, E. S., 54
Rose, Jacqueline, 1, 6
Ruskin, John, 45: *King of the Golden River*, 76, 77, 85

Sadler, Glenn Edward, 12, 38, 46
Sale, Roger, 45, 47
Salmon, Edward, 1
Schiller, Friedrich, 60
Scott, Sir Walter: *Border Minstrelsy*, 137
Selden, Rebecca, 46
Shavit, Zohar, 1
Shelley, P. B., 60: *Defence of Poetry*, 60; *Epipsychidion*, 53, 54; *Prometheus Unbound*, 149
Sherman, Cordelia, 5
Sidney, Sir Philip, 143
Sigman, Joseph, 5, 55
"Sleeping Beauty," 34, 35, 36, 37, 41, 176
Smith, Lesley, 5
Smout, T. C., 141
"Snow White," 36
Spectator, the, 54
Standford, W. Bedell, 27
Stone, Harry, 85
Strauss, David Friedrich, 21

Sutton, Max Keith, 55, 63
Swedenborg, Emmanuel, 144
Symbol, 22, 23, 24, 25, 26, 28, 31, 32, 34, 88, 89, 90, 96, 97, 200, 203

Tam Lin, 140
Tanner, Tony, 43, 44
Theseus, 173, 185, 187
Thisted, Adolph Valdemar: *Letters from Hell*, 209
"Thomas the Rhymer," 140-41
Thompson, Stith, 7
Tieck, Friedrich, 32, 153
Tolkien, J. R. R., 43: *The Hobbit*, 6
Trainer, John, 46
Triggs, Kathy, 168
Tristram Shandy, 112
Turner, J. M. W., 20

Wells, H. G.: *War of the Worlds*, 117
Willard, Nancy, 3
Wilson, Keith, 64
Wolff, Robert Lee, 5, 7, 11, 12, 37, 46, 47, 75, 77, 88, 89, 92, 94, 95, 96, 99, 100, 108, 168, 185, 193, 208
Wordsworth, William, 39, 139, 142, 189: *The Prelude*, 61, 158

Zaitchik, Mark, 208
Zeus, 171
Zipes, Jack: *Fairy Tales and the Art of Subverion*, 80, 85; *Victorian Fairy Tales*, 3, 45, 76